Resolana

Resolana

EMERGING CHICANO DIALOGUES ON COMMUNITY AND GLOBALIZATION

Miguel Montiel, Tomás Atencio,
and E. A. "Tony" Mares

Foreword by
Raul Yzaguirre

the university of arizona press   tucson

The University of Arizona Press
© 2009 The Arizona Board of Regents
All rights reserved

www.uapress.arizona.edu

Library of Congress Cataloging-in-Publication Data

Montiel, Miguel, 1942 Apr. 10–
  Resolana : emerging Chicano dialogues on community
and globalization / Miguel Montiel, Tomás Atencio, and
E.A. "Tony" Mares ; foreword by Raul Yzaguirre.
     p. cm.
  Includes bibliographical references and index.
  ISBN 978-0-8165-2776-2 (hardcover : alk. paper) –
  ISBN 978-0-8165-2834-9 (pbk. : alk. paper)
  1. Mexican Americans—Social conditions.
2. Mexican Americans—Ethnic identity. 3. Globalization—
Social aspects. 4. Popular education—United States—
Social aspects. 5. Group identity—United States.
6. Social ecology—United States. I. Atencio, Tomás,
1932– II. Mares, E. A., 1938– III. Title.
E184.M5M594 2009
305.89468'72073—dc22   2008036912

Manufactured in the United States of America on acid-
free, archival-quality paper and processed chlorine free.

14   13   12   11   6   5   4   3   2

Contents

Foreword

Years ago, when I was the CEO of the National Council of La Raza, my old friend, Tomás Atencio, approached me about sponsoring a "knowledge mining" process that would use a new protocol, a technique that Atencio referred to as *resolana*. The term had an honorable history. In the three hundred or so years of Spanish and Mexican sovereignty and rule over what is now New Mexico, the isolated and insulated Spanish/Indian/Mexican/Sephardic Jewish population developed particular customs and mores and preserved certain archaic Spanish terms; *resolana* is one such term.

Resolana, as I understand its meaning, is both a place and a process, a noun and a verb. It refers to a gathering place where serious dialogue about weighty subjects is encouraged, where knowledge is allowed to flourish. But it also connotes a process of understanding the world at a higher level of awareness. The concept is grounded on a short set of assumptions. Among these is the belief that wisdom is not the monopoly of the educationally credentialed elite: life itself, if systematically and keenly observed, can and does give all of us the basis for making sound judgments about the nature of our world and the meaning of our existence. Another belief is that if thoughtful people take ideas proposed by one group member and in a respectful yet direct manner subject them to reasoned criticism, a more reasoned product will result. Inherently this view rejects, or at least is in opposition to, the Western myth of the solitary genius who valiantly struggles alone to find justice and freedom.

Miguel Montiel, Tomás Atencio, and E. A. "Tony" Mares challenge the reader to examine the ubiquitous reality of globalization through the framework of a resolana. The documentation of knowledge derived from the resolana process is original and timely, and the results are intriguing.

This book gives us a glimpse into a modern-day Camelot where the mythical and elusive Anglo-American common people can join with their Latino and African American neighbors to find common cause in protecting our environment, keeping desirable jobs in the United States, and returning America to fiscal solvency. Through the ancient art of reasoning together, we may just agree that elective foreign wars of aggression are against our national interest, and even that fellow human beings who seek work to feed their families and who make our lives more livable do not deserve to be demonized.

Raul Yzaguirre
Presidential Professor of Practice in Community Development and Civil Rights
Arizona State University

Preface

Miguel Montiel

Resolana: Emerging Chicano Dialogues on Community and Globalization is the fruit of the Motorola Presidential Professorship Community Revitalization Project in the Department of Transborder Studies at Arizona State University (ASU), which professorship I held until my retirement in 2005. This project was inspired by the work of La Academia de la Nueva Raza, and by Paulo Freire, whom the three of us met in the mountains of northern New Mexico in the early 1970s; it is also a continuation of the work Ray Padilla and I undertook while he was at Arizona State University. Beyond everything else, however, it is a tribute to our colleague and longtime friend, Tomás Atencio, whose work inspired and grounded this book.

This book was written in the spirit of a resolana. That is, we began with a series of extended dialogues among the three of us. We met several times for long weekends in my home in Phoenix; in Albuquerque at Tony Mares's home; and in Dixon, New Mexico, Tomás Atencio's ancestral home. We audio-taped our dialogues, transcribed them, then each of us wrote our essays, shared them with one another, and argued over their content. The prologue and epilogue are examples of our resolanas.

Consuelo Pacheco's contributions to all aspects of this project, Caroline Meyer's editorial assistance, and Yvonne Montiel's editing and formatting greatly improved this work. We acknowledge the many contributions of the asociados/as of La Academia de la Nueva Raza whose work over the years led to the maturing of the ideas of resolana and el oro del barrio. We are grateful for the editing expertise of Melanie Chase and Mike Ashby.

We were fortunate to have Kirsteen Anderson as our copyeditor. Her keen eye and affable manner greatly improved our disposition and more importantly, the manuscript. We are also grateful to Patti Hartmann and Kristen Buckles, acquiring editors at the University of Arizona Press, for their most generous support in getting this book to press.

The interviews for chapter 2 were collected as part of a seminar that examined Hispanics' entrance into the twenty-first century and in collaboration with the Profiles of Success Project sponsored by Valle del Sol, a community-based organization. The interviewers were Maureen Campesino, Angelica García, Joe Givens, Estela Ortega, Isaac Zuñiga, and me. Thanks to the many individuals who assisted with this project. Dolores Casillas and Rebecca Ronstadt, who set up the interviews and resolanas; Luz Sarmina Gutiérrez, Valle's CEO, who gave us the agency's support; and Victor Flores, senior government representative for the Salt River Project, hosted the forum. Carol Cabrera and I transcribed the audiotapes. Special thanks to the individuals we interviewed and those who participated in the community resolanas; they are acknowledged in the text.

Diana Arellano, Russ Binicki, Manny Gonzáles, Aída Montiel Jaramilla, Father Luis Jaramillo, Jim Jorquez, Juan Martin, Alberto Olivas, Camilo Tafur, and Maritza Montiel Tafur assisted with the analysis. Jackie Jaap, Rachel López Morgan, Debbie Simpkins, and Wayne Tormala helped edit drafts of the "Resolana in Action" manuscript.

Finally, I am grateful to all those who helped support and fund this project: Motorola, through an endowment; Cordelia Candelaria and Carlos Velez-Ibáñez, chairs of what is now known as the Department of Transborder Studies; Bob Soza, Dean of Students; Nancy Jordan, Institutional Development; and Raul Yzaguirre, Center for Civil Rights and Community Development, all at Arizona State University. If I neglected to mention anyone else who contributed to this project, I hope they will please forgive me.

Prologue

Miguel Montiel: Tomás, let's begin with a discussion of *resolana*. Friends who read early drafts of the manuscript wanted to know what it means and how it connects to *el oro del barrio.*

Tomás Atencio: Traditionally, resolana is a place where the sun strikes and reflects off a wall, creating a place of warmth, light, and tranquility, where villagers in northern New Mexico and in many places around the Spanish-speaking world gather and talk. It is an informal center for communicating. In searching for a Chicano parallel to the Socratic dialogues, I took la resolana and turned it into a metaphor for enlightenment through dialogue. It is a way to uncover subjugated knowledge and to use everyday lived experiences as a source of knowledge. It is a concept that brings light and hope through dialogue and reflection in an uncertain, complex, and rapidly changing new age.

Miguel: Are these sources of subjugated knowledge and experience that are uncovered through resolana what you refer to as el oro del barrio?

Tomás: Yes. But our group at La Academia de la Nueva Raza did not use the terms *oro del barrio* or *subjugated knowledge* when we first started. We began by stating that we needed a body of knowledge for our own education, one that reflected our history. Our ancestors did not land at Plymouth Rock; George Washington was not our founding father; and Padre Martínez was not the villain portrayed by Willa Cather in *Death Comes for the Archbishop*. We wanted those historical distortions corrected. As we all know, the history of our people has been covered up or distorted by the U.S. conquest in the Mexican War of 1848. Our knowledge was subjugated when a whole new set of cultural demands were imposed on us. But as we began to document the stories of the people in order to create that authentic knowledge, we uncovered a body of knowledge that we had taken for granted but was not valid in the eyes of the dominant American society: the knowledge and wisdom of an Indohispanic land-based people. That knowledge and wisdom is what we call el oro del barrio. And through the resolana process of dialogue and reflection, it is uncovered, validated, and used to create new insights and knowledge.

Miguel: Your finding a parallel with the Socratic dialogues is a wonderful insight. That is an old and valued approach to enlightenment. As you know, Ray Padilla and I wrote a book using a dialogical approach, and while we did not refer to our conversations as resolanas, they were influenced by your approach.

Tomás: I think every culture has its "resolana"—or as Ray Oldenburg calls it, *The Great Good Place,* or the "third place"—where people gather to visit and that they use as a place for dialogue and reflection.

Miguel: Perhaps an example from my perspective can explain the connection between experience and awareness. It happened that while I was hiking, a thick fog descended on the valleys of the Phoenix, Arizona, area—a rare occurrence. On my descent from the mountains, I noticed the fog behind me. I had been walking in the fog but did not recognize it until I looked behind me. I have also noticed that oftentimes while hiking, one can clearly see an animal trail from the height of the mountains, but cannot see it directly beneath one's feet. I realized that, like hiking in the fog, we live in confusion, but do not know it until we look back, reflect, dialogue. Our book is meant to encourage reflection and dialogue.

Tony, why don't you talk about your views on resolana?

E. A. "Tony" Mares: Through resolana, I believe we can offer a proactive approach to the environmental, social, and political conditions that are getting worse, not better, in our time. Resolana allows us to reflect on the erosion of our civil liberties here at home and to counter the xenophobic reaction to undocumented workers, mostly Mexican, who come here desperate for productive employment. We are not looking back to a mythologized Golden Age, as some do, but rather we are encouraging communities all around the world to look into their own cultural grab bags to seek intelligent, humane approaches to the problems and issues that beset them and us. Resolana offers hope for the future, a better future, even though at times it may be a very messy future. On a local and on a larger geopolitical scale, we need to meet, talk endlessly, and reach intelligent, proactive compromises.

Miguel: Tony, we refer to Mexican Americans in various ways in this book, but most often as Chicanos, the term we use in the subtitle. What is the "Chicano experience"?

Tony: It is important to be clear about the "Chicano experience." The term *Chicano* was popularized in the movement days of the 1960s. But it is only one of several terms we have used throughout this book to reflect the Indohispanic experience in its totality. The term *Chicano* inspired a whole generation of Mexican American cultural activists, and for some of us that term remains an inspiration. As our cultural awareness matures, I believe we will have a larger influence on education. We want to move education away from indoctrination in the consumer-oriented so-called American way of life and towards a more compassionate and humane interaction with all cultures. Such an interaction between individuals and cultures would be less driven by ideological capitalism and more open to nonideological economic pragmatism. As our Indohispanic cultural footprint leaves a deeper and growing imprint on American society, I hope most if not all Americans will see this as a greater good for all.

Miguel: Tomás, there are multiple ways of talking about globalization. In this book, we do not pretend to make definitive statements about all its complex ramifications. Our concern is the way in which some observers narrowly conceive of globalization and its negative impact on local cultures everywhere. What is your take on globalization and its relationship to the cyber age?

Tomás: Although I am a phenomenologist, I am also something of a technological determinist in that I believe the changes in the ways we relate to the environment—land, water, the universe, the means of production—are the societal forces aiming at some kind of coherency in the interface between humans and nature, between humans and their social constructs. Trade, economics, and globalization are some important embodiments of these social responses. And then we have other fallout from these responses, such as immigration, retribalization, terrorism and unconventional war. In other words, cyber technology is the independent variable and globalization is the dependent one. The cyber age has brought globalization to its current state of development.

Miguel: Tony, the subtitle of the introduction: *No siempre es el león como lo pintan*—what does it mean?

Tony: Literally "The lion is not always the way he is painted"; it implies that the real lion is worse. Or, as we might say in English, "Things are not always what they appear to be." Or, "If at your table there's a lion or two, they might eat you if they're able to. "Or, "Bring a hungry lion home, and he might dine on you alone." Or, "Better for you that the lion is a painting on the wall than that he's actually here." Need I say more?

Miguel: I'm sorry I asked!

Resolana

Introduction

No Siempre Es el León Como Lo Pintan

Ours is an era of ecological destruction, not only of the biosphere, but also of human communities and ethnic groups. Survival of human diversity is a matter of great concern to those of us involved with this book and the activities from which it evolved. Specifically, our focus is on the survival and nurturance of Indohispanic cultures. Yet our concerns are global in scope, or specifically, relate to the dark side of globalization. For globalists, loss of ethnic communities is of little if any importance. As long as goods move freely across borders, questions of human community and diversity are of at best of secondary importance. Global corporate interests are often cloaked in American triumphalism. Single-issue politics—abortion, gay marriage, Second Amendment rights, and the diversion of war—has masked the assault on democratic values, the plunder of the national treasury, and the decreasing buying power of the poor and middle classes, losses in which both U.S., corporate-friendly political parties are implicated.

Political scientists such as Samuel Huntington and Francis Fukuyama have developed elaborate justifications for the imposition of Western, specifically American, values on the rest of the world. These scholars assume a unified American identity that downplays or outright ignores the elements of strife, ethnic cleansing, racism, and military conquest that have been a constant throughout American history.[1] Our vision is opposed to that of these leading interpreters. We assert an American identity that is complex, dynamic, and composed of many complementary and also conflicting crosscurrents.

In *The Lexus and the Olive Tree*, Thomas Friedman describes globalization as the intersection between international politics and the new global economy. The Lexus, a luxury car made by robots, symbolizes the new global economy, and the olive tree, individual and community identity. Friedman claims that countries that have participated in globalization have raised their standards of living, and that any resulting job dislocations have been offset by new jobs in other sectors of the economy.[2] The greatest threat from globalization is to the people who are left out or do not want to change their way of life. In a later book, *The World Is Flat*, Friedman argues that technology is society's salvation. In this work, he extols the Internet connectivity of global corporations, claiming that this technological web has "flattened" the world by leveling the playing field among developed and developing countries.[3] Fixated as he is on technological miracles, Friedman displays no sense of historic infrastructure or of the strong relationship of culture to history. Local cultures may gather under their olive trees if they so wish, he argues, but they will be left out of the technologically sweet solutions to human problems offered by globally connected corporations. We reject this view.

The three essays in *Resolana: Emerging Chicano Dialogues on Community and Globalization* address issues of globalization, value clashes, and the role of la resolana in the lives of Hispanic people in the United States. *Resolana* derives from *resol* (the reflection of the sun) and refers to the sunny side of buildings where villagers gather to talk while protected from the elements. It is our metaphor for awareness.

Resolana's early intellectual development is documented in *Entre Verde y Seco*, a collection of oral history vignettes and in the journal *El Cuaderno*, both published in Dixon, New Mexico, by La Academia de la Nueva Raza (Academy of the New Humanity) at the height of the Chicano movement in the early 1970s.[4] La Resolana was first presented as La Academia's learning model in 1973 by Tomás Atencio, its leading exponent, and by Tony Mares and Miguel Montiel, who along with a group of activists, scholars, and students participated in the emerging resolana process.

La Academia's efforts have inspired a three-decade-long process of documentation of Indohispanic knowledge derived from life experiences. This documentation extends beyond the rural areas where La Academia conducted projects in the 1970s to include projects in San Antonio, Texas, that paralleled the music and arts projects in New Mexico, and oral history projects with Mexican farmworkers in Brawley and El Centro, California. In Arizona, Raymond Padilla and Miguel Montiel focused on how la resolana and the knowledge it uncovers can be integrated with the knowledge and human skills necessary to adapt and transform the institutions of the postindustrial age.[5]

In *Resolana: Emerging Chicano Dialogues on Community and Globalization* we present a Chicano perspective on the globalized world we seem to be blindly inheriting. Our view embraces (a) the wisdom traditional societies bring to bear in their adaptation to the industrial age; (b) resolana in action (community dialogues); and (c) network theory with its dispassionate view of cultural linkages as a basis for community cohesion, the democratic exchange of ideas, and the concerns for a global community. (Network theory, or graph theory, is a branch of mathematics based on the idea that the properties of a network govern how it can be used; for more detail, see chapter 3.)

In chapter 1, "El Oro del Barrio in the Cyber Age: Leapfrogging the Industrial Revolution," Tomás Atencio explores the theoretical groundwork of resolana and el oro del barrio. These concepts emerged from a story of change from an agrarian society to a postindustrial age in northern New Mexico villages. Both are responses to the threats and opportunities presented by the cyber age. Atencio asks, Is it possible for a partially non-Western culture, a culture in transition, appropriately and effectively to take advantage of the opportunities of the cyber age while protecting its core values against the perils this entails?

Atencio conceives of la resolana as a northern New Mexico village experience conceptually parallel to the Socratic dialogues. Both bring to light the knowledge and meaning of lived experience through purposeful exchange. La resolana parallels Paulo Freire's "circles of culture" and discloses the buried knowledge of an older, agrarian culture, not unlike Jürgen Habermas's idea that the psychoanalytic relationship uncovers the unconscious.[6] Dialogue shapes gems out of el oro del barrio and surfaces a collective wisdom that points the way to a life of health, wholeness, well-being, and contentment (*una vida buena y sana y alegre*). These ideas make possible the development of a "learning society," in which learning and knowledge building in everyday life can develop the policy priorities for a postindustrial society.

Montiel's "Resolana in Action: Dialogues on Success and Community" (chapter 2) examines stories of urban Mexican American/Chicano leaders—young and old, men and women—who are "making it," and in the process sheds light on the issues facing their community. Our assumption is that cultural action—our moral compass distinguishing good from bad—must be exercised in recognition of the Chicano experience, el oro del barrio. We assume that uncovering this gold from our community is not an individual but a communal action requiring awareness. The vehicle for this awareness is la resolana.

Because Montiel's chapter consists primarily of a series of dialogues, it is important to elaborate on the meaning of that form of discourse. David Bohm defines dialogue as "a stream of meaning flowing among and through us and between us."[7] Integral to it is the willingness to divulge and share assumptions (or opinions) about the world. Dialogue facilitates clarity of thought, thus enabling people to work together effectively. It is powerful because it enables us to examine our deepest assumptions.

Donald Spoto captures the spirit of la resolana (that is, dialogue and reflection) when he writes

> I contemplate, I think and allow myself to feel—and then reflection occurs: the other re-flects (bends back toward) me. The event or person peers out at me, in a way "speaks" to me, shows me myself, and so I enter into a situation of dialogue. I see a greater reality than that on which I focus, and a greater reality than myself. Connective threads suggest themselves; points of confluence begin to emerge— links between myself and others, between myself and the past. And in this realization, I have the capacity to escape from the chill prison of self.[8]

Thus, the important feature of community resolanas is the process. The resolanas reveal a dynamic, ever-growing community with diverse political perspectives, incomes, and ages; a community with a generational and gender divide; a community pushed by internal and external pressures toward the enfolding of a "Hispanic" nation. Accordingly, our community is not clear on what to call ourselves—Chicano, Hispanic, Mexican American, Indohispanic, or Latino. We describe ourselves as powerless, divided, and selfish; but also as diverse, dynamic, culturally focused, young, vibrant, and an awakening giant.

In *Culture Matters*, Lawrence Harrison and Samuel P. Huntington conjecture that Mexican (and by implication Mexican American) traditional cultural values impede a forward-looking adjustment to the West and its values. We strongly disagree that "adjustment" is a one-way street or that Mexicans and Mexican Americans need to do all the adjusting.

In "A Resolana on Networks: Chicanos, Connections, and Culture" (Chapter 3), E. A. "Tony" Mares reinterprets the concept of la resolana and its application to the broader world of ethnic communities. We began our discussions about this book by asking ourselves Huntington's question: Is Latin America part of Western civilization? We also asked the corollary of that question: Are Indohispanics part of Western civilization? Now that Huntington has clearly told us that Hispanics are a threat to the American way of life, our response becomes even more crucial. He writes, "Mexicans and other Latinos have not assimilated into mainstream U.S. culture, forming instead their own political and linguistic enclaves—from Los Angeles to Miami— and rejecting the Anglo-Protestant values that built the American dream. The United States ignores this challenge at its own peril."[9] The ethnocentrism and cultural provincialism of Huntington's remarks are truly stunning.

We do not see ourselves or our views as a threat to any culture's way of life. Yet there are several questions we need to deal with: Are Hispanics part of Western civilization and to what extent? How do the members of this complex culture relate to the processes of self and group identity, community, the nation-state, and globalization? How do Indohispanics network with each other and with those outside their immediate sphere? Although the forces of tribalism, nationalism, and globalization of the world economy form the deep background of many of the issues discussed, the topic of chapter 3 is primarily the role of networks and networking in the contemporary world.

In his research on Padre Antonio José Martínez (1793–1867), a key figure in early Chicano history (and the dark persona in Willa Cather's *Death Comes for the Archbishop*), Mares noticed that the good priest from Taos had extensive contacts with priests, communities, and government officials in Mexico.[10] This led Mares to think about networks and network analysis. Network analysis, he discovered, allows the investigator to examine the interconnections among individuals and communities and to explore the potential for future development of these connections within a nonideological context. Networks are omnipresent in nature and in society. There are neural networks in our brains, social networks in our families and communities, and a myriad of communication networks. Networks are neither good nor bad; they simply are.

Here Mares examines the appropriateness of network analysis to Indohispanic community responses. By studying the dynamics of networks, we may gain some insight into how la resolana works in both rural and urban settings and into the complexities of dynamic and evolving communities. While thinking about the role of networks in community connections, Mares also became aware of the numerous positive social movements for local community empowerment that have arisen around the world in response to globalization. These movements range from the Zapatistas in Chiapas, to the international slow food movement and indigenous movements in India and throughout Latin America and Canada. By understanding networks, we may gain a better sense of how to connect with like-minded persons and cultures around the world for the benefit of all people.

Applying the resolana process to el oro del barrio offers a more hopeful vision for the twenty-first century. We assume that individuals in all traditional cultures and cultures in transition possess important empirical knowledge and wisdom that may guide us in shaping values and crafting institutions for the present as well as the future. Our intent is to articulate an ideal that people can use to face life with creativity and courage and meaning.

In summary, this book draws insights from the height of the Chicano movement; la resolana—the sharing of knowledge derived from the gold of the community, el oro del barrio—takes root from the seeds of its early intellectual development with a broader, and we feel, timely application for adapting to the challenges of globalization. Our focus is not only on the substance of traditional societies or the importance of network theory, but also on the importance of community dialogues. Ours is a dissenting view of globalization, one that encourages a broader understanding beyond technological advancement and market expansion as the means to greater prosperity around the world.

We propose this analysis with humility. We are aware that abstract generalizations may falsify, or worse still, idealize or romanticize the human condition and our approach to it. We view ourselves as involved analysts of the Indohispanic condition, not as ideologues or founders of political movements.

El Oro del Barrio in the Cyber Age

Leapfrogging the Industrial Revolution

Tomás Atencio

El oro del barrio is not a product of academic philosophers. It is a name given in the 1960s to the values, wisdom, and applied knowledge that assured both meaning and survival to the Mexican American community within the dominant U.S. industrial society. El oro del barrio is both actual and imagined. It is known through the stories people tell. When people tell a story, either from their own experience or one that has been passed on to them, they often add their own reflections and interpretations. Moreover, the story unveils both memories of real activities as well as activities and images of the psyche. Psychic creations, or imagination, such as *cuentos* (stories), *mentiras* (tall tales), *chistes* (jokes), images, symbols, ceremony, and rituals, are integral parts of a community's knowledge foundations.[1] El oro del barrio is not, therefore, uncovered with social scientific methods; it is disclosed and understood through dialogue. The best way I can illustrate el oro del barrio and its importance to the subordinated Indohispanic society is through my own story.

I left my hometown in 1951. In my sporadic short, return visits, I noticed creeping changes in the village: roads were being paved; people with jobs in Los Alamos were building cinder-block houses; domestic water associations were bringing running water to homes; more people had automobiles. I thought nothing of these trends. In 1962 I returned permanently, settled in my ancestral village, and took a job as a child welfare worker with the New Mexico Department of Public Welfare in Rio Arriba County. Now the changes appeared ominous: the region was in the painful stages of profound transformation. Thus started my search to understand my changing homeland.

I began by ruminating on the texts and lectures I had read and heard as a student of social work, recalling episodes of the transition from an agricultural to an industrial society in eighteenth- and nineteenth-century Britain, and the ensuing social and cultural disarray. The conditions in the growing industrial cities fed by thousands of immigrants to the United States after the Civil War and the rise of social work in response to the social upheaval and suffering inflicted by industrialization lingered in my memory. I reflected on the birth of the American welfare state as a response to the Great Depression of 1929. I had lived through that in my childhood and remembered the PWA (Public Works Administration) workers who had dug latrines and built outhouses for rural villagers. As a public welfare worker, I carried out vestiges of these earlier policies.

Interestingly, I found myself in villages that had not fully made the transition to the industrial age. Yet some of them were less than twenty miles from Los Alamos, the birthplace of the nuclear age and the cradle of postindustrial society. In the 1960s, Los Alamos and the ancient pueblos and villages were at the center of this paradoxical transition. Los Alamos had grown out of the industrial age and was rapidly leading the world toward the cyber age; meanwhile, Indohispanic villagers and most Pueblo Indians had their minds and souls in an agrarian society and were barely touched by industrialization. This contradiction stirred thoughts that the Indohispanic and Indian villagers had skipped industrial society and suddenly found themselves in the midst of a rapidly advancing postindustrial age. Remarkably, these preindustrial societies and their traditions had endured to the middle of the twentieth century and had given meaning and social cohesion to their communities.

The jump over the industrial epoch had deprived the natives of the era's bounties and opportunities, yet had saved them from its perils. Villagers had missed the education and training necessary to develop the skills to succeed in an industrial society, but they had kept their culture intact. Ironically, for some villagers Los Alamos provided an employment substitute in the absence of an industrial economy. Welfare afforded a marginal but stable economic prop yet eroded the moral fiber of the community; it became industrial society's predominant legacy to New Mexico's villagers.

One villager and itinerant laborer often repeated to me his analysis of welfare, reasoning that it had introduced canned foods and dried milk to its recipients, which had caused homemakers to abandon homegrown foods and vegetables. Homemakers not receiving public assistance, he complained, were lured to this lifestyle as well, which placed an economic burden on the breadwinner who was still farming. Operating as he was from a male and subsistence agricultural perspective, my friend might not have had all the facts, but his analysis made sense. Women, too, had their say. Taxed to the limits of their time and energy in running households from the products of the land and doing farm chores when their husbands left the village for itinerant labor, homemakers sought relief wherever they could find it. In reality, families gained very few financial resources through wage labor. For some, welfare was the only source of cash in the village itself. As time passed, subsistence agriculture declined; concurrently, Indo-hispanic villagers were drawn into consumption and debt; many sold their homes and land because they needed the money, or just abandoned their inheritance and moved to the cities.

The modernization trend introduced by the railroad in the 1880s and accelerated by itinerant labor away from home and welfare at home made money a necessity but did not provide it through market avenues in the villages themselves. The New Mexico *manito* cultural enclave entered the modern age in the 1930s as an impoverished region,[2] a description the natives found unacceptable. It was a putdown. They did not see themselves as poor: they were living according to their traditions, which were threat-ened by a modernizing society. Within this changing society, the native wisdom and applied knowledge prevailed and the culture endured. This body of knowledge was not written down, it was not systematic; it lived in the people's memories and everyday life activities. As I was privileged to learn this knowledge by listening to people's stories, I pondered whether and how this wisdom could be applied in a society that was just emerging, a society that would otherwise have nothing to guide it but industrial-age values and institutions controlled by its dominant actors. Village culture had endured because industrial institutions and values had skipped over the northern New Mexican cultural enclave.

The homeland I found upon my return home was indeed a different place. My personal and professional vocation was forged by this awareness; my work, as I saw it, was to try and soften the blow to those caught in the vortex of change, and at the same time to rescue the subjugated knowledge that had sustained the community and had given meaning to its people living in an "agri-cultural" settlement within a predominantly industrial society.

In 1968, the counterculture movement discovered the villages. A wise Hispano elder observed that this was the "last invasion of the Anglo. After this," he cautioned, "we will no longer have claim over New Mexico as our homeland." He was right. People sold their land as if they were selling to a relative or village neighbor: below market value. Our inheritance was in fact placed on the marketplace, and soon its value as real estate escalated beyond most natives' reach.[3]

By the 1990s, money channeled into the villages from Los Alamos employment had raised the income levels of many families, transforming a subsistence economy to a wage-earning consumer economy based on a different set of values and thus creating personal and cultural tensions.[4] The postindustrial cultural fallout of Los Alamos onto the manito homeland had triggered a deadly social cancer: drugs. Other postindustrial phenomena, such as Indian gaming, have also entered the region, inflicting both direct and collateral social and cultural damage on Indohispanics and Native Americans while bringing income to the impoverished Pueblo community. Landownership among Indohispanic villagers has drastically decreased during the past two decades, changing the appearance and complexion of the historic settlements.

In launching my vocation, I unconsciously drew from all my experiences and formal education. In my training as a caseworker, I had completed part of my practicum at the Reiss-Davis Child Guidance Clinic in Los Angeles, California, under the tutelage of a psychoanalyst trained in Europe before World War II.[5] After working as a child-welfare caseworker for a year and a half in northern New Mexico, I became a community mental health consultant. Gradually, I turned away from casework to community organization, then known also as community development.

I worked in community organizing for many years but never identified my work or its theoretical underpinnings with any school. Undoubtedly, my social work training influenced my direction. I recall saying very early in my career that community development was not physical development; rather, it was an undertaking to bring people together around shared concerns, values, and visions to enhance one another's lives and to reach toward meaning and plenitude. Community, in other words, provides individuals with meaningful and authentic social security, builds the foundations for a more democratic and humane physical environment, and allows its members to take on a larger and more effective role in public service and social and political action.

In searching for that sense of community in northern New Mexico villages, I found that the social linkages that had kept the community alive were rapidly disintegrating. The extended family had collapsed along with correlated values of solidarity and reciprocity. The only apparently viable social institution left was the *acequia* and its decision-making body, *la comisión*. An acequia is a gravity-flow irrigation canal whose origins are in the Middle East. I focused on the acequia as creating a "community of interest"—a group with common interests and shared needs—which I used as a strategy for organizing.[6] The acequia worked well as an example of a community of interest because active participants in the organization were driven by the shared need for irrigation water to sustain family subsistence farming. On the sociopolitical side of the equation, the *comisión de acequia*, in fact, was a living example of village democracy that made possible peaceful negotiations over the distribution of water, a precious resource in an arid region. From then on, I looked for visions, needs, concerns, grievances, or interests that people shared with one another, all social characteristics of the acequia, in order to identify other communities of interest. Then I assessed what external forces and personal motives might prompt individuals to come together to affirm themselves and protest impediments to their quality of life. The "community of interest" is the first stage in this process. The second stage uses dialogue to deepen the community of interest's understanding of its shared concerns and visions and to discern possible pathways toward common goals and strategies for resisting obstacles to freedom and fulfillment. This process I initially called the "community of solution"; I now call it the "community in dialogue." In "community in action," the third stage, the "community of interest" acts on the knowledge, understanding, and elevated consciousness attained through dialogue.

In addition to the community of interest's legacy as an organizing tool, it also inspired a spiral of thought and action through dialogue and reflection on the action embedded in the individual and community stories. In short, this process leads to a new awareness and respond-ability. The ability to respond implies that action and reflection also foster the commitment, courage, and fortitude to respond to the revelations that occur in this new awareness.

I propose this logic for confronting the challenges of the cyber age. Its conclusion or goal is the revitalization of our community; the path toward that end is reclaiming el oro del barrio, the knowledge of our historical experience as well as the values and wisdom of our ancestors.

La Resolana and el Oro del Barrio

Here is a little history of la resolana and el oro del barrio, the context in which they were thought up and thought out, and their place within the emerging cyber age: In the late fifties, while a college student absorbed in the Socratic dialogues, I wondered whether other cultures and societies used dialogue to find meaning in their lived experience and understanding of their ultimate commitments. I was especially interested in my own heritage as an Indohispanic villager from northern New Mexico. Did our men come together as Socrates and the Sophists had done at the agora, to talk with one another and artfully spar to unmask rhetoric, unveil truth, and reflect on the meaning of their everyday lives? I found no parallels. There was, however, one place where men gathered to talk on sunny fall, winter, and spring days. It was known as la resolana. La resolana is the space defined by the south wall of a building that is shielded from the east and west winds, where the sun reflecting off the wall creates a place of warmth, light, and tranquility. In that place, men have gathered across the years to pass the time of day, exchange good and bad news, gossip, share jokes, and also talk about everyday life, about birth, and about death; they have told stories and shared memories of the past and have pondered the future. In la resolana there was no Socrates, a master at asking questions and fostering dialogue; instead, whoever was most knowledgeable on the subject at hand illuminated and guided the discussion. The counterparts to the Sophists were not the trained teachers in the village who promoted progressive cultural trends; rather, they were tradition-bound *pícaros* (men who survived by their wits), who were moored in agrarian society and lamented the changes that eventually would do away with la resolana and their lifeways.[7] While la resolana obviously originated as an activity of men in a patriarchal society, the process of resolana need not be restricted to males and in fact has not been in its subsequent development.

I did not mention my insight, or fantasy, to anyone for fear I would be charged with intellectual blasphemy for comparing a peasant gathering place in northern New Mexico to the enlightened Athenian agora or Plato's Academy. Yet, from time to time I reflected on the idea. Upon my return from schooling in social work, the vision of la resolana as a possible Indohispanic village parallel to the Athenian models resurfaced.

The possibilities for developing a reinterpreted and formalized resolana rested on an understanding of the culture, its values, and its ways of transmitting knowledge, information, and wisdom. I used my social work position to gain this understanding. As a social worker in a traditional Indohispanic rural area, I listened to the people's stories of the changes in the region and how these were affecting the intimate and spiritual relationship they had with the place where they were born and had lived all their lives. Most of these elderly folks had already reared their children, a good number of whom had left and settled somewhere else, mainly in California, Utah, Colorado, or Albuquerque. A few offspring remained in the villages and commuted anywhere from twenty to a hundred miles to jobs in Los Alamos. Among people I visited I found storytellers, *cuentistas*, who not only told of their immediate experiences but shared stories from the past, folktales, and folk songs. Almost everyone used *refranes* or *dichos*, proverbs or aphorisms, to make a point with a phrase of distilled wisdom. Often they coined their own sayings to express their most profound and meaningful beliefs. *Querencia*, the "meaning of place," for example, would be expressed, "De aquí no me salgo porque tengo que tener un lugar donde caer muerto" (I will not leave because I need a place to die). This was an elderly couple's response to my naive question whether they would ever move from the village to live with one of their children. In essence this phrase speaks of the people's tie to the earth in life and in death. It reveals their profound attachment to the earth, which in turn, disclosed its mysteries to them. Land and people were mutually ensouled, a phenomenon Theodore Abt calls "participation mystique."[8]

Listening to stories helped me understand individual perceptions about life, but I also detected a collective undercurrent, a collective consciousness or perhaps collective unconscious, that told of a people's shared beliefs and views about life. These conversations also revealed the knowledge and skills they used in everyday life to survive.

Life was *entre verde y seco*: it had its hills and valleys. Significantly, these stories highlighted the contradictions in northern New Mexico as well as the tensions and the quest for balance in everyday life; these stories fueled the development of la resolana and el oro del barrio.

The more I listened to people's life histories, the more I connected with my father's tales, which had lulled me to sleep when I was a child. I remembered some of them, but I felt the need for details. I had grown up with a father who was born in 1876, twenty-four years before the turn of the twentieth century; his father had been born in 1838, when New Mexico was part of present-day Mexico. My father's stories about his own life and about his father's and his father's father's connected with a lineage that stretched 150 years into the past and beyond. My father's only surviving brother, Eliseo, was in his late sixties. He had never married, lived alone, and refused to connect electricity to his modest home; he had no running water and had never owned an automobile. He preferred the preindustrial age. He had been a subsistence farmer and itinerant farmworker all his life. He was truly a peasant. One day I walked over to his place and sat on a bench in his room, which served as receiving room, kitchen, and library; he sat on the edge of his bed. I asked him about my grandfather's stories that my father had shared with me; he begged off, saying he had been born twenty-some years after my father and had missed most of those cuentos. Then he reached under his bed, pulled out a leather pouch, and drew from it a neat collection of old documents, stacked and folded in half. "But I have these," he said. They were the "Atencio papers" from the Atencio ancestral home.

I leafed through the fragile papers. The oldest was dated 1776, one hundred years before my father was born and as old as the United States. They were last wills and testaments, deeds of property transfer, and receipts dating up until the 1920s. Apparently, after my grandfather Noberto died, the addition of new documents had ceased. My uncle gave them to me with the understanding that they belonged to the Atencio heirs.

It was a sunny, unusually calm March day. I left my uncle's place and walked back to my home about a mile away. I had to pass by *la plaza*, the site of the main resolana in the village. Some *resolaneros* were chatting there,[9] and I was invited to join them. One asked what I had in the paper sack—my uncle had not given me the satchel. I pulled out the papers. "No me han de creer lo que me dio mi tío Eliseo" (You won't believe what my uncle gave me). The men gathered around while we tried to decipher the ancient classic Spanish script. That activity spun off conversations that lasted until the sun sank behind the black mesa to the west and what was left of the day turned chilly, causing the men to disperse.

In la resolana that day the resolaneros told stories of their families and reminisced about similar papers stored somewhere in the attics of their parents' homes. Others told how documents had been lost or trashed. Most significant for my journey, the papers spurred conversations beyond the relaxed chatter, bringing other themes to the fore, as other activities in the village sometimes did as well. La resolana in my native village that day confirmed the possibilities of resolana, the concept I had envisioned a decade before. Plato's Academy had found its counterpart in la resolana Chicana, with modifications, of course.[10]

A few years later the Chicano movement exploded in the streets of Denver, Los Angeles, and other urban centers, in land grant activism in New Mexico, in farmworkers organizing from Texas and California to Ohio. There were school walkouts in major cities. These events gave rise to Chicano studies as a university discipline. I was then at the University of Colorado, directing a program for migrant workers. Although there is much to say about that experience in relation to the application of the community of interest model, my concern here is with the idea of Chicano studies in universities. Here we are, I mused, missed by an educational system that equipped people for industrial society, and when we are at the threshold of a postindustrial world, the university offers us the ideological drippings of its industrial legacy.[11]

Fortuitously, the rise of the Chicano movement coincided with a growth in writings about the future and the impact of technology on society and culture. I found the writings on technological progress relevant to the future of Chicanos. Lewis Mumford wrote in *The Myth of the Machine* that technological progress would directly affect traditional societies by destroying or burying the knowledge derived from those peoples' life experiences. Robert Theobald warned in "The Cybernation Revolution" that automation would affect the distribution of income through employment, recommending that we must develop a new "human and constitutional right—the right to an income." He also called for a new social ethic generated from within the community rather than one imposed from above. This suggested to me that we must develop values and institutions appropriate to the coming cyber age rather than embracing remnants from industrial society. In *The Technological Society* (1967), Jacques Ellul warned, "Man has lost all contact with his natural framework. He cannot pierce the shell of technology to find again the ancient milieu to which he was adapted for hundreds of thousands of years."[12]

If these futurists were right, why should we Chicanos want access to the waning industrial society? Why should we not prepare ourselves for a direct transition from a preindustrial to a postindustrial age? Why not offer our traditional, preindustrial institutions, values, and ways of knowing and learning as guides and models for the postindustrial age?[13]

I saw the emerging field of Chicano studies in the context of these questions, but I could not envision the university system responding to them and empowering Chicano studies to address them. At that point in my life I saw the establishment of Chicano studies as condescending and, from the Indohispanic vantage point, as a maneuver, the co-optation of a valuable resource. The university was not giving us much, but through Chicano studies it was introducing its students to another civilization: the mestizo, with its legacy anchored in Arabic Spain and pre-Columbian America. Why not bring along its long-subjugated body of knowledge?

It seemed the right time to launch a process corresponding to Plato's Academy, to build a knowledge base from the Chicano experience, paralleling at a different level of conceptualization and action what the Athenians had done in their golden era. I returned to my hometown of Dixon (La Plaza del Embudo), New Mexico, and with others interpreted and created a "new resolana."[14] The collaborators came together under an organization known as La Academia de Aztlán, later renamed La Academia de la Nueva Raza, a name that claimed the Western intellectual legacy (in the adoption of "Academia") and incorporated the idea of a new humanity. The quest for a new humanity was both a vision and a vocation. In naive arrogance and ignorance of the enormous and uncertain task ahead, we proposed to build a body of knowledge from the stories and folklore of the Mexican American—Chicano—people in the Southwest. We would create an alternative educational process that would uncover and compile knowledge as well as raise and expand consciousness. This process would validate our own experience as a basis for knowledge and prepare us for the challenges of the postindustrial age.

As La Academia was evolving I also was an occasional consultant on Chicano-related programs to the National Institute of Mental Health (NIMH). With the same theme in mind of building an autochthonous body of knowledge, I proposed that Chicano mental health programs create a body of knowledge from the culture's history and the everyday life experiences of Chicanos. This knowledge could inform strategies for reaching out to the community with preventive services and also contribute to the development of culturally appropriate therapeutic models.

The name el oro del barrio had not yet become part of my vocabulary. But because of my occasional work with the NIMH, I was recommended as a consultant to a barrio mental health program in San Antonio, Texas, then under the San Antonio Unity Council. In that role I was a learner as well as a teacher. The project introduced me to the idea of el oro de barrio. *Barrio*, which means neighborhood, had often been talked of by some observers with derision and seen as the source of the social problems in the Mexican American community. The young activists in San Antonio turned this attitude around and offered the hidden gems of knowledge, wisdom, rituals, and beliefs in the barrio and its culture as the healing source for their social and psychological ills. Their idea that the healing could come from the community and culture—that *la cultura cura* (culture heals)—was a perfect fit with the goals and ongoing work of La Academia.

With the project's staff approval, I appropriated the term el oro del barrio for La Academia. At the same time, Academia efforts, which had been focused on northern New Mexico, expanded to San Antonio. Under the leadership of Tito Villalobos Moreno, a musician-composer-arranger, and Jesús "Chista" Cantú, an artist, who were collaborating with barrio mental health worker José María "Chema" Saenz and several artists, La Academia de la Nueva Raza en San Antonio was organized.

The concepts of la resolana and el oro del barrio came together. The gold of the neighborhood, reflected in the bright sun of our dialogues, became the currency of knowledge building and consciousness raising. The body of knowledge uncovered in and by la resolana was the people's story, their wisdom, beliefs, values, reflections, joys, sorrows, ceremony and ritual, as well as practical and applied knowledge. The stories and their content became el oro del barrio, and the process keeps evolving as it is applied to diverse experiences.

The Chicano Movement and La Academia de la Nueva Raza

My initial concern that Chicano studies would not respond to the need for an autochthonous body of knowledge did not prove universally true. Chicanos studies programs at UCLA, Berkeley, and California State University at Northridge, as well as the Chicano Fellows at Stanford University moved rapidly in this direction. Chicano colleges built on the existing university model yet committed to alternative learning and indigenous knowledge sprouted throughout the country. The alternative education movement spread among Chicano activists, who challenged the theory and practice as well as the social arrangements of the mainstream learning experience. Moreover, the Chicano movement developed a strong cultural front. The most visible and effective groups were, in some cases still are, El Teatro Campesino, Centro Cultural de la Raza in San Diego, Con-Safos in Los Angeles and San Antonio, the Royal Chicano Air Force (RCAF) in Sacramento, and Octavio Romano's Tonatiuh International and Quinto Sol Publications. Within this cultural movement, La Academia de la Nueva Raza carved out the role and task of recovering and refining el oro del barrio as the basis for cultivating a Chicano consciousness and creating a relevant body of knowledge.[15]

Although there are other approaches to understanding the Chicano movement, I suggest the movement was both driven by and drawn by an emerging ethnic and class consciousness. The origin of the term *Chicano* tells of its relationship to ethnicity and class. Diego Vigil wrote in "Marx and Chicano Anthropology" that the word Chicano originated with the Spanish conquerors' pronunciation of the x in *Mexica* as *ch*—hence, Mechica or Mechicano. *Mexica* was used in the colonial period as a descriptor for all Aztec lower classes.[16] Ernesto Galarza, a scholar and activist, used to say that Mexican Indian peasants immigrating to this country during the Mexican Revolution were referred to as Chicanos, a term of derision. In the movement, Chicano identity emphasized for mestizos the Indian part of their Indohispanic mixed heritage.[17]

Chicanos found their indigenous roots in Aztlán, a mythical place in the region of the Four Corners, where New Mexico, Arizona, Utah, and Colorado come together and whence supposedly originated the Aztecs, who ended up in Tenochtitlán, now Mexico City. The road to Aztlán was the Chicanos' pathway to a homeland—a place both mythic and real to which they could anchor their identity as Indios. The term had political implications as well, for the region of Aztlán also constituted the central part of the southwestern United States, which was annexed from Mexico in the settlement of the Mexican War in 1848. Chicanos were, in theory, reclaiming a captured homeland that also happened to be the cradle of their Indian ethnicity.[18]

La Academia de la Nueva Raza interfaced with the Chicano movement's quest to recover what had been lost to Mexican Americans. Its vision was to create a new humanity out of the pathos that we and our ancestors have endured as strangers in our own land, and out of the faith that sustained our culture and us. In the face of uncertainty in a world bent on unfettered competition in the marketplace, global political conflict between the haves and the have-nots, the clash of cultures, and gross environmental degradation in the name of progress and technological advancement, we accepted the distant dream of La Nueva Raza.

In forging this new humanity, Academia cofounder Luis Jaramillo declared a "belief in the mystery of man because we refuse to accept a destiny that is not ours to forge. . . . La Nueva Raza is both a vocation and a dream. . . . The vocation to bring about that which is beyond the ethnic and beyond poor and rich." For now we are ethnic, *mestizos, mulattos,* and like others with a similar legacy, we must become the 'new cornerstone for democracy.'"[19]

Reaching for La Nueva Raza, Jaramillo argues, is a cultural evolutionary process. Robert Wright, a science writer, and Luis Jaramillo tread parallel paths. Both perceive evolution as a branch of science, but they also see it as a process with purpose, with direction. For Jaramillo the direction is toward La Nueva Raza. Wright is interested in the idea that evolution can be directed by consciousness in living bodies, laying a burden as well as a challenge on the human species to guarantee its own survival.[20] Both reflect the thinking of Pierre Teilhard de Chardin.

Pierre Teilhard de Chardin (1881–1955), a French Jesuit priest and paleontologist, believed in biological evolution and also that there is an evolution of a collective body of thought. In his introduction to Teilhard de Chardin's *The Phenomenon of Man*, Sir Julian Huxley summarizes this idea as follows: "The incipient development of mankind into a single psychosocial unit, with a single noosystem, or common pool of thought, is providing the evolutionary process with the rudiments of a head." He adds, "It remains for our descendants to organize this global noosystem more adequately, so as to enable mankind to understand the process of evolution on earth more fully and to direct it more adequately."[21] Evolution at its next level will lead toward the unity of humankind.

Teilhard de Chardin and Jaramillo offer optimistic outlooks, but neither the noosphere—that is, the development of a common pool of thought— nor La Nueva Raza is assured. These are visions of what the world can be and where it is logically headed. As Wright says, "it is the logic of human destiny."[22] It is up to the "head"—humans—to direct the evolution to the next sphere. This should be our vocation, our commitment to ensuring the survival of the human species.[23]

Wright's work distills Teilhard de Chardin's vision to the notion that societies and cultures have endured, as has nature, because there are no absolute winners or absolute losers among the contenders for survival. Everybody, every cell, every living thing, wins and also loses in a nonzero-sum game. The opposite would be a zero-sum environment where some win while the others lose; there evolution would stop and life would eventually cease.

Those of us involved in La Academia recognized that the cyber revolution would create both opportunities and perils that could either advance the noosystem and guide evolution toward La Nueva Raza or destroy the global ecological and political balance. The most terrifying possibility is a human maladaptation to the cyber age in which some win and others lose, as occurs in the global free market. Community as the source of authentic and meaningful social security is an example of a nonzero-sum approach. Such a way allows for sharing of resources, of meaning; it entails embracing the values of cooperation, sharing, and respect for others.

Turning to philosophy has been logical and natural for La Academia and its legacy, for the biggest challenges of this transformation impelled by technological advances are moral and spiritual. Asociados of La Academia recognized this, as did many Chicano cultural activists. Among them were those who followed the teachings of Maestro Andrés Segura. Maestro Andrés, a Nahuatl spiritual leader, came to the United States from Mexico to assist Chicanos in their journey back to Aztlán. The vision and logic of La Nueva Raza, although derived from Western thought, had a parallel, we realized, in the ideas of this Mexican spiritual leader.[24]

The wisdom of the ancients, as exemplified by Segura, may be invoked as we struggle toward a nonzero-sum world. It teaches that we must look at the other person as our other self. In Mayan this is expressed *in lah kech: tu eres mi otro yo*. A similar belief in Judeo-Christian doctrine is "love thy neighbor as thyself." La resolana and el oro del barrio are pathways toward La Nueva Raza, the dreams, visions, and aspirations of a common pool of thought, a nonzero society.

El Oro del Barrio and the Future

Although Chicanos generally missed industrial society's opportunities and benefits, that loss strengthened the Mexican American community's resolve to survive. El oro del barrio was in part responsible for that strength of mind and will. It is in family solidarity, reciprocity, respect, courage, honor, and *vergüenza* (moral sensibility); in *la vida buena y sana* (a life of health, whole-ness, and well-being) and *herbolarios/as* and *curanderas/os* (traditional healers); in spirituality, ceremony, ritual, faith, and belief in mystery; in querencia (sense of place); in the viability of the economics of frugality, a commitment to self-reliance, and a work ethic that was not tied to employment; in fiesta; in humor; in the virtue of working the land; and in the value of harmony with nature. Most important, el oro del barrio carries the consciousness and meaning of sharing and of community; it encompasses the nonzero-sum idea and its practice.

My challenge has been to interpret these cultural vestiges and to dem-onstrate their value and utility in a postindustrial age, while heeding Alvin Toffler's warning not to invent "a fake romantic past in our rush to judge the present."[25] I arrived at my interpretation by going back to my early days as a social worker and by reflecting on my conversations with my uncle.

That spring when I got the Atencio documents I had another signifi-cant conversation with Tío Eliseo.[26] I sought advice on planting chile and corn. His response was a question: "¿Y 'onde vas agarrar la semilla?" Where was I going to get the seed? I told him, "from an old lard bucket in la despensa [the storeroom], left there by my father at least eight years ago, five years before he died."

"You are fortunate," he said, "because those are native seeds. Son del maíz concho y el chile nativo." He advised me never to use Las Cruces seeds; they are made in laboratories and are not attuned to the seasons. (Las Cruces is the home of New Mexico State University and a center of agricultural research.) "Only the native seeds can adapt to climatic changes," he explained.

He went on to say that the seasons would change in New Mexico around the turn of the coming century, and we would be better prepared if we had native seeds. I was startled by his explanation! Forty years later I am amazed by the accuracy of his predictions.

I listened intently and pondered whether some things of the past would be well suited to deal with a world of climatic changes and uncertainty. As he explained the old ways, Tío Eliseo lamented the changes, pointing out that we were losing our language; that farming—people raising their own food—was also declining. He also talked about the loss of respect and trust in family and community relations. This loss has weakened the core of community. "Ya no hay respeto, ni tampoco hay palabra de hombre" (There is neither respect nor honor in man's word). "In the future," he said,

> We are going to have to live as we lived in the past, when food went from the earth to the kitchen without going through a store. This was possible because the family members worked and lived together. We will return to those ways—when we have to trust each other, work together, and help each other—because "science" will destroy itself and send us to the past. It is destroying nature, the way things are intended to be. We have to save what we can. Start with the seeds.

This made sense: everything starts with a seed of one kind or another. Seeds sustain and ensure the cycle of life.

Tío Eliseo's perspective was not without theoretical or academic support. Lewis Mumford wrote, "Western man not merely blighted in some degree every culture that he touched, whether 'primitive' or advanced, but he also robbed his own descendants of countless gifts of art and craftsmanship, as well as precious knowledge passed on only by word of mouth that disappeared with the dying languages of dying peoples." Referring to Westerners' colonization and technological progress, Mumford adds, "Western man . . . would have been far more successful had he paid closer attention to the cultures he disrupted and destroyed; for in wrecking them he was reducing his own intellectual working capital."[27]

Writing about the end of the industrial era, Robert Theobald has called for new values and institutions for the postindustrial age: "The goals of the industrial era are obsolete. We can no longer afford to strive for maximum economic growth. To do so will worsen water, land, and environmental problems; increase unemployment because of the job-replacement effects of computers and robots; and make the rich countries even more dependent on Third World countries for energy and raw materials."[28]

Theobald was not touting preindustrial modes of life; he was saying we must build institutions appropriate for this coming age because we cannot rely on the institutions and values of the industrial age. Unfortunately, the cyber age is driven by industrial-age values and organized around its institutions. A real concern is that, with America's triumph in the Cold War and its military might, industrial-age capitalism is being adapted to the cyber age, and thus interconnecting the globe but ignoring the need for regulation and contributing to the destruction of traditional societies. Western, or U.S.–style, globalism is zero-sum: one party wins while the other loses.

In its absence of regulation and zero-sum posturing, postindustrial capitalism mimics nineteenth-century unregulated industrial phenomena. The challenge we face is enormous. The peasant reaction to unregulated capitalism in the nineteenth century turned into fascism; in the industrial working class it resulted in Marxism or communism. Out of that also emerged the more benign welfare state, which came to an end with the rise of the cyber age. For years futurists have predicted that the "third wave," in Alvin Toffler's terms, will bring a rise of tribalism and retribalization, terrorism, and other modes of defense by the defenseless in the face of the unlimited power of an unbridled global free-market economy and the exploitation of natural resources—oil and other energy sources—in "underdeveloped" countries.[29] The next encounter on this global economic freeway is certain to be the clash of civilizations. For rather than tempering its global free-market posture, the United States has embarked on a course that would remake the rest of the world into its image of human progress.[30]

In the United States, the middle class is vanishing. This is evident in the displacement of traditional industrial workers, who must seek new employment in the knowledge and service sectors. The former requires additional training and education; the latter generally offers lower-paying, unstable jobs without benefits. Immigrants, both legal and illegal, hold many of these latter jobs. More poignant is the great number of single mothers holding two jobs to support their children and provide the basics and still unable to afford child care or health insurance.[31] We must heed the wisdom of sages like my Tío Eliseo and futurists such as Mumford and Theobald.

Technology and el Oro del Barrio

An important emblem of the cyber age is the computer and its impact on society and culture. Information technology is rapidly changing the occupational patterns that had become institutionalized in industrial society. The blue-collar industrial worker is disappearing in the face of technological advances. Instead of factory workers, society now calls for knowledge workers who must be adequately prepared to hold new occupations. And the word is that preparation is not a one-time effort. Learning must continue in order for the worker to keep up with the changes in the world. There is no class distinction among the knowledge workers; rather, they are "uniclass," even if some make more money than others.[32] Knowledge professionals are generally defined by key components of postindustrial society: information and media technology, globalization, and medical and biotechnology. These knowledge-related professions range from traditional ones such as medicine and law, to the sciences and engineering, software, business, banking, finance and management, higher education, media management, and transportation. Eventually the uniclass will develop into the dominant social class, but it will not be the large middle class of the industrial age; it will be a smaller upper class. The lower classes will probably start where the middle class used to be and scale downward to the service workers, the working poor, the poorly educated, and the single parents formerly supported by the welfare state. The unemployable will be the destitute, homeless, ill, or disabled.

Theoretically, computer technology and the Internet advance democratization and bring equity and equal access to information. They promise a flattening of the hierarchy of information and freedom from control by a few. The digital divide that has denied many nations, groups, and individuals these opportunities seems to be narrowing, at least in the United States, as more ethnic minorities gain access to the Internet. Even so, education, knowledge, and money are necessary to penetrate the digital barrier. Moreover, recent policies associated with the war against terror threaten to curtail much of the freedom made available by the Internet.

As information technology creates opportunities and perils for the workforce, it also changes global economics. Digital technology has spun a global telecommunications network of financial institutions that has transformed industrial society's corporations into enormous monsters. Globalization has made available cheap sources of labor around the world. Fueled by an ideology that justifies industrial capitalism and advanced by free-trade agreements among nations, the globalization of the economy has widened the gap between the haves and have-nots. It has fueled the immigration of workers from poor countries to rich countries, a phenomenon that has been skirted by free-trade agreements promoted by the United States. Furthermore, cyber-age commerce is invading traditional societies, in many cases corroding their languages, exploiting women and children, and attracting consumers, thus causing permanent changes in their cultural patterns.

In the United States, the transfer of jobs to other countries, referred to as outsourcing, is said to be a boon to corporations and even to public agencies, and eventually its positive effects are supposed to trickle down to America's struggling labor force. It creates wealth for a few and lower costs for public agencies, but it also erodes a nation's labor force and threatens the health and stability of the environment. This trend confirms Theobald's predictions, which led him to argue that income is a right and that there is a need to revive the idea of some kind of guaranteed income.[33] Ignoring this trend nurtures the seeds of terrorism and violence from within.

Since the end of the Cold War, transnational commerce, justified by strong ideological forces, has been impelling national governments of industrial economies to dismantle the welfare state and divert health and social services to the private sector. Along with this transition came the demise of the idea of political economy. There is neither the will nor an institution left to level the economic playing field: the zero-sum idea has prevailed; some win, others lose. The nation-state has lost control over its domestic agenda to meet social and human needs. The majority of the populace in the United States is hostage to a health-care system that is a market commodity. Witness the disaster of Clinton's comprehensive health-care plan, the rise of HMOs, the wealth of the health insurance industry, and the countless people for whom health insurance is out of reach. Even Democrats were supportive of this capitalist trend, as Clinton's signature set in motion the removal of the family safety net of the welfare state. This drift cannot be justified by the argument that it saves money, for we see the national deficit skyrocketing beyond comprehension as the wealthy get tax relief. Is this trend driven instead by private-sector forces seeking to further privatize services now provided by the government? There is no policy to address the ethical and moral questions raised by these changes.

The most insidious and dangerous aspect of the global economy is its public relations arm: the media; the same corporations and businesses that control the global economy control the communications industry, the flow of information, and the kind of information conveyed. The growth of unrestrained consumption promoted via the media with the concurrent deepening of credit card debt has created a modern form of serfdom. "Consumership" has replaced citizenship. And since the September 11 attack, the media have been used to defend repressive laws such as the Patriot Act, label those who question the erosion of our civil rights unpatriotic, and justify wars with Iraq and Afghanistan. More troubling is the use of the media to influence public opinion with half-truths and altered intelligence findings. The manipulation of images and of intelligence data has resulted in misperceptions such as that Saddam Hussein had weapons of mass destruction and that he and Osama bin Laden collaborated on the 9/11 attack. These misrepresentations alone have killed more than four thousand American servicemen and women and many more thousands of Iraqis. Meanwhile, we get images of a heroic-looking George Bush clad in a flight jacket emerging from a fighter jet on an aircraft carrier and proclaiming victory over Saddam Hussein's Iraq. Six years later the war continues. It has been redefined as a global war on terror, a tactic to instill fear of another 9/11-style attack and justify ever-escalating expenditures for war.

Tío Eliseo's comments that science was destroying nature were not prompted by reports about global warming or other warnings regarding the degradation of nature. Rather, he had lived, as I had, from the days when we could drink water from the river or the acequia without getting sick, until the 1960s, when this was no longer possible. Since the mid-1940s villagers had recognized the dangers of radiation, as men pushing wheelbarrows full of waste in the Los Alamos National Laboratories suddenly turned ashen, went home, and died. In the villages, meanwhile, children were dying of leukemia. Despite the evidence from Los Alamos and the knowledge that chemicals, including commercial fertilizer, were polluting the land, we had been told that modern technology would improve nature. Biotechnology promised to increase food supplies throughout the world without taking into account the social and environmental fallout from the changes. Genetic engineering would create new seeds and along with them a patent granting ownership of them to individuals and corporations. In time these modified seeds will be priced out of the reach of small farmers in America and underdeveloped countries throughout the world. Moreover, there is no assurance that the introduction of modified organisms into the environment will not have adverse effects on animals and humans. Some experts believe that biotechnology could have long-term consequences through undermining the diversity of nature. The new discipline of bioethics has emerged in response to these threats.[34]

Pharmaceuticals are in many ways related to biotechnology, mainly through the scientific knowledge both require. Although questions have been raised in the *Encyclopedia of the Future* concerning the possible adverse effects of biotechnology on humans and nature, no concerns have been raised about pharmaceuticals. Instead, the predictions are that "by 2020, pharmaceuticals will have played an important role in curing and preventing major diseases. Pharmaceuticals will be an integrated component of health care customized for each of us as bio-chemically unique individuals."[35]

Such innovations are being made possible by new theoretical knowledge of communications at the molecular level that is leading to a technology that blocks out molecular information to prevent disease before it occurs. This technology will be either ingested, via medications, or inserted, via small devices implanted in the body that will have the capacity to monitor a person's condition and prescribe and deliver the appropriate medication to curb the disease. These miniature instruments and drugs will be created and manufactured by a handful of laboratories and corporations throughout the globe. Pharmaceuticals under the control of a select few will dictate a distinct health-care system of customized medicine, rendering our current system of human intervention and preventive public health obsolete and anchoring the health-care program deeper into the free-market economy. Pharmaceuticals will go back to the future, as they will integrate into their services what has been known as alternative medicine, such as homeopathic therapy, acupuncture, and nonprescription drugs, and no doubt indigenous medicines and herbs. At this point, I envision that pharmaceuticals will invade traditional societies and seize their knowledge and herbs via patent and copyright.

It is clear that knowledge drives the cyber age. Daniel Bell calls "codified theoretical knowledge" the axial principle of postindustrial society. In other words, theoretical knowledge is central to the social, economic, and political workings of society.[36] Two examples of the centrality of theoretical knowledge are biotechnology/genetic engineering and pharmaceuticals, the former linked to the modification of nature in order to maintain and improve life, and the latter to the creation and development of technology to prevent and cure disease. But if only a limited number of companies throughout the world will produce the modified organisms of biotechnology and the custom-made devices and drugs to treat the populace, extremely valuable knowledge will be controlled by a few corporations and individuals. This suggests that health care in the future will be provided exclusively through the market, an ominous scenario.

The assertion that codified theoretical knowledge is central to postindustrial society does not invalidate traditional and everyday life knowledge. We must assert the value of indigenous and traditional knowledge in everyday life. We must also be vigilant about who or what controls and defines knowledge and wary of attempts to subjugate particular types of knowledge and their keepers.[37] These brief narratives demonstrate the urgency to develop the appropriate institutions and values that will make the transition to the cyber age more peaceful, just, and civil. We are at the threshold of a dark new age.

How can el oro del barrio play a role in this gargantuan task? If Tío Eliseo were alive today, I would sit on the same old bench and thank him for teaching me about the nurturance of life expressed in the logic of nature and in the ability of the old seeds to adapt to climatic changes. I would also discuss present realities.

Yes, Tío, you are right," I would say, "We must not lose our language; we must reclaim our ways, in which people had vergüenza; children respected their elders; and people respected life and each other, and valued cooperation, trust, and a strong community. We should restore the faith of our ancestors, their ways of health and wholeness, and work with the natural balance in nature to live una vida buena y sana y alegre. We need to question the use of genetically altered seeds. We must preserve water for agriculture and oppose making it a commodity. And we need to be aware of the limitations of modern science and be cognizant that technology cannot solve all our problems, including the ones it might create. Yet, we must also honor the fact that science has contributed immensely to our understanding of nature and to human well-being.

What we need is a way of looking at life, a philosophy, that gives ultimate value to the sanctity of life and protects it so that it can continue. Some years back, my wife, Consuelo, and I were searching our memories for a phrase that describes a state of total well-being, where one feels content, healthy, and whole. Consuelo came up with the descriptive phrase and concept that our people use: bueno y sano.

The concept of una vida buena y sana has undergone considerable reflection and dialogue since I first suggested it as an ethic for the postindustrial society. Since then we have discovered in the folklore the concept of *alegría* (happiness) as part of la vida buena y sana. We now say "la vida buena y sana y alegre," a life of health, wholeness, well-being, and happiness.[38]

One of the greatest social impacts of industrialization on agricultural communities has been the division of labor and the creation of individual employment outside the home, which has had the effect of severing production from consumption. People no longer farm and consume their own food; today they are only consumers. This has altered the family in many ways. The nuclear family has replaced the extended family, and numerous institutions have assumed the roles of community. The values of reciprocity and the consciousness of sharing and community solidarity have been distorted or replaced by individualism and competition. The practice of helping one another has been institutionalized through tax codes and organized charities. The values of honor, trust, and vergüenza have been replaced by contracts and legal agreements. Natural ways of health and healing have been largely ignored or belittled by modern medicine. Community as the source of meaningful and authentic social security has begun to crumble. The game has been changing from a nonzero-sum to a zero-sum approach in which some are absolute winners while others are absolute losers.

From a strictly pragmatic viewpoint, the primary reason for seeking guidance from preindustrial values, institutions, and ways of living—the major thrust of this essay—is that industrialization has disabled or distorted many traditional values and their corresponding institutions. I suggest using el oro del barrio and adopting the concept, vision, and practice of una vida buena y sana y alegre—a life of health, wholeness, well-being, and happiness—to reclaim the values of human dignity, justice, sharing, and respect for nature and to foster a balance between human values and science and technology. El oro del barrio holds vestiges of wisdom that are still vital in many cultures around the world, a treasure that needs to be recognized. It is time to uncover those life-sustaining cultural beliefs and practices and apply them in reenergizing our communities: the future may be yesterday.

La Resolana: A Pathway toward a Learning Society for the Cyber Age

As we open our minds and hearts to spiritual and moral ideals, we also must seek practical avenues to confront the challenges of the cyber age. The vision of a learning society made up of learning communities can be used as an overarching concept for responding to the requirements of the cyber age. The learning society is a strategy for making learning and the uncovering and building of knowledge ubiquitous in everyday life; its two fundamental goals are cognitive learning and consciousness raising. The first entails learning how to use our minds critically to acquire knowledge and practical human skills appropriate for everyday life and especially to meet the technological requirements of the cyber age. The principal skill demanded by the cyber age is a literacy that extends beyond traditional literacy to include technology, information, health, legal, economic, media, eco-, and global literacy.[39] It takes into account not only the cognitive aspects of learning, but also the total field and experience within which the individual lives and moves. Consciousness raising, on the other hand, provides a new awareness of the challenges of the cyber age. These two components of the learning society bear the fruit of a "new awareness with respond-ability."[40]

In La Academia de la Nueva Raza the idea of a learning society grew out of our examination of and reflection on everyday life in traditional New Mexican villages.[41]

From the stories of traditional people, ideas of a new literacy and of consciousness raising emerge. We discovered that individuals learned by doing daily tasks. Young men learned how to butcher animals under the supervision of experienced men. Young men and women learned anatomy as they prepared the animal parts. As the young were carrying out their tasks, they were instructed on the meaning and importance of certain procedures: "Mucho cuidado con la hiel, si quebras la vejiga se contamina la carne. Córtale el nervio en la pierna pa' que se ablande la carne." (Be very careful with the bile, if you puncture the gallbladder, you'll spoil the meat. Cut the nerve in the thigh so that the muscles relax and the meat softens.) And so went the instruction.

Young women learned to deliver babies by apprenticing under experienced midwives. They learned to plaster with mud, make *hornos* (adobe ovens), and weave cloth through observation and practice.

Beliefs, ceremony, and rituals were passed on to young men through the Penitente society, a lay religious brotherhood.[42] They learned the doctrine and ethical commitments by actively participating in prayers, hymns, rituals, and service to the Penitente brotherhood and their families. Young women learned the rites, rituals, prayers, and hymns through participation in female religious societies. They got their practical knowledge about the use of herbs for health and well-being as well as cooking from parents and mentors.

Storytelling was the primary way of passing on life lessons, knowledge, values, norms, and moral guideposts. We believe there is a strong parallel between this traditional educational model and the new model arising out of the needs of a postindustrial society.

So the young learned to understand their everyday life experiences and their culture while incorporating a body of knowledge and traditional values and norms. It occurred to me that if one were to place a canopy over a traditional New Mexican village, one would have a school, a learning community where the skills and knowledge necessary to sustain and give meaning to life in that particular society were taught experientially. Learning and doing were inseparable: one did and thereby one learned. Conversation and reflection usually took place between activities, and the next time the same task was performed an opportunity to apply compounded knowledge from the first experience was created. A growing body of knowledge emerged from such experiences.

This insight brought to mind Paulo Freire's praxis learning.[43] In the educational institutions of industrial society, learning has become separated from practice. And once knowledge has been severed from practice, learning becomes the mere transference of information from those who have it to those who do not. Learning and knowledge have thus become isolated from each other and from action, yet they mesh with each other, like cogs in the industrial wheel.

The idea of a learning society took a leap into the policy arena as I began to ponder the fate of the welfare state—an industrial-epoch institution that some were beginning to call learnfare because of its emphasis on training for jobs—in postindustrial society. Most compassionate individuals would agree that some form of the welfare state, or at least its safety net aspects, must endure for those who fall through the cracks in a market economy. Theobald's idea of the right to an income accompanied by a comprehensive health-care system would be a perfect fit. It seemed to me that as social policy was turning away from the welfare state, the prudent response would be to implement a guaranteed income and a single-payer health-care program and move toward a learning society. The government would make a full commitment to ensure its citizenry would have the opportunity to become technologically literate, especially in media technology. It would also prepare the populace in the use of appropriate (low-tech) and affordable technology that sustains a healthy environment. Such a learning society would also emphasize the arts and humanities. Learning processes such as dialogue would be used to uncover and reclaim subjugated autochthonous and historical knowledge. In addition, the arts and humanities would inspire the psyche, sharpen the mind, and open the pathway to creativity and innovation, the driving forces in a knowledge-based society. Ultimately, this would contribute toward a new awareness and an expanded consciousness. Such a policy, if implemented, would make the general population fully literate.

Recognizing that political economy is not part of the market equation, I realize the idea of a state-supported learning society is utopian. Nonetheless, the idea of a learning society driven by experiential learning seemed like a logical approach for reclaiming the self-reliance of preindustrial society, thus filling the gap left by the welfare state. La Academia de la Nueva Raza encouraged experiential learning by way of storytelling. Its members conducted dialogues with people, asking them to talk about their childhood experiences and their lives as adults and recording these stories on

audiotape. These conversations were framed by the participants' perceptions and interpretations of changes they had witnessed from their childhood to the present. The dialogues proceeded through imagined spirals of
thought and action as we probed for meaning.

This process was described in a Galarza lecture several years ago as
follows:

> The dialogue between a tutor, or collector, and a contributor engaged
> both individuals in a creative process of thought and action. This
> dynamic relationship begins by reflecting on a deed, or action, under
> discussion in the personal history, oral history, or folklore that is being
> documented. I assumed the content of an oral history or folklore was
> based on an actual or imagined occurrence—something that hap-
> pened in the head or in action—that may have been generalized or
> embellished by subsequent reporters of the event. Whether the story
> was factual or not was not important. Our concern was to reflect
> critically on the individual's perceptions, whether these were mental
> images or sensory experiences. Upon reflection, the meaning of that
> account, within a historical context, was revealed and led to subse-
> quent action by the participants in the dialogue. That action could
> be manifested externally or remain within the mind as an intended or
> conceived action. In either case, it is action that results from reflection
> on a previous action. Subsequent action, in turn, becomes material for
> reflection again. This creative process gives birth to a dynamic spiral
> of thought and action.
>
> As more was uncovered, the collector and contributor became
> dynamically linked in a closer understanding of each other's informa-
> tion and knowledge. Language diminished in importance as a tool
> for understanding as the individuals moved from a rational to a more
> intuitive mode. In street language, it was *snapeando.* In northern New
> Mexican street language it was *maliciandola.* It was communication
> with full integrity in the message occurring in a reciprocal exchange
> of words and meaning; and as understanding is fully achieved "the sun
> is shining on everything and everybody is seeing every thing as it is
> at the same time."[44]

After reviewing the recorded material, the narratives were transcribed
verbatim. As we reviewed and discussed the recordings amongst ourselves,
we realized that each narrative was structured around particular themes,
which were what made it a story. We identified those parts in each narrative that clearly clustered under a particular theme, pulled them out of
the transcription, and entered them in a separate text. Estevan Arellano,
our publications editor who had trained in media and communications,

had suggested a scriptwriting/filmmaking approach for the transcription: the narrative was typed in the right-hand column of a page. We identified those stories in the transcribed narrative that fit a particular theme, entered that text in the left-hand column, and labeled its theme. Next, we identified all the stories that addressed a particular theme and compiled them. These were shared with the contributors, who then learned what others had said about the identified theme. The participants were brought together; they talked about their stories and came to a consensual validation and understanding of the meanings of their experiences. This dialogue process, called a macro-spiral of thought and action, became the "new resolana," a process and place for all participants to meet and uncover knowledge, gain understanding, and learn together from their common experiences. As challenges emerged in the community, the community of action would come together for specific action.

What comes out of the group dialogue—that is, la resolana or the macro-spiral—becomes objectified knowledge, knowledge that is committed to print or adapted to other media and is disseminated. Once objectified, this knowledge logically becomes material for further reflection on a wider spiral of thought and action. The micro dimensions produce self-knowledge; the macro dimensions create consensually validated knowledge and meaning. The macro process was truly the contemporary reconceptualization of la resolana.

La resolana is a pathway to knowledge that derives from a dialectal relation between thought and action in the everyday lives of people. To distribute the resolana dialogue to the community in printed form we published these stories in a book titled *Entre Verde y Seco*. The title symbolizes the reality of life itself, a life cognizant of death, a life of imagination and reason, one filled with both green and dry periods. In *Entre Verde y Seco*, we placed the thematic vignettes in a dialectic relationship with each other; one vignette was about the green of life, the other dealt with its dry, or wilted, aspects. The dialectic presentation of vignettes provided a means of exposing the contradictions of life. For example, one vignette told of a great experience in summertime, when a family took its herd of cattle to the forest and experienced solidarity with each other and harmony with nature. The next vignette told of the coming of lawyers to adjudicate the land, who, in payment for their services, got the land itself. In this way, readers learned and raised their consciousnesses. Although they could not change the past, they gained a new awareness they could apply when facing similar circumstances in the future. *Entre Verde y Seco* was another way of expressing the spiral of thought and action.

La Academia published three thousand copies of *Entre Verde y Seco*, many of which were purchased by the Home Education Livelihood Program (HELP) in northeastern New Mexico to use as the textbook for adult basic education. As part of its classes, HELP invited all its participants to gather in the cafeteria of the West Las Vegas School (in Old Town) one evening a month to talk about the stories and themes in *Entre Verde y Seco*. Called the Chicano Town and Gown in order to lure professors and students from the nearby New Mexico Highlands University to listen to their grandparents tell of their experiences and what they meant, the evening was a true resolana, as people delved into the themes in *Entre Verde y Seco* and deepened their understanding through more stories and folktales.

A summary of parts of *Entre Verde y Seco* with commentary prepared for the Galarza lecture illustrates the richness of the story. The presentation follows the life cycle, from birth to death, within which rests the meaning of life. The summary also reveals an emerging body of knowledge from the life experiences of a traditional, peasant society:

> A woman, in her early seventies, mother of four, tells: "I never knew a doctor in my childbearing years—for any of my children. *La partera*, the midwife, *una viejita*, a little old woman, would deliver us; she nursed us to health by holding us to a strict forty-day *dieta*, a period of time when we did nothing. We were kept still and undisturbed, quiet as brooding hens. She nurtured us with lots of *atole, piloncillo, chaquegüe* with milk, and boiled eggs."
>
> Life and death converged in one place during childbirth. My maternal grandfather, who lost his first wife and child in childbirth, tells it this way: "The *partera* would prepare a birthing room by sprinkling it, sweeping it, and placing a sheep pelt—*una salea*—on the earthen floor and hanging a rope from the *viga* [exposed pine joist]. She would order the husband to heat water outside and called el *tenedor*—the holder—a man who would assist the *partera*. When the woman was ready to deliver, she entered the birthing room, knelt on the pelt, and pulled on the rope. The *tenedor* helped by exerting mild pressure on the woman's back with his knee until the baby was born."
>
> "In the adjoining room the husband danced to San Ramón," the patron saint of difficult labor. The dance is a way of getting in touch with the Creator of life, through a spiritual intercessor, to assure a normal and safe delivery. *Santos* serve as intercessors with supernatural forces; they also serve as social mediators and personal supporters. Sometimes the desired harmony with the forces that sustain life was not achieved. At the threshold of life, death triumphed.

The sanctity of life was seen not only in humans but also in all of nature. In describing how she raised her own food, an elderly woman recounts in a detailed description her relationship with the land: "When the days get longer and warmer in the early spring," she said, "I pay someone to plow and to clean the ditches and make the furrows. Then, with my hoe I level the beds so that they look neat and clean, make straight rows, where I dig small holes and there lay the seeds. Then I irrigate until the sprouts show. If the plants of *chile* or tomatoes grow in little heaps and bunched up, I thin them. The tomatoes and cabbage I transplant far from their little brothers so they may thrive and grow beautifully. Then all summer long I spend my days hoeing, weeding, irrigating, and building little earthen mounds to fortify the growing plants until they are ready to yield their fruits." She continues: "The farmer and his or her work are at the mercy of God and of the weather that He may determine for that season. Not always are things the way we plan and hope they will be. What happened this year we did not expect. Rain and hail storms destroyed all we had planted. All that was left were the stems and stalks with small tattered leaves hanging there. And we worked so hard, and it was beautiful, but all was lost. Well, God gave and God took away. And we must accept the good fortune with the misfortune. Nothing of our crop was left, but God never fails. He will see to it that we are fed. We are dependent on His will, and if we have faith, He will provide. God's power can cause the beaten and tattered plants to sprout and yield in abundance."

But the weather and the destiny of the crops were not all left to chance. As in childbirth, where San Ramón is the intercessor, in the toil of the land for subsistence other *santos* were summoned to intercede on the farmer's behalf. "In the summer," another person said, "we would celebrate the Feast of the Virgin Mary. Early in the morning, all together, young and old, we would take the Virgin in procession trampling through the fields, without even causing any damage to the wheat." When times were dry, "we would take the *santos* [San Ysidro, the patron saint of agriculture] in procession through the fields, praying for rain."

This was a life of innocence and simple faith, a reflection of the openness to myth, to primal energy. Fulfillment and freedom were harmonious relationships with nature and an acceptance of destiny.

In the social world there were good times and bad times as well. "People in years past," another woman said, "would help each other. In the summer, neighbors would join to mud-plaster each other's houses. They would invite themselves to hoe and irrigate the neighbors' plots. In the fall, they harvested their crops together and at night would shuck piles of corn and tie *ristras* of red *chile* while they told stories, jokes, and shared the news of the day." That was the green of human experience. But reciprocity was gradually replaced with a formal exchange of goods and services. That was the dry.

"In earlier days," reflected a ninety-year-old man, "we had men of honor. Today I don't think we have any. In those days one man would ask another, '*Amigo*, lend me two dollars and I will pay you when the sun sets.' At dusk the man would return the two dollars, because the word was honored. Not so today. The word of honor is useless. Instead we have complicated documents. People no longer trust."

Reflecting more profoundly about these changes, this man offers an explanation: "The true value of things has been exchanged for a promise—an anticipated life in the future. Our communities and the activities of everyday life have become alienated because our sustenance and our possessions have been purchased and have not derived from an intimate relationship among each other and with nature. We no longer pay for the harvest that sustains us with the sweat of our brows; hence we no longer feel the satisfaction of having done something useful and meaningful. We do not feel the soul of the earth because it has become a disgrace to soil ourselves with its dust. We no longer recognize the miracle—the *milagro*—of food, because we have not bent our bodies over a plant to care for it or to pluck its fruits. Neither do we feel the humility nor the nobility of being human because we neither do the most sublime nor the most base of things. We are satisfied with a life of leisure; with a life of no pain."

"Why has life changed?" we ask. "Strangers—foreigners—have come to our lands with their own styles and manners of being. . . . We have believed what they said because we still have some faith in people." In an ironic twist this observer concludes: "*Semos tan buenos que pa' nada semos buenos.*" We are so good that we are good for nothing. Another way of saying it is: virtues as moral values are useless as instrumental values.

But, "what else do you want?" he ponders. "*Tenemos corazón bueno y sano.*" We have a sense of well-being and wholeness in our hearts.

Despite this fundamental commitment to virtues as moral values, struggle for fulfillment in the social and political domains persisted. The native confronted the intruder. In *El Trovo del Café y el Atole*, a debate in verse commonly used in New Mexican *pláticas* and declamations of years past, Coffee advances his argument of superiority arrogantly:

"Yo soy el Café
Con azúcar soy sabroso

También con carnes fritas
Y con sopapilla generoso
Con bollitos victorioso
Y en puntos bien arreglados
Bien parezco en las mesas
Con huevos estrellados."

("I am coffee
With sugar I am delightful
When served with meat and fried bread
I'm in great demand by all
And alongside little bread rolls on elegant tables displayed
I look distinguished next to colorful fried eggs.")

Atole, the indigenous food derived from corn, significantly rooted in the Indian creation myth, answers assertively:

"Yo también soy el Atole
Desciendo de maíz
Y te pondré mis paradas
Que bien mantengo a mi gente
Con tortillas enchiladas
Con esquite bien tostado
Ahora te daré noticias
Café por comprarte a ti
Ya no se alcanzan pa' camisas."

("And I am gruel
A proud descendant of corn
Ready to declare war on you
For I nourish and sustain my people
With tortillas soaked in chili
With popped corn well toasted
Now, let the whole world know
That my people squander their money just to buy you
And hence have no money left to buy shirts.")

Atole triumphs.

The journey, full of conflicts and contradictions, joy and pain, must come to an end. The storyteller, the listener, all must die as many who told these stories have already died. Death is our shadow—*la doña Sebastiana*—the *seco* of life, but we must confront her, and as another man in Santa Fe said, "think about her at least three times a day," lest we miss living an authentic life.

In the tradition of the Pious Fraternity of the Brothers of Light—the *Penitente*—the departed brother bids farewell through the voices of his surviving brothers, who sing:

De la nada fui formado
La tierra me ha producido
La tierra me ha sustentado
A la tierra estoy rendido.
Adiós por última vez
Que me ven sobre la tierra
Ya me echan en el sepulcro
Que es mi casa verdadera.

(I was formed from no substance
Earth gave me my life
Earth has nourished my life
And to earth I am forever bound.
This is my last farewell
For no longer will I upon the earth be seen
I am going to the grave
My true home and final resting place.)[45]

The images of the Virgin Mary, of the crucified Christ, of San Ysidro that people took in procession through the fields, and San Ramón to whom an anxious husband danced during his wife's labor, were carved from wood by men who were known as *santeros*. They were the community's artists who expressed through the *santo* sentiments of suffering and meaning of an isolated community in a harsh environment. *Santos* were the social mediators among people and the symbols of the religious and mythical dimensions that opened the way for humans to communicate with the supernatural. These men gave the community the sacred objects for its rites and rituals.[46]

With the publication of *Entre Verde y Seco*, people finally had a body of knowledge, a text they could consult when issues arose in the community. They also had a way to understand the meaning of their life experiences. Next, we published "La Madrugada" and "La Resolana." A short bulletin, "La Madrugada," meaning dawn, was a wake-up call alerting its readership to a contemporary problem in the region and linking it to a specific vignette or bit of folklore in *Entre Verde y Seco*, which provided a historical context and connected the current concern with similar situations the community had confronted in the past.

"La Resolana" usually followed "La Madrugada." A one-page flyer written by Estevan Arellano in dialogue format, "La Resolana" used local Spanish dialect as spoken in the traditional resolana of old. It, too, made reference to *Entre Verde y Seco*. The fictional protagonist of "La Resolana" was Pacheco, a master *resolanero* who emerged as the counterpart to Socrates in the Athenian agora or Plato's Academy. In contrast to Socrates, who started by saying he knew nothing, Pacheco understood, reflected on, and expressed well but in modest fashion cultural traditions and meaningful activities in village life. He was a manito wise man—a sage. His readers identified with him. As people read "La Resolana," they would share the content with someone else, thus replicating the traditional resolana. It worked; the people who read or had "La Resolana" read to them understood the meaning of its content. *La maliciaban*, they intuitively grasped its meaning. Whatever action followed was triggered by the thinking and reflexive processes.[47]

"La Resolana" was circulated via village cantinas through a central distribution center, a local bar in Embudo. The Embudo bartender gave drivers of the liquor trucks stacks of the flyers, which were dropped off at bars in neighboring villages. Men patronizing the bars took the flyers home, and the dialogue spread. Thus, the traditional resolana was re-created. It was one of the most effective ways of communicating within our community. Resolana had become, in the words of the O'odham elder, "the sun shining on everything and everybody is seeing everything as it is at the same time." This truly is transparency—full integrity in the message—made possible by dialogue and reflection.

Because the purpose of resolana was to share and democratize knowledge, La Academia de la Nueva Raza published *El Cuaderno (de Vez en Cuando)* (The Occasional Notebook). The aim of *El Cuaderno* was to take the synthesized knowledge to the larger community through essays and creative works inspired by el oro del barrio. Estevan Arellano authored a serialized novel of a picaresque character, Inocencio, and resolanero, Pacheco; he also published poetry that reflected life and thought in the village. E. A. Mares published poetry and essays on the myth of Aztlán and on Paulo Freire. Alberto Lovato, the creator of Pacheco, told cuentos of daily village life in manito Spanish. Lorenzo Valdez, who operated the printing press, also wrote on labor history in the villages. Frank Lujan, the father of Antonio Lujan, another of our asociados, published poems about his life as a railroad worker. In *El Cuaderno* the late Cleofes Vigil published his ancient and timeless *cuentos moralejos* (brief moral tales). Andrés Segura shared the ancient philosophy of the Aztecs, and Luis Jaramillo, his early essays. Chema Saenz and Consuelo Pacheco published poetry. A number of people who were not asociados of La Academia turned to *El Cuaderno* to publish their works. We solicited works of activists such as Enriqueta Vásquez. And we turned to the older stories of deceased New Mexico writers, such as M. M. Salazar whose fable was written in 1881. I used *El Cuaderno* to present the seminal thoughts and insights contained in this essay. Alejandro López, Alberto Baros, Jesús "Chista" Cantú, David Mercado González, Rudy "Diamond" García, Vicente Martínez, Elena Arellano, Juanita Jaramillo Lavadie, and others mirrored to the manito community its experience, knowledge, and wisdom through visual art and photography.

Another way of relating to the community and engaging its members in the resolana process was village and barrio art exhibits. In San Antonio, Texas, Tito Villalobos Moreno brought together a musical group known as Distant Dream that performed in barrio gatherings associated with Los Pintores de la Nueva Raza art festivals and exhibits. The name Distant Dream was taken from Luis Jaramillo's idea of La Nueva Raza as a dream and vocation. The band was best known for Moreno's composition, *"No Tengo Que Ir a la Luna Porque Vengo del Sol"* (I Don't Have to Go to the Moon for I Come from the Sun), which was inspired by a series of paintings of Aztec motifs by Chista Cantú.

La Academia's influence continued to extend beyond New Mexico. In the Imperial Valley of California a replication of the New Mexico Oral History Program was initiated in 1973. José Padilla, a native of Brawley, became acquainted with the New Mexico Academia Documentation Center through the Chicano Fellows at Stanford University, where he was an undergraduate student. He expressed interest in starting a similar project in his hometown. Three of us traveled from New Mexico to Brawley to orient José and advocates of migrant education on the resolana process. Padilla documented the life histories of thirty-six people who had settled in the Imperial Valley between 1900 and 1930. Due to lack of time, post-interview dialogue sessions did not occur, but the documented material was archived at the Academia Documentation Center in Dixon, New Mexico.

There we transcribed several audiotapes and identified life experience themes clustered around a community of interest that would bring people together to engage in dialogue. One salient theme was the experiences of Mexican immigrants finding their first jobs. Our plan, never realized, was to compile a bilingual reader for teaching adults English using the transcribed stories, in effect enabling them to learn English while reviewing and reflecting on meaningful experiences. In 2003, thirty years later, a graduate student from the Imperial Valley studying folklore at the University of New Mexico learned of Padilla's work. Padilla then inquired about the material archived in New Mexico. We identified thirty-three audiotapes and sent them to Brawley to be digitalized, included in a documentation program and made available in libraries throughout the Imperial Valley.

The Brawley project had a profound impact on José Padilla. This experience gave him a meaningful understanding of his roots, and the knowledge he gained was critical in determining his future: It opened a pathway to a life in public service. Padilla, now an attorney, has been executive director of California Rural Legal Assistance (CRLA) for nearly thirty years. His work on the Brawley project is not over; he intends to do a reflective review of his oral history work, which will provide a lens now refined through experience. In the spirit of resolana, this new level in the spiral of thought and action will lead to further dialogue and reflection, and will impel action on current issues such as immigration, employment, and related matters.

Theory and Practice of la Resolana

Reflection on the Academia experience suggested to us that our process for unveiling and reclaiming subjugated knowledge, for learning, and for raising consciousness should be examined in relation to existing theory in order to seek insight into universal attributes of our work.[48] From the beginning of this review, we affirmed that everyday lived experiences from all cultures, regardless of their class status, are valid foundations for knowledge, although they are often denied legitimacy by the powers that be. Even though localized and provincial, the knowledge that emerges through resolana is reflexive learning. At one level, it is an internal self-awareness process that deepens an individual's understanding of the sources of that knowledge, that is, past experiences, sacred knowledge, and myth. As an external, rational, and reflective process that discloses themes from oral history narratives, this knowledge could connect with existing knowledge ranging from ancient times to the most advanced scientific and humanistic theories of postmodern society. In our thinking, although the stories we had collected were set in a local context, their themes were universal. In fact, this process mirrors *The Great Ideas: A Syntopicon of The Great Books of the Western World* , where themes are catalogued and identified with specific authors, providing similar as well as different, or particular, expositions of the same theme.[49]

Early in its development, our resolana process built on assumptions and attributes of psychoanalysis and Jungian as well as Platonic archetypal theory. In developing la resolana as a learning process, we assumed the existence of a collective unconscious or collective consciousness and affirmed that the meaning of its messages—embodied in the story, or oral history—could be discerned through dialogue. By way of analogy, the oral history narrative, carrier of both experiential memory and imagination, parallels the accounts of a person undergoing psychoanalysis. Writing about the psychoanalytic interview as a hermeneutic (interpretative) method, Jürgen Habermas says, "By treating psychoanalysis as an analysis of language aiming at reflection about oneself, I have sought to show how the relations of power embodied in systematically distorted communication can be attacked directly by the process of critique" (that is, through self-reflection). Habermas concludes that "the relation of theory to therapy is just as constitutive for Freudian theory as the relation of theory to praxis is for Marxist theory."[50] Building on Habermas' logic but proposing understanding as the purpose of the discourse, I suggest the role of the oral historian is parallel to that of the psychoanalyst in unraveling the meaning of the oral history messages: the oral historian is to the oral history narrative what the psychoanalyst is to the analysand's communications.

The specific path to understanding the meaning of a story is its themes. When understood in terms of their origins, themes are archetypal (Plato) as well as the building blocks of myth (Jung). Creation myths, myths of death, and those of the eternal return are universal and surface as patterns in people's stories about life, religion, and faith. Life's journey, heroes and antiheroes, love, war, work, water, land, and sense of place are examples of everyday life themes. McLuhan and Powers maintain in their book *The Global Village* that "all of man's artifacts, of language, of laws, of ideas . . . are extensions of the human body. . . . Every artifact is an archetype" (p. 71). I suggest, therefore, that cultural products, including themes in the stories people tell, are archetypes or extensions thereof.

Since I assume that themes are archetypal, there is a logical basis for universalizing provincial thematic content. In other words, a New Mexican story of a picaresque character, a "Hermes archetype," has, for example, its counterpart in Russia. Exchanging these stories and reaching consensual understanding of their meaning are aspects of the democratization of knowledge.

This attribute of the democratization of knowledge can best be illustrated by an anecdote. In April 1994, Gordon Cook, a scholar of Russian intellectual history and publisher of the *Cook Report* on the Internet, wrote that he had read a lecture I had given several years before, entitled "Resolana: A Chicano Pathway to Knowledge." In that lecture I described the picaresque character (the inverted counterpart to the Sophist) as an anti-hero archetype and outlined his importance as a link to el oro del barrio. Cook wrote

> I am struck by the thought that your ideas may be universal. . . . As I read your lecture . . . I was struck by the insight that your very important ideas have relevance to that nation [Russia] as well—especially after three centuries where the state created and educated an elite to serve its own interests and in so doing deprived that elite of any possibility of ever knowing its cultural roots in any meaningful way. The result has been a nation where the *iurodivyi* [also yurodivy], or "holy fool," probably performed much of the same function of the *pícaro*."[51]

Like the pícaro, the Russian yurodivy fulfilled an important role in reconnecting Russians with their buried traditional culture. The yurodivy is to Russian culture what the pícaro is to New Mexican culture. The connection between the Russian and the Chicano experience corroborates that different cultures could potentially come together and understand each other by way of the thematic content of their life stories. This possibility allows for unity in diversity and is consistent with Teilhard de Chardin's noosphere and Jaramillo's vision of La Nueva Raza.

Turning now specifically to reflexive and reflective learning, this aspect was first suggested in the Galarza lecture published in 1988 and applied later that year in two sociology courses that are discussed in the next section of this essay.[52]

Resolana as reflexive and reflective research was applied in a study on how crypto-Judaism shaped New Mexico culture. Crypto-Judaism, a fourteenth-century Spanish phenomenon, came about when Jews converted to Christianity as a means of survival. New converts ostensibly accepted Christianity but continued to practice Judaism covertly. I assumed that new converts and their heirs settled in New Mexico during the colonial period and that as they assimilated into the dominant society lost consciousness of their roots and relegated to memory their secret customs.

I wanted to know if cultural elements of manito society existed that could plausibly be interpreted as remnants of crypto-Jewish practices. The pathway to those elements was the story and knowledge derived from everyday life experiences. This required an interpretive (hermeneutic) and phenomenological framework consisting of two parts: a list of crypto-Judaic characteristics in Spain and Mexico, and a compilation of themes from the story in the contemporary oral history narratives. The story is categorized into themes that resemble the crypto-Jewish characteristics. The greater the similarity, the more convincing the assumption that crypto-Judaism influenced manito Indohispanic culture.

I will select one of several examples of crypto-Judaic practices to explain how this project was both a reflexive process of identifying the cultural elements that were crypto-Jewish practices and a reflective one of uncovering the relevant themes of the oral history narrative. The daily reading of the Torah, a sacred obligation in Judaism, could rightly be seen as a characteristic of that religion. In Spain and in Mexico during the colonial period, crypto-Jews caught reading the Torah were brought before the Inquisition and charged with heresy. Indohispanics' conversion to Protestantism in the late nineteenth century was a theme that emerged in the oral histories of New Mexico. I interpreted that these conversions reflected crypto-Jewish heirs' longing for the Bible, since it was not readily available to Roman Catholics. In fact, most of the literature on Indohispanic conversions from Catholicism to Protestantism, along with contemporary accounts by their heirs, name access to the Bible as a major reason for converting. Some actually say that conversion was specifically motivated by access to the Bible because through the Old Testament they could connect with their Jewish heritage and fulfill their sacred obligations.[53]

When I first saw the term *phenomenology* in a journal of existential philosophy many years ago, I was intimidated. For decades I ignored the word. Then, in the mid-seventies, Pedro David, a sociologist and phenomenologist, heard a presentation on our project, after which he exclaimed: "This is social phenomenology." He went on to explain that he was referring to an application of Martin Heidegger's phenomenology to the social world, an unlikely development because of Heidegger's individualistic orientation. The connection to Heidegger was that we were uncovering "meaning" from the community's experience through conversations with people.[54] I took David's comments seriously, along with his invitation to enroll in the University of New Mexico's doctoral program in sociology which, incidentally, did not promote or endorse phenomenology.

There are several ways of explaining phenomenology. Martin Heidegger, for example, proposed a process of dialogue that uncovers what is hidden as a means of understanding the meaning of being. He wrote that "phenomenon" is what is uncovered "in-itself," and "logos" is the process by which it is uncovered.[55] Resolana could be another word for phenomenology, as it is a process of disclosing experience and its meaning through dialogue and reflection, bringing to light in a place of light what is covered up. Reflexive and reflective learning are phenomenology also. Their principal tasks are to disclose the themes of the narrative and reach consensual understanding, or validation, of the meaning of individual yet similar experiences.[56]

In summary, la resolana as reflexive and reflective learning is based on the following assumptions: (1) life stories are history and sources of knowledge; (2) imagination, visions, and other psychic productions are foundations for knowledge; (3) traditional cultures have indigenous knowledge by which they interpret themselves to themselves; (4) stories consist of themes that are universal while remaining specific to time and place; themes are essential to democratizing knowledge, allowing for dialogue within as well as across cultures, by crossing cultural boundaries and linking cultures through the universal thematic bridge.

I turn now to two case studies illustrating the application of resolana in a university setting. One was a project involving a special-topics class at the University of New Mexico, Department of Sociology, and several rural communities and an urban neighborhood in Albuquerque; and the other was a television distance-learning course, also at the University of New Mexico.

The University and the Learning Society: Two Case Studies

Considering my cynicism about Chicano studies as an academic discipline, it is ironic that I would end up in a university at midlife. I rationalized that I could use its resources and lectern to test and proclaim La Academia's work of the sixties and seventies and determine whether it could be adapted to the university setting. After all, most of the resources for the learning and knowledge enterprise are concentrated in universities. The two case studies illustrate this university experience.

By 1989, when I became a full-time lecturer in sociology at the University of New Mexico, La Academia de la Nueva Raza had been dissolved for a decade. But its legacy continued. One example was La Resolana de Una Vida Buena y Sana in Mora, New Mexico, under the leadership of Antonio Medina; another was my work as a university instructor connecting students to the resolana process and the community.[57] The work in Mora mirrored that of La Academia in the seventies. People shared their stories; they talked about them and then implemented projects emerging from the dialogue. Because Mora's base of operation was a community clinic, a great deal of the work centered on praxis—on traditional ways of sustaining health, such as the use of herbs and cultural practices that reflect a balanced life, hence their motto: "una vida buena y sana."

At the University of New Mexico, I offered a special-topics course on la resolana as reflexive sociology, focusing on praxis learning and action research. As the instructor, I provided the students guidance and ensured their praxis and service to the community were carried out. Praxis learning is learning by reflecting on the experience of serving a community or neighborhood. Action research is the service the student renders. In this course the service was to be in the realm of information and knowledge, with the community determining what information and knowledge it needed. The student and community members then collaborated in the knowledge-gathering task. The community's responsibility was to find a place and create a process for archiving the material generated. Modeled after La Academia's Learning and Documentation Center (LDC), it was to be the action phase of the community-of-interest model, a place for the community to meet for dialogue and to store their products such as oral histories. Moreover, the LDC was seen as a logical and viable step toward the envisioned learning society.

The students' involvement with the Sawmill Advisory Council (SAC) in the Sawmill district in the Old Town Albuquerque area provides a specific example of the activities of the special-topics class. SAC was a creation of the Southwest Organizing Project (SWOP), an environmental justice group in Albuquerque. The critical incident that triggered SAC involved Ponderosa Products Inc., a pressed-wood manufacturing plant that was a remnant of the wood-processing activities that had begun in 1904 on the same site. The emission of airborne toxic particles and the threat of water contamination from the plant unified a group of Sawmill residents in the late 1980s under SWOP's leadership. A couple of years later SAC severed its ties with SWOP, subsequently reorganized and incorporated as a nonprofit neighborhood association, and continued its environmental struggle. It also turned its attention to community physical improvement, getting help from the city through councilmen such as Steve Gallegos and Vicente Griego, who were committed to SAC's goals of paving streets, creating gutters, and building sidewalks. SAC also focused its attention on rehabilitating part of the old sawmill acreage adjacent to its barrio for community- or worker-owned businesses or affordable housing development.[58]

I live in this neighborhood and was a founding member of the nonprofit phase of SAC. Three students in the special-topics class chose SAC as their praxis learning and action research site. The students and I met with the board of SAC and explained the idea of our project, including the vision of creating a learning and documentation center, which I would manage. The students' product—that is, information, reports, interviews, papers, and the like—would be deposited in this documentation center, which would be the neighborhood's own knowledge and information center. A final paper or portfolio critiqued and graded by me was required from the students with a copy for the center.

Max Ramírez, SAC board chair and lifelong resident of the Sawmill neighborhood, and Debbie O'Malley asked for a history of the sawmill industry, which would include area businesses associated with it since its beginning in 1904 as well as a comprehensive story of the people who came as loggers and sawmill workers, most of them from surrounding New Mexico villages. Over the course of five years, fifteen students from this and subsequent classes contributed to documenting the community's history, including even a list of the people who had purchased merchandise in La Tienda de la Máquina de Rajar (the sawmill store) between 1914 and 1917. We talked to residents of the neighborhood about their memories of the sawmill and conducted investigations on the sawmill plant and logging in New Mexico. This material was printed in a bilingual leaflet called "El Pregonero" (which means "the town crier") and shared with the community in the same way "La Resolana" had been in the days of La Academia. A series of murals done by young people under the tutelage of Leo Romero, a sign painter and muralist from the neighborhood, rendered images of that history.

The most significant class project was Mark Suazo's award-winning honors thesis on the history of the sawmill and the application of the resolana process to praxis learning. Out of Suazo's work came an after-school learning project that used the acequia that runs through the neighborhood as the basis of the learning experience. The acequia and the life of the community around it became the foundation of the project syllabus and curriculum. In working to understand the acequia, students learned about local history, arid lands, biology, and ecology, all in relation to practical, everyday life experiences, while also improving their literacy skills. Unfortunately, the heart of the project was lost upon the departure of the university student who had written the curriculum. Nevertheless, the acequia project, which had started as an after-school program, continued successfully for some time.

In a far more significant move, the thesis, then in progress, was put to use by SAC when the Center for Community Change (CCC), a nonprofit housing technical advisory organization, requested information about SAC. A summary of the thesis was sent together with a brief proposal, and within weeks the CCC had assigned a consultant to work with the community toward the purchase of twenty-seven acres of the old sawmill site for affordable housing.[59] The land was purchased and the Sawmill Community

Development Corporation (CDC) was incorporated. A decade after the students had left the scene, the old sawmill site had become an award-winning and exemplary land-trust project of affordable housing.[60] And Debbie O'Malley, a sawmill resident, SAC founder, and the person who led the Sawmill Community Land Trust's (SCLT) development, eventually became an Albuquerque city councilwoman. In this position, O'Malley advocates for housing land trusts and for responsible urban development.

Although SCLT was initiated to offer affordable housing to young people who had grown up in the Sawmill neighborhood, most current homeowners there are not from the area; it is an integrated housing development with a mixture of ethnic and racial groups, a diversity reflecting a large portion of our society in general.

The Sawmill CDC became the legal entity for the SCLT. Its board of directors is composed of trustees, who own the houses, and of at-large representatives, who are members of the community. The idea that knowledge in the community enlightens as well as empowers was validated by this project. The learning and documentation center initially envisioned was never created, but the concept endured and was expanded to include service as well as learning and documentation. It took the name Resolana Service Learning Documentation Center (RSLDC), as it was integrated into an AmeriCorps service-learning project. In the Sawmill barrio the idea of an RSLDC has lain fallow, waiting to be cultivated. The most encouraging sign, however, is that a University of New Mexico service-learning program has been picking up where the project left off some years ago. Some material generated by the students is still available for the service-learning program to organize and archive. In another turn, a graduate assistant in the Office of Community Learning and Public Service (CLPS) at the University of New Mexico was assigned to oversee the development of an RSLDC in the Sawmill neighborhood. This effort has initiated a Sawmill digital database for documents, audio, and film. The surge that occurred during the summer months of 2006, thanks to student volunteers from the Bonner Foundation, has come to a stop as CLPS seeks new leadership and financial support. The center is eying a home in the SCLT to further the vision of transforming its residents into a learning community.

Turning now to the second case study, Resolana Electrónica was an electronic bulletin board created in 1995 by David Hughes, a retired army general committed to connecting small communities and nonprofessional people to the Internet, and Carmen Gonzáles, then a doctoral student in education and technology at the University of New Mexico. Managed by Ms. Gonzáles, the demonstration project linked several northern New

Mexico villages engaged in a resolana service-learning project of Ameri-Corps volunteers.[61]

After the project ended, I appropriated the Resolana Electrónica name and applied it to a distance-learning course that used both television and the Internet for teaching, learning, and knowledge building. For several years the University of New Mexico had had a distance-learning program using interactive televised instruction. It offered courses to outlying rural communities in New Mexico, southern Colorado, and eastern Arizona through satellite and community downlink sites hosted by a community college or public school. Courses in education, communications, public administration, psychology, and engineering were offered, but there were no sociology courses. As in the praxis course, I took an established sociology course and redesigned it to achieve the goal of democratizing knowledge through telecommunications technology. I called the course "The Sociology of New Mexico: Viewing New Mexico through Colores and Seeing New Mexico through Resolana."

"Colores" is a successful, high-quality KNME-TV film series on New Mexico history and culture. Granted permission by KNME-TV to telecast films for my course, I selected those related to four specific themes in the class syllabus. I taught the course for four consecutive semesters, until I left the university.

For three semesters the course was telecast through the University of New Mexico's TALNET, the university's teaching/learning network channel. That was an encouraging experience which confirmed the principle that knowledge, knowledge discovery, and knowledge building under the auspices of a public university should not be limited to those who matriculate. Moreover, it showed the value of pedagogical approaches that reach the on-campus population, the students in outreach sites in rural areas and Indian reservations, and the viewers not enrolled in the class who view the program at home. This approach was greatly enhanced by the Colores films. The course gained popularity in the Albuquerque Chicano community. One informal group of Chicanos, the *resolaneros* from Old Town Albuquerque, on occasion would discuss it in the park or at a restaurant hangout on the day after the class.

The course illustrates resolana as reflexive and reflective learning. The subtitle, "Viewing New Mexico through Colores and Seeing New Mexico through Resolana," alluded to the process of presenting New Mexico through film; "viewing" referred to the films, "seeing" implied grasping intuitively the meaning of New Mexico's historical development, and through "resolana" students were to understand New Mexico by building on one another's knowledge and individual life experiences and by collecting life histories from the community to learn how it interpreted itself to itself. They would expand their own knowledge, correct prejudices, add new perspectives, and tell their own stories about New Mexico.

The course had two intersecting pathways. One explored New Mexico's cultural productions—the ideas, beliefs, art, and philosophies of Native Americans, Indohispanics, African Americans, Jewish merchants, and Anglos—from the early frontiersmen and traders to the scientists who ushered New Mexico into the postindustrial era. The other pathway examined and interpreted the impact of the scientific and technological revolution on New Mexico natives and discerned ways of using the technology for educational purposes. Class discussion was enriched by information and images from Colores films, a comprehensive reader containing thematic articles, and guest speakers who shared their experiences and reflections. Students also could participate in Internet dialogue hosted by Robert Theobald's Transformational Learning Communities and Transformational Change program in Spokane, Washington.[62] The fundamental beliefs of the indigenous peoples and those who followed were examined, as was the military and scientific complex along the Rio Grande corridor. Los Alamos developed the atomic bomb; the Kirtland Air Force Base laboratory provides security and conducts research; the Sandia National Laboratories conduct research for the U.S. Department of Energy; and Rio Rancho's Intel plant produces microchips for computers worldwide. We focused on how these scientific advances had propelled a Latino backwater directly from a preindustrial to a postindustrial society, and pondered their role in educating the people who had missed the opportunities and benefits of industrial society. Could this technology further the goal of democratizing knowledge? This framework for understanding social change guided the course.

We also heard via a Colores segment from Fred Begay, a Navajo physicist who had been drawn to the study of theoretical physics through his native religion. He demonstrated the similarities between Navajo myth and theoretical physics, an ancient tradition and a modern science, both of which, according to resolana assumptions, are extensions of the same archetype.[63]

Did the resolana approach work in this university setting? There is no question in my mind that most students liked the approach used in both courses. The majority of them were not comfortable with the idea of starting with their own knowledge or creating knowledge from their own experience. This was most obvious in the sociology of New Mexico course. Most students felt they had to know something objective about the history of the state and would not risk talking about their own perceptions. Dialogue, or conversation, was difficult for most students, and not many used the Internet to share their ideas. I believe this situation reflected their previous traditional educational experience in which knowledge is handed down from teacher to student in a hierarchical model. The distance-learning course showed great potential for reaching a wide population in our path toward a learning society. The university must consciously reach out to the wider community if in fact it is going to be a player in creating a learning society.

The praxis learning and action research course worked very well in the Sawmill district of Albuquerque. Students working in rural settings completed their class projects, but they did not get the same attention that students in the city did. Students in the Sawmill barrio engaged in dialogue with community residents, collected material, and wrote papers and portfolios that were left with the SAC. This process created a consciousness of the community's history. The Sawmill example was turned into a pattern for AmeriCorps service-learning programs in the Sawmill and in various northern New Mexico villages and pueblos in 1995–96. The program was reborn at the University of New Mexico when Michael Morris, senior staff member of the northern New Mexico project, organized the Community Learning and Public Service (CLPS) component of the College of Education.[64] It sponsors an AmeriCorps project and also gives students at the university and Central New Mexico Community College (CNMCC, formerly Albuquerque Technical-Vocational Institute) an opportunity to learn while they serve through a youth civic engagement curriculum. The resolana approach serves as a theoretical base for the CLPS program. A central feature for a university-based resolana process would be a "model" documentation and learning center in the community under the sponsorship of a university.

The Resolana Service Learning Documentation Center (RSLDC)

The two preceding case studies illustrate, in the first instance, collaboration between a university class and community groups in learning, action research, and democratization of knowledge; and in the second, the university's extension to the community through telecommunications technology to contribute to lifelong learning and the spread of knowledge. Such cooperative endeavors are two pathways towards a learning society. The RSLDC is another. An organic model, the RSLDC grew out of La Academia de la Nueva Raza as a structure embodying la resolana in the making of a learning society.

The idea for an RSLDC came out of practice. When La Academia de Aztlán was conceived in 1968, a *torreón* (adobe tower) that I had added to my home in Dixon became the first center.[65] A small group of Academia enthusiasts met there to discuss the concept and to imagine what a center for creating a body of knowledge from our own cultural and historical experiences would be like. The most vexing challenge was underwriting this tantalizing vision.

In 1969, the United Presbyterian Church, USA, convened a group of Chicanos, including myself, to serve as "interpreters" of the Chicano experience to the church's General Assembly in San Antonio, Texas. By week's end the interpreters had formed a kinship and had reached consensus on the vision of La Nueva Raza, a vision that also had achieved legitimacy with executives of the church and had been embodied by the Presbyterians' Nueva Raza Caucus.

In New Mexico La Academia de la Nueva Raza was incorporated as a nonprofit corporation. Most of the early Academia asociados were staff members of the Living Lab, a project of the New Mexico Home Education Livelihood Program (HELP) in Peñasco, New Mexico, directed by Facundo Valdez, an Academia founder. At the next Presbyterian General Assembly in Chicago in 1970, the Nueva Raza Caucus delivered its report to the assembly in a sermon by Padre Luis Jaramillo. At the conclusion of the assembly's annual meeting, we were notified that the Caucus would receive in the vicinity of $200,000 to assist Chicano groups in their struggle for social justice. La Academia de la Nueva Raza received a third of that amount. On receiving the grant, our dreams, ideas, and plans were transformed into objectives and tasks. First was the purchase of portable cassette recorders and two reel-to-reel recording machines. Documentation of people's stories began immediately, prompting the need for transcription and, in order to return to the community its own story, for publications. Other demands were made on our space and time. La Academia de la Nueva Raza thus quickly outgrew the torreón.

At about the same time a four-acre plot of farmland and an old adobe house on the northeast corner of the old Plaza del Embudo, owned by a local family, became available. Two Academia asociados purchased the house and surrounding land and made it available for use as an Academia center. A group of asociados from the Embudo/Dixon, Taos, Mora, and Española areas, who eventually formed the core staff of the emerging center, began the much-needed repairs and the transformation of the nearly two-centuries-old adobe residence into El Centro de la Academia.

The old house consisted of five contiguous rooms running from east to west, marking the northeast corner of the outer rim of the plaza. The east-end room was the kitchen. Next to the kitchen was the main room; it served as an entryway from the outside as well as the main bedroom and sitting room for the middle-aged bachelor who lived there at the time. It had a small wood-burning stove in the corner. Access to the kitchen was from this room. The kitchen had a door and small window at the back, on the north side, and an old wood-burning cook stove. At the east end was a small staircase leading to the attic, which eventually was used for storage. The kitchen was cleaned out and turned into a place for publications materials as well as for the finished products—that is, *Cuadernos*, "La Resolana, and "La Madrugada." In time we bought a secondhand offset press and placed it in the old kitchen; the kitchen then became known as the pressroom.

We discovered that a narrow nonbearing adobe wall had been added as a partition separating the main entryway/sitting room from a small bedroom. The partition came down, exposing a window to the north and doubling the size of the room. The small wood-burning stove was left as a main heating source. We also connected butane LP gas as a backup with a heater that kept the whole house comfortable in the winter. In the middle of the room we placed a homemade four-by-eight table with a plywood top and four-by-four legs. There we wrote our reports and crafted proposals. That's where we did publication layouts and collated issues of *El Cuaderno*, "La Resolana," and "La Madrugada" to distribute in the surrounding villages and mail to subscribers. We sat around that table with people from the community who stopped by to talk, and had more formal conversations there with northern New Mexico and southern Colorado university students as well as Chicano Fellows from Stanford University. In that room we met with Paulo Freire, Pedro David, and other special visitors. Formal presentations were given to small groups. The space was also the setting for dialogues about the material we were uncovering. Food and drinks were shared in that room. We had Chicano movement posters, local photographs, and Academia asociados' sketches and drawings on the walls. On several occasions we hosted village art exhibits and fiestas, the first such events in this isolated community and its environs. For those exhibits the entire house was used. Many times the room served as a crash pad for visitors who stretched out their sleeping bags and slept there. The room, in fact, was an enclosed traditional resolana.

Originally, the next room to the west, which had an entry door and a small window on the south wall, was to be partitioned lengthwise to create a bathroom on the north and a small bedroom and storage space to the south. The planned bathroom (an existing outhouse out back served as the only restroom) became the file room and documentation section as well as an embryonic library. In addition to audiotapes, we stored literature, periodicals, and newspapers related to the ongoing Chicano movement. Gradually, we started a collection of Latin American liberation theology materials; works of Ivan Illich, Paulo Freire, Orlando Fals-Borda, and others; and publications on U.S. civil rights and education. Eventually, the Spanish-language collection set the trend for the library. We acquired part of University of New Mexico Professor Rubén Cobos's collection and continued to obtain books from Mexico and Latin America. The storage part of the room became a transcription and typesetting room. Since it had a door to the outside and usually someone was working on transcription even though the rest of the building might be empty, this also became the front office where visitors entered the center.

Last in the string of rooms was the oldest one in the house, probably dating back two hundred years or more. Its vigas were dry, and the *latillas* (battens) of ax-hewn cedar were brittle; the ancient ceiling freely filtered fine dirt from the roof. This room had been the *troja* (granary), a storage place for staples, dried fruits, and other foods. The walls were nearly two feet thick and had no windows. A crude door at one time had opened to the road. It was so well secured that we left it closed and patched it over with adobe while leaving the frame exposed. A year or so later Guillermo Chávez Rosete, a Chicano/Indio roving activist and artist from El Centro Cultural de la Raza in San Diego, stopped by, stayed a few nights, and painted the Virgen de Guadalupe, the patron saint of Mexico and a widely recognized movement icon, within the old door frame. On the west wall hung a large crucifix carved by Cleofes Vigil, a famous folklorist, storyteller, and woodcarver. On the floor in front of the crucifix was *la carreta de la muerte*, a cart carrying a sculpted skeleton with a bow and arrow carved by Horacio Valdez, the famed santero. On one corner was an Alberto Baros santo; opposite it was an abstract piece by Estevan Arellano. Only two of the carvers were or had been Penitente brothers, but we decided with all due respect to call that room *la morada*, the brothers' spiritual home and chapel. It had a small adobe fireplace in the corner and adobe *banquitos* to sit on. It was a place for meditation, reflection and relaxation, and it also became a home for our growing production of woodcarvings.

In everyday parlance this building was *el centro de la Academia*; in my emerging theoretical work on la resolana I first called it a community documentation center. As reflection and dialogue continued among us, we noted the main room was truly an enclosed resolana in its redefined role where everyday life conversations as well as formal dialogue took place. Thus we added "learning" to the concept, and it became a learning documentation center.

On the external wall (of the kitchen/pressroom) facing east where the sun's rays touch in the early morning, Estevan Arellano and Alberto Baros constructed an adobe *banco* (bench) against the wall and created a comfortable place to sit and talk. On the wall the word "RESOLANA" arched over an image of the sun. This was the final statement before La Academia dissolved in the late 1970s. La resolana will always be anywhere the sun strikes against a wall and people can sit and talk, whether it is branded, is trademarked, or is just there.

A few years after the first center developed, a group of asociados purchased another old house on the southwest corner of la plaza, diagonally across from the Academia center. It had been Dixon's second post office in the late 1920s and early 1930s. My uncle Epifanio, then the postmaster, had owned the building and also operated a small grocery store. It had living quarters attached for his children to use in the wintertime since it was close to the Presbyterian Day School they attended. The place fell into disuse and eventually was sold by his son to the Academia asociados. The old post office and store became an annex to hold the growing library and documentation that had outgrown the original center. This building eventually became a village library under an independent board of directors. While the interior of the building has been restored and modernized, the exterior remains unchanged. Jaime Valdez, an Academia artist, painted San Antonio on the wall. This image of the village patron saint endures, albeit weathered and worn.

The thought of adding service to the concept of a learning and documentation center was driven by action research. Students engaged in action, or participatory, research essentially are providing a service to the people involved in the research, namely, knowledge, information, and the literacy skills they need to uncover their own knowledge. Service-learning is a view of the same idea through a slightly different lens. Therefore, when we created an AmeriCorps program in 1995, the project was named "Resolana: Learning while Serving." Sponsored by Siete del Norte, a community development corporation in northern New Mexico, the project operated in the Sawmill barrio in Albuquerque and in several northern New Mexico villages and pueblos.

Thus was born our idea of the Resolana Service Learning Documentation Center as a vehicle for arriving at a learning society. Our designs for an RSLDC as a resolana for the cyber age derive, therefore, from experience, reflection, and imagination. Its further development, if it is to continue, must follow the same path of experience, reflection, and imagination. We proceed cautiously, nevertheless, aware that the idea of a learning society is fundamentally utopian and represents a step into an uncertain future.

The most visible and perhaps most important part of the Academia learning documentation center was the main room, where we gathered to visit, talk, and work. In summer the room was cool, kept comfortable by its thick adobe walls. A cyber-age RSLDC will need a comfortable, warm, and tranquil space that carries out a similar role, attracts people, and fosters openness. It could be billed as the "classroom of the future," where dialogue is the way to knowledge. Any center should have at least one such space. And in place of the old telephone, electric lights and bulbs, wood stove, and butane heater, this updated center would have modern but sustainable and environmentally sound conveniences. It would have computer hookups, a video screen, and video and audio recording capabilities. In today's world of digital media and other technological innovations, this space would include a theater-in-the-round for dialogue and actual as well as virtual presentations, for both the generation of knowledge and its diffusion.

The press room with its old offset press and two small tables, and another small room for transcription and typesetting, would in a contemporary RSLDC be transformed into a fully equipped multimedia communication facility. It would have the technology for conducting interviews, recording dialogue sessions, digitalizing stories, photographs, and other historical materials, creating virtual productions, and recording theatrical performances and other creations; in other words, it would be made capable of developing one of the most important skills for negotiating the cyber age: technological literacy.

The RSLDC has been billed as the "library of the future." Although this brings to mind different images for different people, to us it means that it carries out the traditional functions of a library—circulation, reference, special collections, archives, and periodicals—while adding local knowledge through a community-documentation process, integrated with socially created global knowledge. The learning component is literacy and the goal is the democratization of knowledge. In other words, documentation is both a knowledge-discovery process and a learning experience. The library of the future, therefore, not only stores and disseminates "finished" knowledge, but also fosters the social creation of knowledge through face-to-face interaction and through the virtual community, or resolana electrónica, made possible by the Internet.[66] All this is facilitated by the convergence of the media/communication center, the theater, and the enclosed resolana, or meeting space.

While the focus thus far in envisioning a resolana for the cyber age has been communal and group oriented, individuals using the RSLDC should have the privacy of individual work spaces, much like carrels in university and research libraries. Studios for artistic productions should also be available. Just as creative artistic work was a part of La Academia, la resolana for the future should have a cyber-age gallery and museum.

Given that experiential learning and new literacy are central to the resolana process, practices, conditions, environments, and equipment for conducting experiential learning must be part of the RSLDC. Participants in the RSLDC must have the necessary equipment to investigate nature in all its manifestations and dimensions. Garden space must be available. The creation of a heritage orchard as part of a library reflecting a two-hundred-year tradition of apple growing in northern New Mexico provides a "text" to "read" and understand nature through land, water, plants, and trees. Beyond that, the heavens can be examined and understood through telescopes, bringing in another dimension of agriculture: archaeoastronomy. Finally, there is the microscopic world and its particular lessons and riches.

Hospitality was a natural outgrowth of the openness, warmth, and generosity of la resolana in the Academia period. We never envisioned the center becoming a crash pad, but it served that purpose when individuals connected to the Chicano movement came to visit. Several members of the RCAF, a Chicano art group from Sacramento, stayed at the center and the library and documentation center annex for more than two weeks. It makes sense to provide comfortable accommodations for visitors, along the lines of artists- or scholars-in-residence in the industrial-society tradition. Along with lodging would be a kitchen for both service and learning. Cuisine and culinary activities are also avenues for innovative experiential learning related to life sciences and environmental and nature studies.

As business has incubation centers to develop and test prospective enterprises, the RSLDC should have similar endeavors. The content would differ, as the RSLDC would seek innovative ideas in learning methods, knowledge building, new literacy, action research, consciousness raising, health, and sustainable technology; develop them; and share them with communities involved in similar activities.

Long before the 9/11 attack, some futurists were already painting scenarios of a postindustrial rise in religiosity and consequent craving for spirituality. Radical fundamentalism was already flourishing within Christianity, Judaism, and Islam, spewing intolerance and the seeds of hatred and terror. A rise of spirituality occurred among Chicanos claiming Native American spiritual traditions and, in the general population, there was growing interest in non-Western beliefs, for example, Buddhism. La Academia proposed the idea of a new humanity, a pull toward fulfillment in a just society. In the proposed RSLDC, space would be set aside for spiritual reflection, meditation, ceremony, and dialogue about moral issues in our society.

An RSLDC is the administrative hub of la resolana. It is important to note in this connection that it is the social as well as physical structure that embodies la resolana in all its manifestations and applications. A vital part of any endeavor is organization and administration. Rather than being run by a hierarchical model, however, the RSLDC should operate by consensus and coordination. Its various components would be coordinated by persons competent in the relevant fields or subject areas.

To further illustrate this point, I refer to an indigenous model of the O'odham people of southern Arizona. In setting up a health department under the direction of the tribe, various program directors funded by the Indian Health Service reached into their own traditions of addressing health problems and found not only medicine men and health and healing practices, but also a body of wisdom and knowledge for making decisions and addressing problems in their community. The O'odham people use the metaphor of an earthen pot (in their language *bith haa*), with all the ingredients and water boiling and stirred, seasoned, and watched over, producing a well-cooked and seasoned pot of stew. The bith haa is defined by its function, which is to provide the space and environment for a dynamic process to take place. Its contents are integrated with each other as the dynamic process of cooking occurs. The analogy of the bith haa illustrates the dynamics of a group process, similar to that traditionally used by villages to define problems and make the decisions necessary for solving their problems and achieving their goals. It has been seen as a systems approach with structural flexibility, much like the Porterfield model, which "allowed skills to be drawn from wherever they were available from whatever source and to participate in teamsetting focused on a defined task or set of tasks."[67]

In relation to the administration of an RSLDC, the first and most important feature is that administration be horizontal rather than vertical and hierarchical. Second, decisions are reached through dialogue and consensus. Third, communication is characterized by full integrity in the message, by "the sun shining on everything and everybody is seeing everything as it is at the same time." Fourth, project leaders are chosen based on their particular knowledge and competencies. Fifth, all project coordinators, tutors, mentors, and participants in the organization are allowed the fluidity and flexibility to come together when necessary to review and assess goals and objectives as well as to analyze problems and develop action alternatives. While the bith haa metaphor is not meant to suggest the direct application of a Native American model to an RSLDC, it is a pattern from which one may derive a progressive and truly democratic process consistent with the demands of the cyber age: based on networks as opposed to hierarchy.[68]

There are many other possibilities for making knowledge ubiquitous and lifelong learning a lifestyle. We must not wait for governmental or market initiatives to make the first move. Community organizations such as those built on the legacy of the War on Poverty; affiliates of the National Council of La Raza; neighborhood associations; service, charitable, and faith-based organizations; and cultural centers and museums are all potential documentation and learning centers.[69] Even families could provide the basis for such centers. We must embrace the idea that literacy, knowledge, knowledge building, and learning are services society must offer along with other human services.

Subjugated Knowledge in the Cyber Age

When la Academia de la Nueva Raza was created in 1969, its founders had not heard of Michel Foucault (1926–84) or Samuel P. Huntington. Both are important in relation to my topic here. Foucault, a French philosopher, is central to my analysis because of his work on the subjugation of knowledge and the "insurrection of subjugated knowledge." La Academia's work is, I believe, an example of that phenomenon. Huntington, a longtime exponent of culture as a variable in the politics of development, must be taken seriously because of his concern about the growing Mexican American presence in the United States. He warns the American public that if not checked, this trend will result in two Americas, with dire social and political consequences for the established English-speaking white American Protestants.[70]

In *Who Are We?* Huntington lists six factors that will bring about this change. The last relates to "historical presence" and is the most relevant to New Mexico and the other states that were annexed by the United States in 1848.[71] In brief, Huntington states that because of this historical fact, today's immigrants believe they have a right to their ancestors' land. This position was clearly articulated by activists in the Chicano movement and their slogan "our return to Aztlán!" I am not sure that today's Mexican immigrants to the United States have that in mind. But it may become a factor for those coming to the Southwest as the United States increasingly criminalizes illegal immigrants. Nevertheless, Huntington reminds us that there is a historical side to the subjugation of knowledge that has not been examined in the story of resolana: the impact of conquest and annexation on the historical and cultural knowledge of New Mexicans since 1848. In view of Huntington's assertions and the tremendous impact his work has on American foreign policy, and in this case domestic policy as well, I would be negligent not to address the subjugation of our historical knowledge of struggle by at least telling the cultural history of New Mexico after annexation. In telling this history I will highlight education as an apparatus of knowledge; everyday life knowledge, including language; and the invalidation of sacred, cultural, and historical knowledge.

I began this essay by describing the social and cultural background and the circumstances that led to the development of la resolana and el oro del barrio. It is an insider's understanding and description of northern New Mexico as a preindustrial society catapulted into the cyber age. This Indohispanic cultural enclave missed industrial society, I have argued, and consequently preserved its traditional wisdom and knowledge. This knowledge was not, however, consciously stored away for a later day, rather it was gradually covered up or invalidated after 1848. The Treaty of Guadalupe Hidalgo, an important document subtly misrepresented in primary and secondary school curricula, gave all Mexican citizens in the seized territory the choice of leaving New Mexico and resettling in what was left of the Republic of Mexico or staying in their homeland, accepting U.S. citizenship, and leaving behind their previous status. They had one year from the time of the mutual ratification of the treaty to decide. Those who did not declare their intent to keep their Mexican citizenship within a year would automatically become U.S. citizens.

Not all Mexicans took the offer. Some moved to the Mesilla Valley north of El Paso del Norte; they however, found themselves back in U.S. territory when a strip of Mexican land along the established border was acquired by the United States in 1853 through the Gadsden Purchase. Others settled in villages farther south in Mexico where their progeny still reside, but the majority stayed in their homeland and adapted to the changes as best they could.

Changes did not occur only through the gradual course of cultural diffusion. It became clear to Anglo settlers in the New Mexico Territory that they had a critical mass of Mexicans who claimed New Mexico as their homeland and whose culture, religion, values, and language were distinct from their own. At the same time, they were citizens and had a right to vote. What should the American victors do? Educate them! Educate them to be American. One approach was Protestant missions.

"In 1877 the Home Board [of the Presbyterian Church] created the Department of Schools to work with 'the degraded and deluded women and children of Utah, New Mexico, and Arizona.'" At the Presbyterian Church's General Assembly in 1881, the case for mission support in New Mexico was made as follows: "Those Mexicans in New Mexico, Arizona, and southern Colorado, without an exception scarcely, bigoted Romanists, speaking a foreign language, 130,000 of them are American citizens. They have a right to the ballot box. Yet they cannot even read the ballot that the priest puts into their hands. So ingrained is their tremendous ignorance and superstition, that scarcely an impression can be made, except by undermining through education."[72]

This statement and its accompanying convictions underlay the attempt to change the existing culture and belief system in the Southwest; education, a method for the creation and the validation of knowledge, was the principal tool. In the process New Mexicans' cultural knowledge was invalidated within the emerging Anglo society, and their historical knowledge of struggle was covered up.

By the close of the 1880s, the Presbyterians were operating twenty-four day schools with forty-eight teachers in northern New Mexico and southern Colorado. Most of the teachers were Anglos, with two or three newly converted natives.[73]

Protestants were not the only ones concerned about the "uneducated" new U.S. citizens. Following annexation, the Catholic Church severed New Mexico's relationship with the Diocese of Durango, Mexico, and created a vicariate apostolic, "a provisional mission diocese," with French-born Jean Baptiste Lamy as vicar.[74] Within two years the Diocese of Santa Fe was created and Lamy was promoted from vicar to bishop. Traditional religious beliefs and practices—religious knowledge—came under scrutiny and in some cases under attack by both the new Catholic Church and Protestant denominations.

The most obvious cultural clashes within the Catholic Church were between Padre Antonio José Martínez and Bishop Lamy and between the Lamy church and the Penitente brotherhood. For Martínez, a scholar, political leader, and educator as well as a priest, the issue was not theological; his preoccupation was cultural and political but manifested itself in ecclesiastical squabbles. Martínez readily accepted the U.S. Constitution, included the right to religious freedom in the incorporation of the Penitente brotherhood under the territorial laws of New Mexico, and argued that Catholic parishes had the right to select their priests. The conflict between Lamy and Martínez escalated. Anglo newcomers and some Mexicans sided with Lamy, demeaning New Mexican popular, or vernacular, Catholicism and traditional culture. The best examples of this are Willa Cather's *Death Comes for the Archbishop*, where Martínez, through a fictionalized character, is portrayed as the villain and Bishop Lamy as the hero; and Charles Lummis's *Land of Poco Tiempo*, whose target was exposing secret traditional religious practices.[75]

The criticism directed at the Penitente brotherhood was more abrasive and cruel. Its secret religious practices during Holy Week, which included flagellation, were callously exposed and condemned. Besides its primary religious function, the brotherhood also fulfilled important social, cultural, and political roles. It ensured community solidarity by providing social and economic support to its members and protecting communities from interlopers and intruders, which meant Anglos, including Protestant missionaries intent on proselytizing. These activities bred acrimony among all newcomers. Bishop Lamy barred priests within the diocese—most of them natives and protégés of Padre Martínez—from participating in the brotherhood. Most ignored the edict. Some of the brotherhood leadership opted for Protestantism. The Presbyterian denomination was especially attractive since it governed itself according to the principle of self-rule as opposed to the Catholic hierarchy. Those who accepted Protestantism and became Presbyterian in opposition to Lamy could not have foreseen that what started as a Hispanic Presbyterian Church would someday lose its ethnic identity and become merely Presbyterian, namely Anglo, but open to diversity. In any case, the attack on the Penitente brotherhood was also an assault on sacred knowledge.

With the penetration of the railroad into New Mexico in 1880, the Euro-American presence increased, especially in areas where the railroad established shops. Such was the scene in Las Vegas and Albuquerque, New Mexico, where new towns were created and the descendants of the original settlers retreated to the old town districts, which became impoverished barrios—and, today, tourist attractions. Smaller communities such as Belen and Socorro in the Rio Abajo also were centers of railroad activity. In northern New Mexico, the Denver and Rio Grande Railroad, a narrow-gauge railroad nicknamed the "Chili line," meandered from southern Colorado to Taos Junction, a railcar switching point, on to the mesa northwest of Taos, and down the gorge to La Naza, where a major station was built.

This depot was less than five miles from La Plaza del Embudo—now Dixon—which eventually became the Presbyterian center of educational and medical services for the region. The major station was Española, some fifteen miles from Embudo and the gateway to Los Alamos from the north and east.

The railroad took from New Mexico its lumber and minerals and brought in industrialization; a free-market economy; more missionary teachers, doctors, nurses, businesspeople, educators, executives, managers, mining engineers, sawmills and their managers; and along with them an alien culture, language, religion, social class, and values. New Mexico became stratified in a different way; the Mexican upper class of *hacendados*—wealthy in land, livestock, and cash—slid to the upper middle class, while a handful of well-to-do Anglos were at the top. The predominantly landholding peasantry landed at the bottom as marginal wage earners. Money and income became necessities.

After annexation, people began losing their native tongue, a principal conveyer of culture and knowledge, but they were not learning the new one effectively, which placed them at a disadvantage. Missionary activities were therefore a mixed blessing; on the one hand, they introduced New Mexicans to the American ways they were compelled to acquire; on the other hand, New Mexican cultural and intellectual heritage, rooted in Spain and Mexico, was ignored and gradually buried. Before 1848 New Mexicans had faced south for their intellectual nurturing. After 1848 they faced east, toward a different language and culture, a different body of knowledge. The gradual alienation of the people from their historical and cultural knowledge continued piecemeal but steadily, finally reaching a point of no return with the founding of the Los Alamos Lab during World War II.

In 1891, New Mexico created a Territorial Board of Education, impelling the Presbyterian Church to close all but eight of its schools, since public schooling would now be available. The indoctrination process continued, seeking not to "missionize" as the mission schools had done, but definitely to Americanize. The Mexican Revolution of 1910 increased immigration to the United States, most people using the city of El Paso, Texas, as their passage into the United States. From there immigrants fanned out to California and other southwestern states, including New Mexico, some traveling north following the crops as migrant farmworkers and settling in Midwestern cities. Although most immigrants were inclined to preserve their culture and language, the League of United Latin American Citizens (LULAC) made a concerted effort to favor English in the schools at the expense of Spanish. The home could take care of the native language, LULAC leaders reasoned. The trend toward English monolingualism pervaded both the public and parochial school systems; Spanish-speaking students were punished for using their native language. U.S. cultural and historical knowledge prevailed.

Although Spanish and Mexican legacies and the landholding peasant society with its traditional worldviews endured, there was a continuous erosion of the language, values, and beliefs. In the 1920s the likes of Willa Cather and other writers and artists, along with an army of archaeologists and anthropologists, uncovered this waning culture and its quaint wisdom and bodies of knowledge, but none of these riches were returned to the communities from which they had come. The knowledge was shared among scholars or used in novels, thereby becoming distorted and rendering life experience invalid as a basis for knowledge.

The entry of the railroad and other industrial developments into New Mexico lured many New Mexicans to labor as railroad workers, miners, shepherds, and farmworkers away from home. The stock market crash in 1929 and the ensuing economic depression sent the day laborers and first-time wage earners back home to their abandoned farms to be supported by Federal Emergency Relief Administration (FERA) programs, which served up to 60 percent of Rio Arriba County residents. The Civilian Conservation Corps (CCC), which offered job training and jobs to young men, the offspring of displaced laborers on emergency relief, took up the unemployment slack and also acculturated young men to institutional military life. Most CCC members moved on to the military as America entered World War II. This trend sealed the ongoing acculturation and Americanization while further eroding the traditional subculture crafted from the Indian and Spanish union. Its mestizo knowledge of struggle had been relegated to memory. With the nonviolent penetration of the railroad had come industrial society and a free-market economy, eroding the traditional village values of reciprocity, sharing, communalism, harmony with nature, and honor, and finally climaxing with the 1990 heroin epidemic in the villages where the Los Alamos laborers, housecleaners, and some technicians came from.

Los Alamos, the home of the Manhattan Project, the country's program to develop the atomic bomb, had a history long before it acquired fame as a war facility in the 1940s. Originally the place of *álamos*, cottonwoods, the area was awarded to Pedro Sánchez from Santa Cruz de la Cañada in 1742 and later acquired by Ramón Vigil. Los Alamos's thick forests were exploited after the "Chili line" made the land accessible to lumbering in the

1880s. Yet it remained a homestead for local Indohispanics, who carried on high-country farming and stock grazing. In the early 1900s rich folks purchased a portion of the land grant to establish the Los Alamos Ranch School. The federal government purchased the land in 1934, and in 1943 it became property of the War Department.[76] Los Alamos became a secret government facility that employed many construction laborers from the villages to build the facility and service the infrastructure for the emerging community of physicists, engineers, weapons scientists, and other technical experts. Between 1943 and the 1960s the percentage of PhD holders among the general population of Los Alamos became extraordinarily high. Its public schools boasted the highest achievement rates in New Mexico. It had many Protestant churches besides the one Catholic Church, and it had the lowest crime rate of any city its size. Los Alamos was thus everything the purveyors of the legitimated body of knowledge valued and sought to advance through the educational system.

The subordinated body of knowledge, and specifically the knowledge of struggle, had been totally suppressed. The explicit act of suppression is most notable yet most subtle in the public school curriculum and the media. It took the aggressive action and loud rhetoric of Reies López Tijerina to spark the insurrection of our subjugated knowledge as he exposed the injustices of the Euro-American landgrab by bringing the provisions of the Treaty of Guadalupe Hidalgo to the attention of Indohispanics. This is the official document that describes the legal actions for the taking of our ancestors' homeland, which rendered us a conquered people having to negotiate for more than a century to recover our land grants and water sources, ostensibly protected by the treaty. It is all about the spoils of the Mexican War and the subjugation of our history of struggle.

What happened? One thing is clear; when the Manhattan Project came to Los Alamos, most of the villages and pueblos were not part of the industrial age. Obviously, industrialization had affected the villagers, but there was no industrial wage labor in the region and no way to participate economically in the bounties of industrial society. Native northern New Mexicans were marginal consumers. Los Alamos provided some jobs, at the lowest level of occupation but at relatively good salaries for small land-holding subsistence farmers. Sale of rural land accelerated in the 1960s; most young people were thus not only separated from their culture and totally deprived of their historical and cultural knowledge, but were also cut off from their land. At the same time, the U.S. education system had been successfully alienating young people from their culture but had provided neither the incentives nor the opportunities to acquire the human skills necessary to survive and thrive in a rapidly advancing technological society. Thus has grown the notion that northern New Mexico was missed by industrial society and drugged by the cyber age.

Traditional Knowledge in the Cyber Age

Traditional knowledge was subjugated but not totally blotted out from people's memories. La resolana and el oro del barrio provide an approach for recovering this knowledge and validating everyday life experience as a basis for knowledge. They also offer ways to democratize knowledge, which guarantees its perpetuation and continuous development and thwarts its subjugation.

I turn now to a cursory view of other voices calling on traditional knowledge and wisdom for revitalizing our communities in the cyber age. In describing the impact of Los Alamos on northern New Mexico's villages, Arellano quotes Wendell Berry, who lives in Kentucky: "I am convinced that the death of my community is not necessary and not inevitable. I believe that such remnant communities as my own, fallen to the ground as they are, might still become the seeds of a better civilization than we now have."[77] From the Piedmont in Europe we hear from Carlo Petrini and Enzo Bianchi, lamenting the weakening of the "long established traditions, lifestyles, and ties between people and the land." They acknowledge that these traditions reflect the people's shared humanitarian values, which are embedded in a way of life that is rapidly changing. These communities and their culture cannot survive or be re-created, but in fact, they "have a lot to give and teach our urbanized society," asserts Petrini. Bianchi adds, "What we have to do is somehow recover a form of social life that is typical of our towns and villages. . . . We have to think how we can reinject life into these communities, looking back to the past and providing a means for communicating with others, understanding what living together really means."[78] Peter Van Dresser, a Depression-era decentralist and an early activist for sustainable communities conducted a successful experiment in sustainability on a three-acre plot in El Rito, New Mexico, in the 1960s. After removing himself from the New Mexico State Planning Office, he produced a "counter industrial" plan for the highland region of northern New Mexico that built on its natural ecology and its traditional culture.[79] Theodore Abt, an engineer and Jungian analyst, has outlined the threats of industrialization to land-based people in the Swiss Alps in his book *Progress without Loss of Soul*. These acts and ideas represent el oro del barrio from other cultures. They stand for traditional wisdom, indigenous and local knowledge that must be validated and reclaimed as legitimate local and popular knowledge that can guide us as we rebuild institutions and reclaim values for the cyber age.

But honoring the power of local knowledge to revitalize our communities has not been without its challenges. The central concept of democratizing knowledge means uncovering the knowledge from everyday life experience, objectifying it, connecting it with other intellectual achievements, and ensuring it is never alienated from those from whom it came. But we ran into a troublesome paradox as we were developing la resolana as a learning and consciousness-raising process in the 1970s. What happens to everyday life knowledge once it is reflected on and objectified? Is it decolonized knowledge? Is it in the marketplace of ideas to be exploited and recolonized? Despite these concerns, we proceeded, convinced we were doing the right and ethical thing.

La resolana shows that knowledge from everyday life experience can be reflected upon, and that a body of knowledge can link with universal knowledge and as such is transmissible to others. Ortega y Gasset has written that knowledge acquired from life experiences is part of life itself, and that it forms automatically: "It is the kind of knowing which is at once, and of itself, living. At the same time it has the inconvenience that it cannot be transmitted to anyone."[80] The basic assumptions of la resolana that themes in the stories of life are both specific to time and place and universal leads logically to the conclusion that empirical knowledge can be communicated and transmitted, not only within but across cultures. This is what is meant by the democratization of knowledge. The few examples given earlier of shared understanding of traditional values among people of different cultures and in different parts of the world attest that knowledge from everyday experience can be transmitted and exchanged, thus preparing the ground for the creation of a learning society. We need both a learning society and the ethic of una vida buena y sana y alegre.

La vida buena y sana y alegre is a philosophy of life, an ethical belief that defies Western philosophical discourse about the nature of good. Well-being and a wholesome life are about plenitude, justice, happiness, and being at peace with oneself and others. It honors, respects, and seeks harmony with nature and is rooted in a faith and a belief in a power beyond us. It is an ideal that can guide and sustain us as we face the challenges of the cyber age.

Resolana in Action

Dialogues on Success and Community

Miguel Montiel

When I started the community dialogues project I discuss in this chapter, the first person I talked with was José Ronstadt (a Los Angeles news anchor on Spanish-language television and my friend of forty years), who advised me that people would be more inclined to participate in a project that called for extensive community involvement if it had an economic or emotional appeal. Over a period of four years, our project attracted more than one hundred participants, and its appeal, we believe, was due to our approach: that, through stories and dialogue, individuals can work together to enhance self-esteem, self-worth, success, adaptation, and transformation in a global-ized world. *In the Birth and Death of Meaning*, Ernest Becker explained that culture's main task "is to provide the individual with the conviction that he is an object of primary value [by making self-esteem possible] in a world of meaningful action." This is society's way of providing a "vehicle for earthly heroism" (p. 27)

This chapter tells stories of struggles Latino leaders face in "making it," and their interpretations of the issues facing the Latino community. The Hispanic community is often described, on the one hand, as fragmented and beset with multiple problems—depressed, powerless, demoralized, isolated, poor, undereducated, plagued by violence and drugs, and with depleted resources: a community whose available solutions cannot keep up with its growth. On the other, it is characterized as family centered, hardworking, religious, and resilient (*aguantadora*). In the previous chapter, Tomás Atencio argued the core problem facing Chicanos is the disharmony between Euro-American and Chicano values. One set instrumental (e.g., goal oriented), legitimate, and systematic; the other moral, nonlegitimized, and unsystematic, but linked to myth—the primal forces of society that serve to give meaning to cosmic and social phenomena. Atencio uses the idea of la resolana—sunlight reflecting off the walls where men gather to talk—as the metaphor for enlightenment. The spiral of thought and action that evolves from individuals to groups leads to consensual validation objectifying a body of knowledge from everyday experiences. Cultural action must be based on the Chicano experience uncovered through personal history, oral history, folklore and art—el oro del barrio.[1] This chapter is a search for el oro del barrio among Chicano urban leaders. More than an attempt to characterize the Hispanic community, this study illustrates the power of dialogue in community building. Our hope is that their stories will inspire others to engage in similar conversations.

Part 1 reports on interviews with Hispanic leaders conducted by students—graduate and undergraduate, Hispanic and Anglo—who participated in a Chicano studies seminar on globalization.[2] The interviews explored the challenges Hispanic leaders face in light of the new millennium. We asked about their life accomplishments; their struggles in "making it"; about the forces, trends, attitudes, and influences that shaped their lives; and about the strengths in the Hispanic community that will help it face these challenges.[3]

Based on their stories, I wrote a piece on education, immigration, family, and community and sent them copies, inviting them to join in a series of conversations—dialogues or resolanas—on the issues raised. These resolanas are reported in part 2 and include resolanas with the same leaders discussing issues that emerged from their encounters with students, followed by resolanas with additional participants: with young leaders, between the two groups, and in an open meeting with community members.

I refer to these dialogues as resolanas to provide a connection with the Atencio essay. We could, however, also refer to these ever-expanding encounters as dialogues, conversations, or *pláticas*. Our intent was not only to illustrate the power of dialogue, but also to develop, through stories and dialogues (resolanas), an "insider's" look at the circumstances facing Hispanics as we enter the twenty-first century.

Rollo May writes that stories (or myths) are "self-interpretation of our inner selves in relation to the outside world. They are narrations by which our society is unified. Myths are essential to the process of keeping our souls alive and bringing us new meaning in a difficult and often meaning-less world."[4]

Part 1: The Fruits of Our First Resolana

My search for Hispanic leaders led to Valle del Sol, a community-based organization in Phoenix, Arizona, that sponsors a "Profiles of Success" lun-cheon honoring individuals for their contributions to the Hispanic com-munity.[5] We asked Valle staff to identify twenty individuals who had been honored in the past eight years. Valle contacted them and got their consent to participate in the project. We interviewed most of the individuals that the Valle staff had selected (along with two additional people whom we felt had made extraordinary contributions to the community). Their accomplish-ments are obvious: important jobs, contributions to institution building, community awards, wealth, and successful families. They generally come from large, traditional families, have suffered discrimination in some aspect of their lives, have attended schools populated mostly by Mexican students, and believe in giving back to the community. Still, their narratives reveal a great diversity of life experiences and worldviews.

The group of leaders selected included María Vega, PhD, a pioneer in the development of bilingual education in the high schools; Arthur Othón and Armando Flores, vice presidents of Arizona Public Service (APS), the principal utility company in Arizona; Jess Torrez, private investigator and activist who exposed racist police policies; Tommy Espinoza, executive director of the Raza Development Fund, the bank of the National Council of La Raza; Mary Rose Wilcox, member of the Maricopa County Board of Supervisors; Danny Ortega, community activist and partner in a large law firm; Ernesto Calderón, president of the Arizona Bar Association and member of the Arizona Board of Regents; Sophia López-Espindola, founder and executive director of Mothers Against Gangs; José Cárdenas, lawyer and administrator of a large law firm; Toni María Ávila, community activist; Elizabeth Valdez, MD, psychiatrist and founder and executive director of a health clinic; Rocci Maynes, PhD, migrant education pioneer; Ed Delci, longtime community activist and educational counselor; Gilda Ortega Rosales, former corporate executive, now a school district administrator, and a tireless political activist; and Ed Pastor, U.S. congressman. In their stories, the Hispanic leaders mirror the complexity present in the com-munity's history and diversity.[6]

I start with observations and insights about what we learned from the interviews, rather than with what we were told. My objective is not to influence your interpretation of the material, but simply to make the material more accessible. After reading the stories and dialogues in parts 1 and 2, I encourage you to revisit the interpretation and continue the dialogue. It is important to note that the following observations are based on a group analysis that included the authors, friends, and students. This approach is consistent with our resolana process.

In *The Revolt of the Masses*, José Ortega y Gasset once proposed that our lives could be imagined as a shot from a rifle. We are free to make decisions, but those decisions are made in the context of the trajectory of our lives, the beliefs and life forces into which we are born. From this perspective, we can perhaps better understand the forces and challenges in the interviewees' lives.

As the group of analysts read the transcripts, many questions came to mind: Is "success" a matter of luck or accident? Do people truly chart their own course? Are our lives and what happens to us more a result of circumstances than we care to admit? If we have attained knowledge and understanding, is it transferable and how? Is it possible that the Hispanic vision of the world is not in sync with Western culture? What else do we need to know about these individuals' lives that would help guide young people to prosper and learn how to become "aristocratic" (individuals of virtue, men and women who demanded much of themselves)? How do we encourage people to slow down and seriously consider el oro del barrio in our fast-paced, globalized world? What would happen if we were to gather these individuals to discuss their stories with one another and seriously contemplate these questions? Is it possible from these resolanas to develop a curriculum for living more fully?

You will find these men and women to be complex individuals who, in spite of difficult circumstances, have planned and sustained successful careers. They have contributed much to their communities, and although integrated into the dominant culture, they have maintained the cultural values of their home community. In other words, they have emphasized the importance of culture and family in their private lives, and they have resisted assimilation and oppression in their public lives. Their views of success run along personal lines—family, marriage, parenthood—and along occupational and political lines—profession, jobs, community service, and public affairs. Interviewees viewed their own roads to success according to two main perspectives: The "defining moments" perspective spurs people to achieve; the "family and values perspective" is tied to mentor influences, that is, attitudes toward self and others.

In many of these stories, less than ideal early lives blossom when hit with adversity, a transformation from the negative to the positive that is often accompanied by anger. These stories describe oppression. A student progresses through school, yet he cannot read. There are stories of politicians who learned about discrimination by living in union towns or through pivotal events that jolted them into another reality. In one narrative, a mother teaches her son to be aware of injustices and, later in his life, this wisdom guides him to action at a critical point in his life. Other narratives tell of people who are fired for taking stands against discrimination and subsequently realize that they alone must bear the consequences. Courage, focus of purpose, preparation, and perseverance seem to be the central virtues expressed in these stories. There is an element of the heroic in them.

Education is valued and stressed. Regardless of whether their motivation to "get ahead" and contribute to the community arose from anger, courage, or a set of cultural values, these leaders had to lay the educational foundations necessary to take advantage of the opportunities life presented. Nevertheless, there is a shared feeling that the school system has failed the Hispanic community—if not them personally, then the community at large—in terms of poor teaching, lack of respect, and failure to create a smooth transition for newly arrived immigrants.

"Getting ahead" is difficult for Hispanics. In addition to the obvious difficulties of overcoming poverty and obtaining an education, there is a hidden dimension to "success": the need to market oneself. In order to get into school, to get a job, or to advance in life, one has to sell oneself. This type of self-promotion runs contrary to traditional cultural roles. Does behaving in this manner not come naturally to many Hispanics because it does not mesh well with their cultural patterns? Nevertheless, these individuals learned how to navigate the labyrinth of their complicated surroundings.

In some ways, the "movement people" of the sixties operated like priests in poor parishes: they had to raise money but did not feel good about doing so. Similarly, these leaders had to compromise with "the system" to keep the movement alive. They justified their behaviors by pointing out that if not for their sacrifices, society might never have changed. Acting "white" not only helped in "getting ahead," it also enabled them to contribute to the greater good. Unfortunately, "getting ahead" was not always compatible with remaining true to their real selves. At the organizational level, community development agencies moved from an advocacy stance in the tradition of the NAACP to business–social services enterprises with a broader, community orientation. In switching perspectives, did these agencies abandon their responsibility to serve as a moral compass for society? If so, whose responsibility is it to advocate for the public good? And what are the dangers of relying exclusively on "the system"?

These leaders repeatedly point to "luck" as important in their success. This may be a sign of humility, in that it diminishes the role they played in shaping their own destinies. There are many other factors that influence success, such as whether or not they grew up where they were a "minority" and how the consequences of their minority or majority status affected them. What were the effects of growing up in a town composed primarily of Hispanics, in segregated barrios of town, or in Mexico? What did these various individuals experience in the Army, the university, or the workplace, where minorities are discriminated against?

Migrant workers' stories raise very interesting issues. For example, these leaders maintain strong traditional values. Like the Euro-American middle classes, they are mobile and know how to adapt to various places and circumstances. In their case, mobility is not a liability but an advantage. In spite of their poverty, migrant parents somehow provide the necessary support, and perhaps more important, convey the expectation that their children will remain in school. In this case, the most important gift that parents can give their children is to expect them to go to school and ensure that their children graduate. The standards and expectations of their parents seems to have a great impact on the young.

How do some people manage to create an environment that sustains their passion for life? It takes great strength for a woman to inspire or push her son toward success, or for a mother to shape the direction of her family by moving out of the housing projects. Such strength is reflected in one woman who sees childrearing as central to her being and in another who developed a support mechanism for mothers who lost their sons to violence, as she did. In the latter case, we can assume that the woman's defining moment was the death of her son, yet there is really no explanation of how the healing took place or of how she managed to gain the pride in her own accomplishments that is manifested in her story. What makes her situation different from that of women who suffer similar losses but never recover? This woman reminds us of many Hispanic mothers who have overcome obstacles to create great things out of virtually nothing. This phenomenon was evident in the early phases of the Chicano movement, when such women did the frontline work, fought the battles, but their efforts were rarely recognized. Some of these narratives provide us with a sense of the price women pay for their strength, including divorce and societal and familial rejection. Some may also feel an element of guilt when others confront them about their life choices.

One politician's story begins with a change of perspective that came when she confronted the racism of the university outside her town and began to refine the organizational and political skills first learned from her family's union background, skills that she later honed to become a successful politician. She talks about her family and how proud she is of them, but gender issues are not central to her story.

In one story, the rules of university accreditation in the United States prohibit a Mexican woman from practicing medicine. She later becomes an eminent teacher. In the process, she had to confront many hurdles: hurdles created by her status as an immigrant to a country that did not value her education; bureaucratic hurdles within an educational system that blocked her path to becoming a teacher; and ethnic and gender hurdles faced by women of her generation. She dealt with more than her fair share of the world's injustices. Still, she was not intimidated by those hurdles, by medical school in Mexico, or by the educational bureaucracy in the United States. Nor did she become embittered. Why not?

Some of the stories are very emotional. They resonate with the experiences of many successful minorities who at one point in their lives were told—explicitly or subtly—that they should go to trade school. How did those who lost their parents as teenagers still manage to become strong individuals? The formula for success is reiterated time and again: family, friends, and other types of support plus the courage to deal with adversity lead to success. Religion plays a prominent role in some of the stories.

There may be a pattern in these stories with regard to gender differences. The women seem to organize their stories around central themes or cores, weaving all the other parts to this core as in a spiderweb. In contrast, men seem to tell their stories chronologically. Their narratives flow in a single direction: they begin with a defining moment in their lives, such as an experience of racism or discrimination; move on to their education; and then describe a phase in which they justify their actions with a feeling of self-fulfillment.

One woman's story, for example, begins with the cultural expectations of the Hispanic community when she was young—getting married and having children, staying at home, and not pursuing an education—then evolves to the development of her career goals, her self-fulfillment, and the realization of her family aspirations. It is not uncommon for highly educated minorities to distance themselves from their community in an effort to escape the wrath of being marked as "affirmative action minorities." How and why did these individuals follow a different trajectory of maintaining close connections with their community? Many of the narratives demonstrate a sense of history. Interviewees speak about raising their children to know who they are, where they came from, and what their role in society should be.

What about the identity issue raised so eloquently by the Mexicans who came here as adults? What do they see about Mexicans born in the United States that concerns them so? Clearly, schools and other institutions were neglectful of many Mexican Americans (and other Hispanics) from segregated neighborhoods. Yet the youngsters were sheltered in their communities and only later realized that racism and discrimination existed in the "outside" world and that the institutions, particularly the schools, that supposedly existed to protect and guide them had cheated them. It seems that the low expectations for achievement directed toward Hispanic schoolchildren has had devastating effects in the Hispanic community. What about the darker side of Mexican history and culture, the painful colonial history of the mistreatment of our indigenous ancestors? What about the conditioning that has taught us to be passive, perhaps racist, and demeaning of women? And what about the sense of inferiority articulated by Samuel Ramos more than sixty years ago?[7]

Community Leaders Speak with Students

What follows are the stories shared in the resolanas between students and community leaders. I read the transcripts, discussed them with students and colleagues, identified themes, and collated stories around these themes. Themes fall into several major categories: (1) making it in the Anglo world; (2) defining moments; (3) family and values; and (4) major challenges: (a) education, (b) leadership and politics, and (c) immigration. The section concludes with the challenges of adapting to the new society.

Making It in the Anglo World   I do not attempt here to define the idea of making it. For my purposes, it is sufficient to assume that their being honored for their contributions means that in the eyes of the wider community, these interviewees have made it. When we think about someone having made it, we tend to make that judgment based on factors such as income, type of job, level of education, and employment. One question I asked myself was, Do the depictions of success in these stories conform to those outlined by conventional wisdom and self-help books: staying ahead of the competition; listening to advice; presenting a good image; not being afraid of failure; staying focused; possessing negotiation skills; controlling emotions; using proper body language; and having concern for friends, family, and personal pride?[8]

The first steps toward making it are influenced by family, friends, colleagues, teachers, and occasionally one or two enemies. Dr. María Vega, who grew up in Mexico, described the powerful influence of her father: "In my home, there was no bread, no food. We were very poor. But we had no scarcity of education. When our father arrived home, he'd say, 'Is everyone ready to go to school? Let's see your papers and pencils.' Today, it is not like that. My parents envisioned that I could become a doctor."

Vega completed four years of medical school in Mexico, but after marrying and immigrating to McKinney, Texas, she was unable to practice medicine because she could not take the required examination in English. Working with her husband and church members in McKinney, she founded the Latin American School to educate the children of laborers who picked cotton, "a barbaric task," as Vega described it. "The parents left for work at six in the morning. The oldest was left in charge of the younger ones, thus keeping the oldest child from going to public school. Once there was a house fire, and a father and five children died. We needed to act. My husband said, 'No more of this. The little school will open tomorrow.' And so we opened the little school." Vega and her husband operated the school and later opened a health clinic before moving to Phoenix, Arizona, in 1959.

Vega talked about her struggles to continue her education in the United States: "The studies in Mexico were very difficult, and my parents had made great efforts. When I went to Arizona State University in hopes of working on a master's degree, I overheard the registrar say, 'She's a Mexican who's here because she wants the degree given to her without putting in the work. The university in Mexico is no good.' They placed me as an undergraduate, a sophomore. I had already taken many hours of every science course possible, but they didn't know what courses to give me." That registrar later tried to prevent the Phoenix Union High School District from hiring Vega as a teacher, claiming that "she had not completed her studies," but they hired her anyway. She recalls the pain of those events: "I cried a lot because they wouldn't accept my studies from Mexico."

Making it often involves at some point a revelation about being Hispanic, Mexican, Latino, or Chicano in a non-Latino world. The word "shock" is used repeatedly in many of these stories, as if this revelation catapults people into a new reality. Arthur Othón recalled, "I came from the school of hard knocks—dropped out of school when I was a junior in high school and joined the service. I got a GED in the service because if you didn't, you were sent to Vietnam. I didn't experience racism or discrimination until I went to high school, because we were all in the same barrel—poor." Othón related that in school, Anglos were encouraged to study geometry whereas Hispanics were steered toward "vocational and body and fender work and painting cars." In high school he recalls many conflicts between blacks and Chicanos, and how the Anglos in the Army made him "feel less than I was." Early on, he recognized "that the discrepancies and disparities between communities and how young people are treated were the issues and battles that would shape the direction of my life."

Othón's family was upset when they learned that he had left his state job and its security (steady paychecks and benefits). "You must be out of your mind!" they said. But Othón wanted to help his community and its youth and felt he could best do so by becoming director of the community-based organization Chicanos Por La Causa (CPLC). "There was a time in Phoenix when, if you were walking on the sidewalk and an Anglo was walking towards you, you had to step down and let them pass. . . . These were very black and negative times, but now we are accepted and everyone knows we are here." He broke ground when he was named executive assistant to the mayor of Phoenix and took on the challenge of serving as a liaison between the Hispanic community and the mayor's office.

Othón remembered an old black man who advised him to "kiss ass 'til you can kick ass." Whenever Othón complained about his frustration that minorities did not get their fair share of community dollars, this was his friend's constant counsel. "My friend's advice worked. I was very 'yes sir, no sir,' until I had the strength and the power to say that this belongs to us and our community and we are going to kick ass!"

Defining Moments   More than the accomplishments of Hispanic leaders per se, our interest was in what spurred them on, what moment or moments seemed to define their path toward success. Some of these experiences involved an adverse or traumatic event—an act of discrimination or the death of a loved one. Other accounts describe a gradual unfolding from a set of core values or moral foundation handed down from family or the culture. Jess Torrez, for example, spoke of the values his family instilled in him and how they interacted with various incidents of discrimination, incidents that eventually led him to take a stand against the Scottsdale Police Department and their unwritten "no n***** zone" policy.

Torrez grew up in the sixties. His father worked as an upholsterer and his mother worked for the Arizona Civil Rights Commission. Torrez recalled his mother's stories about civil rights violations against farmworkers and Native Americans. She read to her children from a book about Joaquín Murrieta, a legendary miner turned "bandit" after his claims were stolen during the California gold rush. Torrez related that he thought things were fine until he became aware of the struggles his mother confronted at work.

He began to wonder why the books he read in school were always about "white kids," even though the kids on his block were mostly Mexican. He remembered lifeguards at the community pool where he swam "saying that the kids from the elementary school couldn't come to the pool unless it was the day that they emptied the water. And they had to take two showers before they went into the pool. And I knew it was because they were Mexican. I was 'okay' because I swam on the swim team. Those were things that stuck with me." His mother died during his junior year of high school. He attended college as a tribute to her.

Besides his marriage, Torrez said his legal fight was the most significant and defining moment in his life. Torrez's story went something like this. He was fired from his position as a police officer for blowing the whistle on the Scottsdale Police Department's "no n***** zone." This name refers to a part of town where, unless they were carrying yard equipment in the back of their vehicles, people of color were stopped if they crossed an imaginary "white" boundary. One day, some police officers stopped three Mexican adolescents for no apparent reason other than that they were Mexican. Torrez voiced his objections, and the trouble began. "It shut a lot of doors for me," he recalled. He was thirty-eight, past the age when he could apply for a federal law enforcement position. But he knew no other kind of work. He had a wife, three children, and a mortgage, and as he described it, he didn't know what he was going to do. His situation reminded him of an old saying in police court: "One 'oh shit' erases all those 'atta boys.' And it was very true. There was nothing that I did that made a difference in being fired and labeled. I was blackballed, couldn't find a police job."

Torrez filed suit for unlawful termination, alleging violation of his civil rights. Two and a half years after Torrez was fired, the trial took place. During the first three weeks of the trial, the only people in the courtroom were his family, an occasional friend, and one or two other interested individuals. Then toward the end of the trial, one of the police captains stated, "Oh yeah, we [the Scottsdale Police Department] have a 'no nigger zone,' but every police department in the country has one." All of a sudden the media jumped on the story. Torrez thanks God that on the day the captain made his statement, there happened to be a newspaper reporter in the courtroom. It was standing room only in the courtroom after the reporter ran a story about the captain's remark. Torrez described how shocked he was to learn that these zones were a common topic at police chiefs' conventions. These zones, Torrez recounted, "are the same thing as no Mexican zones." Torrez explained that the captain's admission helped his case, even though the jury never heard it because the judge felt it was too inflammatory. There was more: "We later found out that the judge got his judgeship because the city's attorney had cleared the way for him. He should have excused himself from any trial where his friend was the lawyer, but he didn't."

Ed Delci, volunteer and former employee of the Peace Corps, a respected community activist, and now an Arizona State University student counselor, knows about taking stands and suffering the consequences. After graduating with a degree in Spanish and Latin American studies, Delci's goal was to become a Foreign Service ambassador to a Spanish-speaking country. He came close to realizing his ambition when he became a Peace Corps regional director in Peru. In Peru, Delci developed a strong relationship with the U.S. ambassador, who sought his "counsel" and "credited" him for handling delicate situations with the volunteers. However, when the Nixon administration reneged on its promise to pay for the volunteers' education once they had completed their tours, he resigned his post never to return to the job he loved so dearly. He explained that in some ways the actions of the administration in Peru foretold what was to happen in Chile in years to come.

Tommy Espinoza, whose experiences of discrimination similarly became defining moments in his life, talked about what drove him to succeed: "I was always driven at first because of what happened to my father [who was discriminated against at work], and a dog incident [an Anglo dog-catcher beat his dog], and although it sounds minor, it really impacted me. The last time my father tried to get a promotion, he was almost defeated, and it really upset me. I remember telling him, 'Don't give up.' By the way, I was always getting kicked out of school. I was always doing terrible in school, and I was always a troublemaker, so it was not my position to be telling my dad [anything]."

Espinoza described how racism drove him to succeed. "At one point I was a racist. I saw the damage that racism caused my own father and to some degree myself. It was a negative force because it was more geared at anger versus love, which is a much stronger energy." Espinoza recalled organizing a walkout against the company he worked for in his youth because it was discriminating against one of the Mexicanos. He learned, he said, that it was "okay to organize and to be a leader, but there is a price to pay—I got fired."

Mary Rose Wilcox gained her political acumen from witnessing her father's involvement with unions; she learned the power of organizing. "When you organize for a purpose, you change things." Her father became the first Mexican American shift supervisor at the mine in Superior, Arizona. One of his functions in this role was to serve as a liaison between the workers and management. Initially, this created resentment among his coworkers and neighbors, but in the end he managed to advance the miners' interests.

Wilcox described the shock she experienced upon arriving at Arizona State University in the mid-sixties, where the only three minority girls out of one hundred new students were assigned to the same dorm room: "What is going on?" I wondered. I'd been in student government and knew a lot of the kids that were coming to ASU because I'd been involved statewide. I knew people of all ethnic groups, and it was a real surprise. We ended up rooming together for two years in that dorm. But it was a major eye-opener." She expressed her belief that racism is subtler now; it has gone underground, but it is just as damaging. Still, she added, it gives her hope when she sees young people from a variety of racial groups interacting with one another.

A second defining moment came later in her career when Wilcox was first elected to public office. Other Hispanic officials, she reported, ostracized her because she refused to make any politically motivated appointments. Although the isolation was difficult, it was, she realized, "the best thing that could have happened because it made me strong and independent."

María Vega also experienced numerous confrontations with American schools. There were five thousand students at Phoenix Union High School when Vega started teaching there. She noticed the Anglo students got A's, the black students C's, and the Mexican students F's. The director of registration, an Anglo, asked at the time, "Just what are you going to do with so many silly, crazy people? They never study, they're lazy, and they're *burros*." Vega countered that the students were not getting what they needed. "They have brilliant minds. Let me give them a new kind of class—Spanish for the Spanish speaking—and you will see a difference," she argued. It was 1961. She was given five classes. Vega recalled starting her first class of bilingual students:

"'Buenos días, ¿Cómo les va?' Their mouths dropped. 'Good morning, Teacher.' No 'teacher,' soy tu maestra—and I began to call the roll, Pablo Gonzáles, Juanita Chávez, . . . 'Hey,' they said, 'We're all Mexicans.' 'That's right, we don't speak English here, and if anyone does, you will be fined.'"

"Within nine years, we had four Hispanic teachers. The director and I became really cooperative. It was wonderful. They gave me students who only spoke Spanish but did not read Spanish, and they advanced easily. They spoke both English and Spanish."

One of Vega's students, attorney Danny Ortega, talked about how his teachers influenced his life: "They were kind to me. It's amazing how a little love will go a long way. But in terms of education, my major event was getting a twenty-five-dollar scholarship from the Vesta Club."

His education, Ortega stated, allowed him to achieve economic independence for himself and his family. He recalled his father, a migrant worker, saying, "El cabrón que no quiera ir a la escuela, se va a levantar a las cuatro de la mañana a trabajar conmigo." (The lazy bastard who doesn't want to go to school can get up at four in the morning to work with me.) Well, Ortega loved to sleep, so there was no way he was going to get up at four in the morning to go to work. He went to school instead.

Tommy Espinoza also reflected on the positive influences his education had in defining his life: "In the sixth grade, I found out that I couldn't read. I had just been promoted and promoted and promoted, and my teacher was very upset. He took the time to stay with me after school and tutored me—and bribed me with a baseball glove. He touched my life for the best."

Not unexpectedly, school experiences did not always represent a positive defining moment. Ernesto Calderón recalled a teacher who told his mother that by encouraging him to go to college, she was giving him "unrealistic expectations." He remembered how angry his mother was after her conversation with the teacher—and her quiet act of defiance: "My mother sent that teacher a copy of every graduation announcement and newspaper clipping until the day the teacher died." In contrast to his early school experiences, Calderón remembers "Northern Arizona University being a wonderful time away from home. I don't remember anyone at NAU saying I couldn't do anything. On the contrary, all my teachers and advisers at NAU said, 'You can do anything.' . . . They made me feel like I was doing them a favor by going to NAU, when in fact, they were doing me a favor by educating me."

At times, a person's own family prompted the defining moment. In a moving interview, Sophia López-Espindola reminded us of a phoenix rising from the ashes of abuse, brokenness, and the violent death of her son as she described her commitment to reaching out to other grieving and oppressed women. Mothers Against Gangs is López-Espindola's greatest accomplishment. The idea, she said, grew out of the death of her son. "It made it seem that no one gave a shit about my son's life, that he was just another Mexican who died—another statistic. And I showed them that my son's life was important . . . that he meant a lot to a lot of people. I helped our people understand the system and helped them with the grieving process. And I also let women know that if you don't have degrees or if you're not rich or whatever, you can still do whatever you want in your life—that a 'nobody' can become a somebody if they really, really want to be that somebody, and that we shouldn't allow anybody to hold us down."

Family and Values   Many community leaders spoke of their families as accomplishments in and of themselves. In describing the good things Mexican culture provides, Cárdenas observed, "It's hard to find parallels in the culture at large. There seems to be an ability to focus on family and culture in a way that adds something to the experience of being Hispanic." Preferring to talk about his family rather than his significant career accomplishments, José Cárdenas listed his marriage to his wife, Virginia, a Mexican native who comes from "a very strong family," and his Catholic upbringing as major influences in his life. "We're regular churchgoers, always have been." Cárdenas, who lost his father when he was only fifteen, explained that family is important "both in terms of keeping us humble, so that you don't get a fat head because you think you've done a lot, [and instilling] a work ethic that we both got from our families. You combine those, and you do have a better culture. It doesn't mean that we don't have a lot of problems. That's part of it."

Similarly, besides her involvement in politics, Toni María Ávila referred to marriage and motherhood as important accomplishments. She described becoming a mother as "creative." She proudly mentioned that she watched her son graduate as an engineer and become a wonderful person.

Responsibility—taking responsibility both for one's own behavior and in general—was an often-mentioned family value. Armando Flores spoke about his mother's influence: "She would never accept any excuse for C's or even B's, that it was the teacher's fault or anyone else's fault other than mine. She had a very sharp tongue and let us know that, when it came to education, under no circumstances was there any possibility of compromise." The results of his mother's efforts were impressive. He went to twelve years of Catholic school even though the family could not afford the tuition. His sister worked in the cafeteria for her tuition, and he worked after school and on Saturdays pulling weeds and cutting the grass on the football field. But he received a quality education through parochial school then went to college. He still has his acceptance letter to the University of the Pacific, where he did his undergraduate work. He never thought he could go to a private school, far less college, any college. Receiving the letter saying he was admitted was one of his most emotional experiences. But once he got started, no one was going to stop him. All he had to do was get through the door. He had significant opportunities in the business world and today he is an executive vice president of APS.

"My strong values have also contributed to [my] being a good husband and father and a good member of the community, somebody who is able to recognize the good fortune that he has had and to recognize the responsibility and obligation to give back to the community—to support and assist those who have not been as fortunate." He explained that there is more to life than titles and money. Sometimes he wonders how he did it all.

U.S. Congressman Ed Pastor got his love of politics from his grandfather Jess López, who was active with the Alianza Hispana Americana and from members of his family, who were involved with the unions in Miami, Arizona, a segregated mining town where he was born and raised. He recalls his teachers telling him that he should know that "the doctor's son has to get good grades. We're going to give him good grades so he can go to medical school, and you're going to the mines anyway." This did not stop him from pursuing his passion. And despite the inequality in school where "they were at the lowest end of the totem pole, the unions, Hispanic organizations and the positive attitude of my folks never caused us to give up and say they are better than we are." It is important to have an "anchor to sustain self-esteem—feeling good about yourself and having a very caring family and people around you to nurture you and your education."

Although he got in trouble in high school, he still managed to go to Arizona State University. In 1974, he graduated from law school. While he was preparing for the bar exam, however, his brother was killed in an automobile accident. Too upset to take the bar exam, he went to work for Arizona Governor Raúl Castro. In 1976 when his friend Joe Eddie López decided to vacate his seat on the Maricopa County Board of Supervisors to run for the U.S. Congress against another Hispanic, Tony Gabaldón (they both lost), Pastor ran for López's seat and was elected to the Board of Supervisors in 1976. In 1991 he became a U.S. congressman. He told his interviewer that the "biggest favor you can do for yourself is to educate yourself to the highest point you can achieve . . . because it is the thing that nobody can take from you . . . and only you can decide that you're going to do it. You can say I'm going to do it for my family, I'm going to do it for my girlfriend, I'm going to do it for César Chávez, but in reality it's for you. But once you have the education, you have a good foundation. You never know what's going to happen to you in life." He never dreamed of going to law school or becoming a U.S. congressman, "but when the chance came, you know what, I was able to go forward because I knew I had the foundation. And without the foundation, then I would have said, 'Well, I guess I can work in the mines, or the post office' . . . which are good jobs, . . . that doesn't mean you give up everything, but you have to be careful. You make little sacrifices."

Gilda Ortega Rosales, a tireless advocate of voter registration, highlights the importance of politics and the centrality of gender in her life. In the sixties, women who aspired to go to college (and high school in some cases) "were not encouraged, either by the educational systems and in some cases by their families. [Culturally] a woman's primary responsibility was to get married . . . and rear children." Her immediate family (migrant farmworkers able to provide no more than food and shelter), however, did encourage her, and she knew that if she wanted to "have more and make a difference in my own quality of life as well as that of my family and my community, I needed to do more than just graduate from eighth grade." At an early age she knew that she "needed to get good grades so that I could get scholarships. I was very fortunate in that the government still was providing substantial financial aid to economically disadvantaged students. I was in the top ten of my high school graduating class, which provided a Regents Scholarship that paid for my tuition as long as I kept a B average. I had loans, worked part-time throughout the school year and into summer to continue the funding of my education as well as helping my family." During her early years, her family offered support by providing her with a set of expectations that inspired her to pursue an education. Later on, her family, her husband, her job, and her employers supported her desire to go outside of her home and become involved in the community. The support she received from the people around her made it all possible.

Elizabeth Valdez, a psychiatrist, provided another perspective on family life in the Latino community. The community, she pointed out, faces challenges because of the dramatic increase in single-parent homes and dysfunctional families. "Kids don't feel loved and valued; there are few resources for families to heal." One of several problems is the language barrier. When the children of immigrant adults learn English but the parents do not, a role reversal occurs. The parents lose authority and the children become embarrassed by their parents. Valdez and other leaders warn of the violence, anger, and depression that such situations engender. The self-centered philosophy of American culture, Valdez asserts, is another source of stress on the family. Because the culture is "me-focused" not "we-focused," it detracts from the family and family relationships. There is a need, Valdez pointed out, for more English as a second language programs for parents and proactive programs to help return strength to the family. Valdez also described her vision of programs that would enable women to foster community and coalition building, to take full advantage of women's energy and strength.

Mary Rose Wilcox echoed the need to create stable home environments for children. The great numbers of working parents and single mothers make it imperative, she emphasized, to involve grandparents and extended family members in rearing children. Sophia López-Espindola experienced the negative side of family life. Members of her family put her down. "My husband used to say that I was stupid, that I was dumb because I had a lot of kids. Even my father would tell me that no one would want me and that no one would give a shit about me. That was my upbringing—we're just supposed to have kids, stay home, be stupid, be whores, and have babies from different fathers. But that's not what we're supposed to be. Hispanic women have a lot of talent, if they learn to use it. There's a lot that we know how to do. I always told my daughters and my sons that when I got married I learned to become a mechanic, a plumber, a construction worker, and a bookkeeper because you have to maintain your home."

López-Espindola recalled, too, the many family problems she faced as a little girl, problems that eventually led her to a foster home. "And when I was growing up, I swore I would never let my kids live the way I had. I never really had anything that was really, really mine until I had my son. And when I had him, it was like the best thing in my life, because for the first time I had something that belonged to me."

One of López-Espindola's vivid memories is of her grandmother getting a flush toilet. Before that she had to use a homemade outhouse. "It was a wooden box that my grandfather made," López-Espindola remembered, "and we had to throw the water hose through there, and in the winter it was cold. When my grandmother got a toilet that actually flushed, it was the happiest part of my life."

Almost all of these community leaders pointed to the strength of their family ties as a crucial source of support in pursuing their career and life goals. Tommy Espinoza told his interviewer, "We shouldn't lose track of our biggest asset—that we are close to family . . . because when we need help—monetary, psychological, or whatever—we can usually count on our family; there are cultures that don't have this." He emphasized the special place of mothers. "In this generation, the beauty of our culture is the love of our mothers. The broader society has a tendency of using women in a most negative way."

Mary Rose Wilcox pointed to other important lessons learned within the family. "One of the things my mother taught us was that anything you do will come back to you. If it's good, it will come back. If it's bad, it will come back. So you make your own destiny." José Cárdenas talked about the importance of love and caring in families, "We're very proud of who we are. We have high self-esteem, and we love our music, our culture, our food—we love everything about us. If we take the high self-esteem, the ethic of hard work, the family nucleus—those are the things that are really going to propel us in the future."

Major Challenges   Community leaders also addressed the challenges of education, leadership, immigration, and a multitude of social problems. I do not present their comments in order to analyze these problems in depth, but merely to provide a framework for the resolanas that are reported later in this chapter.

Education   Attributing their own success to their education, many of the Hispanic leaders we interviewed asserted that improving education should be the preeminent goal of the community. Education for the Hispanic community encompasses much more than the three R's. As Ernesto Calderón pointed out, education in the community calls for multiple strategies, for there are negative forces, including racist legislators "that don't want to educate Latinos, but if Hispanics don't have the capacity to really educate the kids, then we are part of the problem instead of the solution."

In articulating some of the educational needs of Hispanic youngsters, Mary Rose Wilcox proposed a more broadly structured educational system, one that would reach beyond the schools and into the homes. It would include teaching children how to deal with conflict, how to avoid gangs, and how to develop alternatives to violence and firearms, which are too widely accepted in the community. Ideally, María Vega added, the curriculum would include teaching children to "have pride in themselves, know where they came from, where they are going, and what they are doing in this world." "Likewise," Vega continued, it would be important to "ensure that everybody learns English. It doesn't matter how you learn it, bilingual education or immersion." A proper education, Tommy Espinoza explained, would include instruction in finance, credit, and asset building, or "we will become nothing but consumers." Ernie Calderón pointed to the value of investing time and money in creating scholarship funds to provide opportunities for youngsters who want but cannot afford to go to school.

Several leaders stressed the importance of a sense of history in the education of young people: "I wish," Vega said, "I could be young again so I could move things around some more. I see those of you that are at the university as needing [to teach] the true history of Mexico. It's wonderful that the Americans give money to maintain the missions, but do they know who built them? I remember taking my students in the bilingual program to Tumacacori. What a wonderful place! One of the girls saw a metate there and asked, 'What is that for?' I told her that her grandmother ground corn on it when she came here to Tumacacori. She asked, 'My grandmother came here?' I said, 'Yes.' She was amazed. She was my student in 1971, and she's my friend today. She discovered that her grandfather had lived in Tubac.

Today she remembers with regret that she was kicking the walls of the place, not knowing that perhaps her grandfather had helped build the walls."

Dr. Rocci Maynes suggested the educational system is unprepared to handle the increasing number of Spanish-speaking children. There is a lack, Maynes pointed out, of qualified bilingual teachers. He recalled instances of bilingual teachers spending time "teaching children how to make tacos." Sometimes teachers used incorrect spelling, he added, and mispronounced Spanish in their classes. Good bilingual education does not mean not learning English. It is important to learn English, Maynes emphasized. English classes should be started in preschool so that children are not at a disadvantage in school, but it is just as important that children and their parents understand that Spanish is as legitimate as English; children need to be bilingual.

Leadership and Political Participation   In addition to the challenges of education, community leaders pointed to the need for leadership in different segments of society—in politics, business, religion, and the family. Danny Ortega observed that though the names have changed since the sixties and seventies, the same issues remain, albeit in more complicated form. The political battlefields have moved from the agricultural fields and the educational institutions to a larger arena, where only the wealthy and highly educated are able to "swing the bat." Education, economics, health care, housing, immigration, and language are some of the more important issues facing the "Hispanic nation." Ortega pointed to the many distractions— the Internet, entertainment, sports, computers, television, radio—that are diminishing the support system in the Hispanic community.

Tommy Espinoza talked about organization, advocacy, and partnerships as critical for correcting "our lack of voice and our traditional mentality of silent suffering." First, Espinoza proposed, there is a need to motivate leaders in all contexts—in business, government, and church; in organizations; and in families—to envision a future where Latino universities "teach multilingual programs and incorporate immigrants from all over the world to find ways of helping finance third world countries. We need to start thinking of ourselves as tools of change for the future, for the whole world and our country. And that needs to be articulated by everyone in leadership positions."

Arthur Othón expressed the belief that organizations should pay greater attention to advocacy: "In the old days, Chicanos Por La Causa used to play an advocacy role; it was the one that would stand in front of mayors and the legislature and city council saying that discrimination and unfair treatment were not going to be accepted in our community. We don't have that today." He voiced the opinion that Chicanos are "going backward." Othón pointed with particular concern to the influence that state and other monies have on Hispanic organizations. "The evolution is that we start something for the community, then the majority community funds it and wants to take it over . . . and we lose the sensitivity and the *corazón* [heart]." He expressed his feeling that people are too comfortable working for corporations like Motorola, APS, and the banks, "so they are not out there fighting. . . . We are still very underrepresented." Othón also called for a broader-based dialogue around issues of leadership in all spheres of life, including partnerships with banking, financial, and government institutions.

Leaders also expressed disenchantment with the related issue of political participation in the community. Gilda Ortega Rosales talked about the importance of politics in the Hispanic community: "In the last ten years, I have been very disappointed again at the level of participation of our community in an election. Voting is not a priority. It's very sad, very disappointing, and we can't continue in that manner." Rosales suggested the need to "educate immigrant children at a very young age about the importance of political participation so that they can understand it. If they don't, it will be our failure, not theirs."

José Cárdenas stated that community participation is central to his life. Involvement is a tradition in his law firm, he said; it is expected and it's good for business. He also mentioned that obligations to his friends often lead him into community undertakings. As a lawyer, Cárdenas said, he believes he has been provided with leadership opportunities that otherwise would not have been available to him. Indeed, he sits on the Arizona State Foundation and hosts a weekly television show about Hispanic issues.

Immigration   Community leaders also discussed the challenges posed by ongoing immigration from Mexico and other parts of Latin America. While acknowledging the complexity of the Hispanic community, Mary Rose Wilcox spoke of the new wave of Latin American immigrants and the fear it has created. There is infighting, Wilcox explained; Mexican Americans see themselves being displaced in the workforce by immigrants. She points out that the Mexican American community is a "changing, evolving culture, with second-, third-, and fourth-generation Mexican Americans and 600,000 immigrants in Maricopa County alone, half of whom have been here for less than five years." There is a need to work with the immigrant community on issues affecting their lives—immigration laws, treatment of undocumented workers, education—because they are our own people."

On a related note, Rocci Maynes pointed to the "need to calm the immigrant bashers, racists, and bigots" and "convince people with facts that immigrants are contributing to the economy of the nation. They came to work, not to be on welfare." Maynes added the dominant society's belief that legal and illegal immigrants drain the U.S. economy is a major misperception that needs to be addressed. He pointed out that, for the most part, immigrants take jobs nobody else wants.

Elizabeth Valdez alerted us to the importance of understanding not only the numbers of immigrants but also the various reasons they are coming: "I don't want to generalize, but there are many that are really outcasts from Mexico, from El Salvador, and from other places. They are involved in drugs, they are involved in crime, and they are involved in other issues. And this is a paradise for dealing in drugs and for crime. And it is very unfortunate that [those] undocumented immigrants continue the bad business that they were already doing in other countries. I feel bad about that. But what we need to understand is that there are sociopaths, there are people who are not obeying the law in those countries. And very unfortunately, they are coming into this country. And that gives a bad image to the majority of immigrants. We are not about committing crime."

Ed Delci commented that many of the undocumented Central American refugees have been fleeing the wars instigated by U.S. involvement in Latin America. This involvement has given rise to organized crime, especially among those with connections to Iran-Contra activities under Colonel Oliver North.

Many community leaders expressed concern over the growing contention in some quarters that there is at present an "invasion" of undocumented immigrants. These claims are generally couched in terms of immigrants' supposed inability to assimilate into "western civilization."

Adapting to the New Society Elizabeth Valdez, who visits her family in Mexico on a regular basis, is a keen student of life on both sides of the border. On the subject of social problems, Valdez expressed her view that the Hispanic community seems to be divided into three groups. The first is educated, recognized, visible, and identifies with its culture. The second group is at the other extreme—lost, marginalized, and neglected. The third, the one in the middle, is "too quiet . . . detached" from the segment of the community that is "struggling, in jail, burdened with unwanted pregnancies, suicidal, or on drugs." She observed there seems to be a crisis of identity—"the force of pride in who you are"—among many Chicanos. "We who came to the U.S. already educated and with a sense of who we are or what we can accomplish or what we can give back to society don't have to struggle with what a lot of Mexican Americans have to struggle with."

Armando Flores explains, "We do not have the political clout that we should. We already have significant numbers but since we don't vote (and don't vote together on the issues) no one takes us seriously." He sees the need to establish a balance between the Anglo culture and one's personal Hispanic identity, and while he is proud of his heritage, he recognizes that the corporate world (of which he is a part) is founded on a white male culture. "It does not mean that we need to compromise our values; it means that we need to recognize what the other culture's values are and bridge those as best we can. It is a challenge every day."

All the community leaders we spoke with expressed a strong desire to serve the Hispanic community. Tommy Espinoza suggested, "We need to grab hold of our religious spirit and our religious roots. Our grandparents or parents were in the same situation at one point or another. . . ." One articulated the sentiment of most: "If the Hispanic community worked together, it would make a difference." One leader said he wanted his children to "enjoy the better things in life, but I also want them to understand that they must give back to the community, so that others can enjoy them also."

Jess Torrez's view is, "If you want it, you've got to take it. . . . We as a minority need to get together with other minorities and have a stronger voice. We are so lacking in that. We do not have a voice in this community." He expressed his disappointment in Hispanic politicians who did not speak out when he was fired. It was a black clergyman who raised his voice against the city but "there were no politicians or anybody who came to my trial to say, 'Hey, you can't do this!' You can't fire a Mexican cop for standing up for three Mexican kids that were face-down in the dirt for no reason. Scottsdale spent well over a million dollars after my trial to get surveys done, to bring a cultural diversity officer in there. I mean they got a huge PR firm to get them back on track with the publicity."

In an effort to bring greater recognition to the strengths of the Hispanic community and its members, Rocci Maynes wrote a series of booklets highlighting the accomplishments of Hispanic writers, actors, athletes, and others. Maynes stated that he hoped not only to change the perceptions of mainstream society, but also to change negative self-perceptions and increase self-esteem among Hispanics themselves. He said that his wish to show that Mexican Americans are worthy and capable people was one of the motivating forces that led him to pursue advanced degrees and to work hard in his career. His success, he said, has only increased his desire to be involved and help others.

Part 2: Four Resolanas

Part 1 examined the stories of Hispanic leaders who "made it" and, in the process, shed light on the issues facing their community. When I read their interviews, I wondered what would happen if we were to gather these and other participants in ever-expanding resolanas. That musing led to four community resolanas, which are recounted in part 2. The first, in which the individuals interviewed by the students participated, dealt with whether the differences in this community are a result of diversity or fragmentation. The second resolana's major theme was the generation gap from the perspective of young leaders. The third was a dialogue among Tommy Espinoza, Nancy Jordan, and Danny Ortega, longtime leaders in the Phoenix community, and the group of young leaders who attended the second resolana. Its themes were leadership and the generational and gender challenges facing the community. The final resolana began with presentations from Tomás Atencio, Tony Mares, and me and concluded with a general discussion with the audience.

The challenge of presenting these dialogues in written form is to edit them so that they are readable while respecting the participants' original voices. The general rules I followed were to delete material that required background knowledge, to delete repetitions and asides unrelated to the point at hand, to correct some but not all grammar, and to keep it short. The editing is extensive.

Earlier I offered an analysis of the initial interviews but did not explain how these dialogues were conducted. The resolanas in this book, unlike the resolanas that take place in the villages of northern New Mexico, were highly structured—participants did not just drop by, they were selected because of their leadership and public service interests, and there was a beginning and an end to these encounters as opposed to the ongoing flow of life in the villages. I am not the only one to adapt the resolana concept in various ways. Tomás Atencio transformed the idea to written form by retelling stories—el oro del barrio—in pamphlets aimed at raising the level of awareness of issues central to community concerns. In similar fashion, Paulo Freire's liberatory education, crafted in rural Brazil, focused on the power arrangements between classes and the organization of "circles of culture" where, through dialogue, people realized that they were the creators of their own culture and history. Our resolanas, mirroring these "circles of culture," identify "generative words" or "themes"—power, leadership, machismo, diversity, healing, organizing, gender, and generational gaps—and various types of reforms to address challenges facing the community. Consistent with Freire, in *Debatable Diversity* Ray Padilla and I used a dialogical method of a shaped conversation aimed at greater efficiency in social action. In all these methods, there is an inherent tension between an individual's conception of reality and the alternate perceptions of other participants, which are elaborated through dialogue.

It is through this process that consciousness is transformed. This process is illustrated in the resolanas that follow, and it is the analytical process we use in interpreting the theme of fragmentation. A similar analytical process could be used in analyzing other themes such as generational and gender gaps, leadership, or service. Whether the dialogues influence behavior is an open question. (In chapter 3, Mares analyzes these stories from a network perspective.)

My intent in conducting these resolanas was to let the process identify the central issues in our community. I knew that whatever questions I posed would influence the direction of the discussion. Yet I also realized that groups need some direction to get started. This is one of the dilemmas built into the resolana process. The sessions always started with an overview of the project: the seminar course on globalization, the role of Valle del Sol, and the idea of la resolana that set the rules for the discussions.

A Resolana with Community Leaders:
Fragmentation and Other Concerns

MM: The interviews conducted by the students surfaced two primary issues: (1) the importance of family and culture, and (2) the characterization of the Hispanic community as fragmented, disorganized, and powerless.[9] Let's start with the issue of power.

Do We Have Power?

TE: We do have power. What we fought for in the sixties and the seventies has been accomplished. I remember when we did not have access to law firms, to health care, to utility companies, and to universities. The next generation, especially immigrants, have the same fire in their gut that we had in the sixties. It may not be going in the "right" direction, but there is leadership.

ED: Power brokers see us as homogeneous rather than the heterogeneous community that we are. They think of power, money, or political strength rather than the role we play within our community or in the larger community. The misconception diminishes our community's accomplishments.

Community: Fragmented or Diverse?

MM: Is our community fragmented?

ED: What are outside groups trying to achieve by saying that we are fragmented?

DO: When we disagree, I do not see fragmentation; I see differences as positive. We are no more fragmented than other groups. We are promoters of diversity—we accept everyone for who they are, irrespective of the color of their skin or gender, but we don't promote it among ourselves. In times of crisis our community has responded beyond our expectations. It is unfair to think that the only way that we can attack those problems is through a unified effort and through a leader or a group of leaders who are going to deliver us to the Promised Land.

We have to take responsibility for why we [as a community] are not as effective as we should be. We have arrived. Our community hasn't, and those of us that are saying we are fragmented are taking a very negative view of our success. We had a cause once; we had a mission once because we had nothing. . . . Now we have a lot and because we do, we have lost sight of what that cause is. We can refocus on what we are trying to achieve [the greater good rather than personal success], or as a community, we are going to continue to be, as you call it, "fragmented."

Too Young or Too Busy to Contribute?

TE: It is not until you get to be fifty or sixty that you can focus on community because [before that] you are [busy] going to school, building family, careers—this takes time, energy, and maturity. In the next twenty years, we will see Latinos in positions of power: the U.S. Senate, the House, and conceivably the White House. That is real. The challenge is to translate what we have learned to the next generation.

We live in a capitalist society. How do we sensitize that system to our values? And that is the rub—between economic and cultural values. We tend to look at everything as consumers—bigger house, bigger car—and this is what we teach our kids. How do we take the value system that [is reflected] in everybody's comments about family and service, and translate it into our experiences? That is the challenge.

Should We Be Satisfied with Our Progress?

JT: I am not satisfied—we have so much more to accomplish. We are so far from being equal in every realm that nothing less than equality is going to satisfy me. I don't see us ever getting behind anything anymore. It concerns me. Maybe the road has been plowed and the seeds have been planted, but I do not see a field of roses. I take my children back to where I grew up, but it is hard for them not to forget just because it makes it easier when someone else walked the path. Maybe I am more on the militant side.

I was ingrained with this "silent sufferer" mentality—just take it. When I was in the midst of my lawsuit, my grandmother told me, "M'ijo, just take it." I could have taken it and gone on with another police department, but I was too stupid and headstrong. I see [this mentality] from the people from Mexico. When Mexican kids are "patted down," they say, "Do what you want to do to me; I can take it. I'll go to the joint." That is where they think their place is rather than looking beyond that, and we need to let them know that if someone mistreats them, someone will say, "You were mistreated." I still work as a defense witness, every day someone gets screwed and it is a person of color, and until we've bridged that, I don't see any parity at all.

Hunger in the Belly

AO: When we were younger, we had discrimination that was blatant. We could feel it. It hurt us. The discrimination now is more subliminal. They are more educated in what not to say, what not to do, but we are still discriminated [against]. Our kids in school, except for the *mojaditos*, do not feel the hurt, the hunger, or the need to make a change or to get out in front. I guess they just take it, but they don't feel the way we felt. When we were involved in Chicanos Por La Causa, we had a goal, a mission. We had to get to where you had to put *raza* in different places, different positions. There was a hunger that is not there the way it used to be, because our kids are not discriminated [against] as blatantly as they used to be. They are not going to let them achieve any more than "X" level, but they will not see it because they do not have a hunger and the negative feeling about it.

Our community is diverse. We fought and now we are everywhere. We are Republicans, conservatives, liberals, and educated. We are in different places so we are spread out. [In the city council election] we tried to get behind raza and we lost. We split: half went with the African American and half with the Chicano. That is why we talk about being fragmented. We can't muster enough support to get behind an issue. The last time we did was the "English only." We do not have that hunger. How do we explain that?

Is There a Hispanic Nation?

EV: There is fragmentation and there is the richness of diversity. One of the main problems is that some of us have arrived at positions of privilege that are very well deserved, but I don't think we have embraced the next generation. I came to this country twenty years ago when I was forty years old, well educated. There is a lack of involvement [from those who are] successful. There is fragmentation between the Mexican Americans and the new arrivals—¿tu qué sabes?— about our Chicano struggle. You come from a different country. You don't know the issues. It has taken me twenty years to be accepted as a Mexicana. We have not been embraced, and I think there is a big loss.

There is a difference between a Mexicano living in the United States and a Chicano. We need to reconcile those differences. There are Protestants, Catholics, educated, not educated, all kinds of differences. The gap between successful Chicanos and our community is incredible. There is no one there. Andan solitos papando mosca [We find ourselves alone catching flies]. I am a woman. I am not [a] man; that is one disadvantage. I am not Catholic; that is another disadvantage. I am educated; that is another disadvantage. There are a lot of macho, male-oriented things that we need to be aware [of]. We apply a double standard for [those that have] not been able to achieve what we have achieved. On the other hand, there is incredible beauty [in our] diversity. We no longer fit into one profile, [but] it is lonely to be in a leadership position if you are a Mexican woman. That is not just my reality, but that of many others.

We see the people from South America getting together [organizing]. They are the ones who are going to use the power, the ones who are going to be elected—the ones getting into the schools—and not the Mexicanos. The problem is that they are not addressing the problems in our community, the Mexicano community. We need to understand that they come as refugees. They have different standards. We come undocumented or as immigrants. Most are low income and come to work on different kinds of jobs than people from Central America. It is our duty to mentor and embrace new blood. There is a vacuum.

One or Many Voices?

JC: I think that [fragmentation] is heightened by generalizations that are applied to the Hispanic community. For example, if Bill Post [the CEO of APS] took a position on an issue and Valerie Manning, the head of the Arizona Chamber of Commerce, took a different position, no one would say that the "white" community is divided. They would say that big business has a different view on this issue than the chamber, which represents mostly small business. And the problem is that when people [in the Hispanic community] have different views, people say that the Hispanic community is divided, but they don't drill down to see what kinds of divisions are being talked about, and people who would otherwise be allies won't get involved because the Hispanic community can't come together. These generalizations are a problem, and it is a different version of stereotyping. We need to not say that the Hispanic community is divided just like you would not say the white community is divided. What are the differences here? What is the basis for these different opinions? One would then identify the mutual interests that are shared between big business and small business. The important point is [to decide] "I should get behind this issue" or "these are legitimate differences and we will not be together on this particular issue."

EV: The key is to educate the larger community [about our diversity]. Why should we have just one voice? It is our duty to educate the public, but it needs to start in-house. If someone does not think and look or speak like you speak, then you are out of the loop.

Healing

EV: We need to do some healing and come together. We [including "the boys"] are victims of the same system. In accomplishing our personal goals, we have detached from the needs of the community. I think there is a lot of *chisme*—if someone goes up, we are the first ones to pull [him or her] down. We are our own worst enemies. It does not mean that there is no support system, but until . . . we clean our own *trapitos* [dirty linen], it will be a big struggle. We want people to recognize our diversity, but we are not validating our diversity. There are a lot of spiritual things that are reflected in our everyday lives. ¡Caramba! There is so much to be done—the juvenile system, the health system, and the educational system, but we have to recharge our batteries.

TE: There *is* a spiritual healing that needs to occur, and I don't necessarily mean in a religious manner. I argue that the Catholic Church has been a powerful tool in working for our community. The Virgen de Guadalupe [has served to] evangelize the Americas. We need to capture that spiritual side even if the institutional church sometimes shuts its door on us. Once you have embraced your spiritual side, no one can take that away from us. Danny Ortega and I have actually done exactly what you just said. We went through years of picking and stabbing at each other, and we went through a spiritual retreat, a *cursillo,* where we both asked each other for forgiveness. It was very powerful. I look at Danny from a whole different angle. That needs to occur.

There have been a large number of Mexicanos that have come here who are well educated and are powerful instruments of change for our community, but we do not embrace them. On the other hand, there have been Mexicanos that have come to our community with a chip on their shoulder, *Chilangos* [people from Mexico City] or whatever, and view Chicanos negatively.

National Council of la Raza: No Longer Mexican but Latino

TE: The National Council of La Raza [NCLR] is no longer a "Mexican American" organization, and they want to change the name and have changed the logo. They want to "demexicanize" [the organization]. Now, it is terrible if you are a Mexicano. What is happening is that the Salvadorans, Puerto Ricans, Chilenos came here under different circumstances. They see us [Mexicans] as the target. In their mind we "hold them back," so like we organized in the sixties and seventies against the "system," or Anglos, they now look at us as part of their problem. I don't think they should become our enemies. I think we need to be smart enough to organize and deal with our community issues and embrace that diversity. There are many Latino groups [who] feel that we excluded them. They don't want an inclusive agenda. This is a [political] challenge.

Are Chicanos Backsliding?

TE: If you compare where we were when we were organized and where we are now, we should be outraged. We have had successes; I agree with that, but the issues have gotten much larger than when we started. Education has gotten worse. The justice system has gotten worse. We are taking the worst hit with the younger generation. They are the ones that are really going to pay the price if we don't challenge those institutions.

Their and Our Agenda

JT: I know some of what it means to come from Mexico, but my agenda is completely different. If other Latinos want to target me, you know what? Bring it on. I don't know why we need to "play nice" because they come with money or with an education. They got that money and that education off the backs of their own people, and I would be no better than them if I embraced them as my peers. My grandparents came to this country [as] kids in tow and they were workers, and I will challenge anybody to find a Mexican national who is on a street corner with a sign saying, "We will work for food." They are all at Home Depot waiting for a job and humping for fifty dollars a day. I take umbrage at that. Nobody is going to tell me that I don't deserve a place at this table. We don't deal with each other like the Chinese, like the blacks, or like the Irish. That is what kept us from getting ahead. Yes, there are Los Abogados [Chicano lawyers organization] and the Bomberos [Chicano firefighters group], but what do they do as a group? The reason they started is because they needed a voice as a group for protection and it has not changed today.

And as far as the National Council of La Raza, and please don't take this wrong, tell me what they have done in the last ten years. Have they ever stood up and said, "We as a people get screwed every day?" We don't have politicians that do that, but the one that I know got shot. [An irate taxpayer shot and wounded Maricopa County Supervisor Mary Rose Wilcox.] I give Mary Rose all the props in the world because she is one of the few who will stand up and say, "You know what? You screw us every day." I don't see any politicians, businessmen in power, or anyone else that will say that. It frustrates the hell out of me.

Energizing the Community

TE: Take that anger and that frustration and refocus it. We have to refocus and reenergize ourselves to the struggle in our community or someone else will do it.

AO: How do we energize our community? I can tell you about my frustrations with the Mexican Cultural Center. For nine years I tried to get it off the ground for the Mexicans, not Chicanos, to set it up, and we could not get people to help. I have been a little successful with health issues because we have gone to the federal government, but we had to fight to get a health center in South Phoenix, Tolleson, and Maryvale. But it is a lot of blood, a lot of sweat and tears. There is a point when you say, "I am tired," and you try to get young people into the Chicano Political Action Group and half of them support an Anglo.

JT: Blacks are the squeaky wheels and they have gotten the grease. Pin a black kid down, he is the first one to be yelling, "I am black; you are doing this because I am black." Pin a Mexican kid down, and he will say, "Take your best shot at me."

AO: How do we energize our community to take leadership positions— that they need to fight, they need to stand up and be vocal? We do it in our little ways and try to give resources, but it is not enough.

EV: "Los héroes están fatigados [Our heroes are fatigued]." That is why we're talking about healing and being able to regain that willingness to do something, but we need to recognize that we are very tired.

The Need for a Bigger Vision

DO: This discussion is part of the problem. We have no big vision. We get into criticizing each other about NCLR or Los Abogados and all this negative stuff and anger against our own people. If we could just direct that against the powers that really keep us down. How tough I am does not mean a damn thing to the world. It is the vision that I have about a mission to improve the lot of our community. If we could look at it in those terms and could make improvements, who benefits does not matter, whether Salvadorans, Cubans, blacks, whites, or poor people. We spend too much time on the small stuff, and the reason is because we don't take the time to know each other.

You can go to the Internet and find out about NCLR and you will eat your words. The point is this: It does not matter what NCLR does or does not do. What matters is, What am I going to do to make this a better world, to get the kind of equality I am talking about? without dealing with whether NCLR does anything or not. You have wasted thirty seconds of your life on something that does not matter.

The Lost Art of Organizing

DO: We need a greater vision, a selfless vision. We are the worst teachers about that, and that is why we have a crisis of leadership with young people. We have sent them the wrong message about where we need to create change. Let's look at organizations like Valle del Sol, Chicanos Por La Causa, Hispanic Chamber of Commerce, Friendly House, and ask how many of them have committed any time, money, or resources toward organizing— true organizing. This is what they did when they started. Today, they do not get involved in any organizing, because there is no sense of the greater good and the need to inform and bring people together and to have these kinds of discussions. We are not committing resources and money and time to that. Our children know nothing about that. Until we direct them in that fashion, we are going to continue to talk about fragmentation, and we are going to have a generation of "fragmenters" to continue the fragmentation.

EV: I agree, but if we don't have self-criticism and assess where we are, it is very hard to move. [It is not enough to] have a vision; you need to assess where you are so you can take solid stepping-stones to get where you want to be. We can have dreamers, have a vision, but it [is necessary] to have a conscious assessment of where we are and straighten and examine our deficits. I do not agree that looking at negative things is a waste of time. Of course, you must look forward. We [Latinas] are drained. Most of us are in the menopause stage, and that is an incredible stage to be in. What does menopause have to do with leadership? Believe me, a lot.

Healing the Community

ED: It has a lot to do with lack of energy. Our next generation is complacent. We don't want our children to fall off the bike, [but we need to] let them fall off and get skinned and [realize] that they can [get] back on. If we don't have a sense of direction, all we are doing is hurting ourselves. And by reiterating our flaws and internalizing them, we never get out of [that rut].

EV: Can you continue moving forward without healing first? We need to step back and regroup, have the vision and the energy to continue, but we are not a group yet. We need [to] take away those things that separate us and have a common vision.

Building Parks for Everyone

DO: We don't need to do that. If we need a park in my barrio, let us build it. It is going to benefit Guatemaltecos and others, and I am not going to worry about whether she likes me or he likes me. Let's build that park, and in the process you know what is going to happen? I think people will have something to aim for, something to work for. And then you move on to another project and another project.

EV: But are we ready to build that park? Do we have the strength, the vision, and the means to do it? I am suggesting that we regroup. Healing does not take that long. You saw what happened between the two of you when you healed. Why will it not be productive for others? You pulled together through a healing process. It is my perception that it does not have to be one or the other. We need to do a lot of things, and we don't have the luxury to wait too long—*Despacio que voy de prisa* [Slow down, I am in a hurry].

Apologists

ED: I have never accepted being an apologist—we have nothing to apologize for. And far too often because of religion, we denigrate our past rather than value our contributions. We are so ingrained with faith that we lose sight of who we are and accept the blows. There is a lot of value in turning the other cheek and in being nonviolent, but when Chávez said nonviolent, he did not say step back. He never apologized. If they did not gain the full victory, they marched forward—that is the important part. We have raised our children to be complacent—*para no aguantar*—and I think that is wrong. We need to encourage them to keep moving forward [and do away with] the *pobrecito yo* syndrome. We need to push for that rather than seeing ourselves as problems, and if we are a problem, we are a problem to ourselves.

EV: I did not want to portray a problem. We need to heal and not to say I am sorry to anyone. If we have to say I am sorry, we would need to have the power of forgiveness. It is not about being a fighter; it is simply to recharge batteries. It is not the *pobrecito* in me. It is a reality check for those who are discouraged. There is nothing wrong with being tired.

Becoming a Leader

TE: I would recommend that regardless of religion, you go through a process of finding yourself. In the beginning [of the movement], one of the things that sparked a rallying cry for CPLC was Phoenix Union High School—it became the focus for energy that everyone embraced. I did not know Rosie and Joe Eddie López [political activists], but watching them on TV got me so energized that I got involved. We are [at] a point where there is more energy than we realize. There is a yearning in our community to move things. If you want to be a leader, you have to be a servant. It is time we do something like that; it would work.

Tending Your Own Garden

TE: The ills of the community are reflected in our families. I have a little of all the problems that we claim we are all trying to fix in my family. My *abuelita* is always telling me to take care of my own back yard before fixing the ills of the community. We do have access to power in certain circles. How do we use Arizona Public Service, Louis and Rocca [Law Firm], and ASU to focus on a major vision? We need to think big. It may be education or whatever this core group would be willing to embrace.

The Generation Gap

CM: As the youngest, I am in the minority. It is very disheartening when people my age talk about the gap that exists. Is it their [the older generation's] fault for not helping us? Is it our fault for being complacent? I don't know what the answer is.

There will always be fighting among different groups—white people, black people; there is fighting among each other. The focus should be on educating younger people in the community who want help, who want to be educated, who want to be leaders. There are gaps between the different groups. That is the way it is going to be, but there should not be a gap between the older, seasoned leaders and those of us who are reaching out. Maybe it is not our fault. Maybe it is a collective fault, but that needs to change, and that is where you have the power to change. And I humbly give advice where you guys need to make a change.

Obligation to Mentor Future Leaders

DO: Our group has the biggest obligation to do what she just said because we have the experience, the economic stability, and we understand what the fire in the belly was about. And as most of us are looking at retirement— winding down—instead of asking ourselves, How many years do I have left? [we should ask], What legacy am I going to leave behind [at] a point in my life when I could do the most? It does not matter if your commitment is in education, housing, mental health, law enforcement. Those of us who have been in positions of leadership, those of us who have "made it," should focus on development and mentoring of leadership—on the fundamentals of leadership.

We have sent the wrong message on what it means to be a leader if it means "I get": I get to be elected, I get a job, I get notoriety, I get an award, I get, I, I, as opposed to what people get from what you are doing. And if what you do for a living benefits many people, that is okay. We have not talked about giving for the sake of giving or creating change, at any level, anywhere. It can range from leading a march of a thousand people to teaching a child how to read English. To me those equate because if you teach someone to read, you never know if that person will be leading the revolution twenty years from now. If we do anything in the next fifteen years, it has to be in developing and mentoring selfless leadership.

Reaping the Benefits of the Movement

AE: I want to respond to what has been said [about the gap]. I am [a] brat of the movement. I grew up leafleting, and that was great; that was fun. People in our generation got lazy, got comfortable. We saw the glitzy part of the leadership, and so [people like us] crash and burn because we don't have the substance and training that you people experienced. And not to make excuses, but you were busy making the trail. I understand about the need to heal. How can you expect to help others if you can't even take care of yourself? I understand what you are saying about the healing, and healing among yourselves, too, the fighting among each other. It is also our fault because we did not reach out and ask how to be effective leaders. Maybe our parents did not want their children to have to go through what they did, so they focused on [our] going to school and getting an education. I am not saying right, wrong, or indifferent. Now I am reaping the benefits, and my children are reaping even greater benefits, because these people have matured from the selfish to the serving stage, and thank God my children can benefit from their mistakes and successes.

CM: No one has reaped the benefits more than me. My father made it up the ladder like the people at this table. When I asked him if he wanted me to get a job, he said, "No, mi'jita, your job is to go to school. You don't need to work." Now, I wish I had not listened to my father. Now I am behind other people my age, because I don't have the work experience that they do. They tell me, "You are so lucky," but am I? I am not. Will your children reap the benefits because of that gap? Yes, we have reaped some benefits, but where has that gotten us? What have we done?

AE: We need to take the responsibility ourselves and not blame these people, because we did not ask for the chance. You should not expect things to be given to you. We should have the respect and ask them to show us, teach us. I am thirty-seven years old, and I am barely asking my dad, "Teach me. Show me."

Bridging the Generation Gap

DO: We have to be available; we cannot be too busy. It bothers me that people think that you are not someone they can go to. After [my presentation] at the Hispanic Leadership Institute, individuals asked me if I was willing to talk with them. God almighty, what are we doing wrong? That is a bad message! We need to get around the table because we cannot deal with these issues in a speaking forum.

JC: We need both good leaders and followers. I don't view myself as a leader. I do view myself as a follower, so that when some of you call and say, "I need this," I say 'okay.' I think this is very important. I am not that pessimistic about the younger generation, because I am actually impressed with it.

Becoming a Scholar

RM: It took time to learn to study, learn to carry a book, little things, and finally I learned to do all that and it worked. My attitude shifted, [and] after that I got into a mode of helping the community. I got involved in teaching because I wanted to teach Anglos Spanish and culture. My goal was to teach literature and linguistics at a college and retire. I got involved with the migrant child education program and I have been in it for thirty-eight years, and it was meaningful—helping these kids. I talked to the migrant parents who could not speak English, and [told] them that they had to give the impression to their kids [that] they were concerned about them learning English. Otherwise, they [would] not make it in school. They asked, "¿Qué hacemos"? I told them, "Whenever your son is working on his homework, go up to him and ask him, '¿Cómo se dice salero en inglés?' He will respond, 'Salt shaker, Mom.' This fosters the attitude that English is okay."

[Addressing one of the young women]: We can't even agree on bilingualism. There are differences of opinion, and it goes on and on. What about the vision of building a park? I worked with the National Child Migrant Program that follows the crops from the Rio Grande Valley in Texas across Louisiana to the Midwest and on to the central and eastern [migrant] stream, the thirteen western states where Mexican and Mexican Americans [increasingly] hung around. Now they are in New York working on the sugar beets. It was Puerto Ricans; now it is Mexicans and Mexican Americans. It has really grown.

Strengthening Organizations

RM: We need a national organization like the NAACP; LULAC [League of United Latin American Citizens] has been around since 1929, the year I was born, and I am still waiting. They are a nice group, and now and then you hear of a conference and that is it. I don't hear any support nationwide for the people. The NAACP is verbal. We have to be verbal; we have the numbers. Now we are the largest minority. We are going to get larger. That is why I had ten kids [Laughter].

I have always been concerned about the southwestern states. [Congress used to spend more money on migratory birds than migrant children.] We started meeting like this and started pushing for Mexican Americans to become state directors, and before we knew it we had a clique of Mexican American state directors. We would go before committees of Congress and fight for the program, and we went from $7 million to $350 million. It took a lot of work but we had to fight. We could not sit back and be nice. Today, we don't have a migrant [program] state director because people [stopped fighting].

I have been going to La Perla restaurant for forty years because I enjoy talking to the people there. I write letters for the people that want to become

American citizens. They are married and are doing well. They are good workers. You cannot judge a group by a few. What does the newspaper do? It gives the impression that [undocumented workers] come to steal or kill. They are coming, and we are going to have a large group, and we have to be ready. A lot of young people want to get involved but they don't know how. They get lost.

The Next Step

NJ: I had the opportunity to observe some of you in this group when I came to Arizona in the seventies at a time when there was a very cohesive group, very focused, very strategic, [very successful]. I have seen the evolution, and I am moved by some of the same issues. One of my concerns is the lack of women involved in leadership positions—that has been one of my causes for a long time. How can we use our institutions, how can we move forward to get that vision, and to get that strategic impact that we need? What should we [do] as a group, or what can we do to help us get to the next level?

AO: We need to make ourselves available to the younger folks that want coaching or direction, or just want to sit down and discuss these issues. How do we do this? That is where you guys have the power to do that, and we have the power to help.

Listening to One Another

MM: These dialogues present us with an opportunity to listen to one another. When one steps back, when one says, "I am going to listen to what Danny is saying without trying to anticipate what he is saying, I am not going to anticipate, but just listen, and Danny is going to do the same thing. And somehow our ideas merge, a consensus is created."

TE: You have created a vehicle that worked—you got me to stay up until two o'clock in the morning. I think you hit on something that is key. I am sitting here listening and I am not accustomed to that. We had an opportunity to know one another in a different way. The narratives moved me; they were powerful.

Leadership Models

DO: What we are doing is evaluating our leadership models—how the leadership of the past is different from the present leadership, and how that leadership might or might not be having an impact on younger people. Has anybody ever thought of sitting down and assessing the various leadership models—MALDEF [Mexican American Legal Defense and Education Fund] Leadership Institute, Hispanic Leadership Institute, Valley Leadership? We have more institutes now than ever, and somehow we feel we have fewer leaders. The question is to focus on different subjects. You started with fragmentation, which went right to leadership. You focused it, and now we need to have these discussions in different areas by different leadership. I think what you have more than anything else is a group of leaders from an activist standpoint. I think these resolanas will have a different set of [ideas] from leadership in education, mental health.

Leaders and Followers

JT: I don't consider myself a leader. I did what I did because I had to do it. My leadership and the people that taught me morality were my parents. I did exactly what was expected of me at that point in time, and it was not machismo, bravado; it was what was right. They taught me what was right and you will, at one point in your life, have the opportunity to do the same thing, and there will be times when you stop, times when you step back from that and there will be times when you step up from that. I should have said that up front, but if this was a leadership meeting, then I probably should have excused myself from that because I don't consider myself a leader. I lead a family of five, and those are the only ones I care to lead. I will leave three healthy young adults when I die and that is it. I did my crusade. If we don't sit here and self-examine and say what we have done, where we have been, we just fool ourselves, and we are no better than a group of guys who go to the Fraternal Order of Police and pat themselves on the back. I see a lot of good things from the younger people coming up, but it will be a test in time, and that will come when the line is drawn in the sand for the individual. For everyone here it was a different point in time.

RM: You say you don't consider yourself a leader, but sometimes people around you will look at you [as being] in a leadership role, even though you don't realize it.

CM: I wish that this discussion [had occurred] with all of you and with ten others my age, because you would really see that we do want your help, that we have reaped the benefits.

A Resolana with Young Leaders:
Views on the Generation Gap

MM: The central issue in our previous resolana was whether our community was fragmented. Cristina talked about the great distance between older and younger leaders, and suggested that a dialogue would be useful to both sides. Today, our resolana concerns young leaders.[10] Cristina, why don't you set the context?

CM: At the first meeting there was confusion about why the gaps existed. Some older people felt that younger people weren't asking for help. The young people at the meeting spoke about older leaders not engaging and saying, "Hey, I can show you the way." You are at a point where you have made your way in life, but unfortunately for the younger people, we are not; we're fighting different battles. One of the biggest weaknesses, at least for the young people, is not having that togetherness, that connectivity between the older leaders and the younger leaders. In coming together we can figure out why this has been occurring and think of a remedy.

Sharing

ED: I encourage students to work together in student organizations because people learn more through direct experience than through the theory they get in the classroom. As adults, we expect students to respond at the same level, without their having the experience. We are sharing these experiences so that the circle of influence can be expanded.

The Conflict between the Generations

MM [in response to questions about the idea of an intergenerational conflict]: I am most familiar with the work of Ortega y Gasset, the Spanish philosopher. Each generation carries with it, for lack of a better word, "baggage." We are born into a certain epoch, into a particular family, in a certain year. A person like me who is sixty years old comes with baggage that includes Mexican immigrant parents, first-generation college-educated, influenced by the sixties, and educated at the University of California. I view the world differently than, let's say, Cristina, who is Mexican born, well educated, not poor, and twenty-seven years of age. Each of us looks at the same world with different lenses: a person in his sixties, one in her forties, and one in her twenties each views the same event in a different light. Not only are we, let's say, captured by the time, captured by our family, but we are also in a sense captured by our age. I don't have the same kind of ambition and vision that many in this room have. I have a different vision, and much of it has to do with the fact that I'm sixty years old. I'm towards the end of my life, towards the end of my career. Ortega's point was that divisions among the generations are what create social change. Great conflicts between generations create crisis. That's the idea of the generation.

RC: Well, we find that you are not as ambitious as we are! How do I motivate you to be as ambitious as I am [and not give up], to make sure that you push the envelope for me? I got here three years ago, and [after graduating from the University of Arizona] had nobody to look to. How does our group start doing business with the big guys, the "good ol' boys" network? I had to start from zero. How do I motivate you to do things for me? If I build some type of value for you, I guarantee you're going to help me. And that is where we fail as a younger generation.

If an Anglo calls a friend: "By the way, my son is graduating from college. Yeah, he graduated with a 2.5 GPA, but he needs to be one of your senior reps at Smith Barney." I guarantee you he's going to get that job. In turn, this guy is going to give him some type of job kickback from his other job. That's how corporate America goes to bed, and it doesn't happen in the Latino community.

CM: I want to comment on what Ricardo just said. I made it sound that the younger people were expecting [the older leaders] to help us, that we deserved it—that was not my intent. We have a responsibility to each other, and it's not, What are you going to give me? but How are we going to work together for the community? The reason we have a generational gap is because everybody assumes that other parties owe him or her something, and that's not the way it should be. That's what we have to work at, and that's what I mean about bringing this connectivity back to our community.

Mentoring

MEC: When I was twelve years old, Tony Sotelo [a well-known Arizona union leader], took me on my first peace rally. Later we started forming circles of friendship, and I discovered my role in life—to serve my community. We were involved when Ed Pastor was running for Congress, and he knew that students were key. The students mobilized in Tempe, at the University of Arizona, and it was through those circles that we met [community leaders], 'cause everybody had the same agenda: we wanted to get a Chicano congressman elected. And together we were able to do that.

RC: There's always a sense of the "godfather." One [leader] can't represent us; for us to have one or two or three leaders is a joke. That's the problem. We don't all think the same. I know I don't, but that doesn't mean that we don't have the same spirit. I know people in leadership positions [who] have very big egos, and young or old, they are not going to relinquish [their power], and we keep feeding into this hierarchical notion.

Whom to Look Up To

MHD: How do you instill in the younger generations that they can do things and give back to the community and get educated when there are no real leadership role models here in Phoenix? It's hard, especially coming from a different city.

ED: In César's model, there are no individual leaders; everybody contributes. A non-English-speaking person would be charged to go from Los Angeles to Delano and organize a boycott in Chicago. "How do I get to Chicago with one tank of gas?" People quickly realized that there was a network throughout the community that helped that caravan along. We always tend to look for that one person who can be our anointed leader, and as long as we apply that model, we are going to have this conversation repeated.

I Am Not a Leader

JT: I think that what drives politicians is far different from what drives me. I appreciate success, but it is like that Janet Jackson song, "What Have You Done for Me Lately?" I don't make a career out of being a professional Hispanic. I'm here; I'm just doing my thing. So people do things for their own personal gain, and we are no different than Anglos, blacks, and Asians.

Hopefully, you will never know what it's like to be called a "spic" in school or a "wetback" or a "beaner," even in your professional career. . . . In my generation, I went through all those things. I know my daughters, at twenty, won't have to worry about that. We've advanced past that, not that those things are not still said behind closed doors, but certainly it is not as open as it used to be. One has to take personal responsibility and, Cristina, there may come a time when you will make a decision to stand up for what you believe, and it may cost you a great deal and you may never recoup from that.

What's Mine Is Mine

JT: I just will not pay homage to anybody. I was born in this country. I don't expect anything, but I will take what is mine. We need to stop thinking that we're second-class citizens and to expect what is our due. Parents should be telling their children, "This is yours. You have to go out and take it, because nobody is going to come and give it to you." There were people who paved the road, but nobody sat there while I studied [or] worked hard. Nobody in the world can tell me, "Well, we did all of that for you; you only got there 'cause of this." Bull. I worked hard to get it, and I am going to work hard to keep it. We talked last time about people coming from Guatemala, the Dominican Republic, whatever. I don't care where they come from. This is mine; I was born here. My parents were here and . . . my ancestors were here from Mexico. It's great that people are out there doing all of those things. I'm not a joiner. If you want to label me, I'm a revolutionary.

CM: When you say that you will take what you want, from whomever, are you referring to people outside of your community or within your community?

JT: Both.

Community Fragmentation Revisited

CM: I'm not criticizing you [referring to Jess Torrez], but because a lot of people have the same views that you do, our community becomes divisive politically. I was touched and disgusted by what happened in the Phoenix City Council race; I haven't forgotten that. [Many Hispanics supported an Anglo over a Chicana that was running; the Anglo won.] When Congressman Pastor ran, everybody rallied their troops [because they wanted a Chicano/Hispanic], but unfortunately [it was different with this situation].

Monica and I have expressed our desire to [seek a national post with the National Women's Political Caucus]—both of us want to be on the board. I chose to leave myself out of the running not because I don't believe I'm qualified, but because I [saw] strength in a counterpart, I will say, "Go ahead, I'm going to support you," and I think that's what needs to happen.

JT: There's not just one leader now, there are multiple leaders, so you can make a choice. You can feel good about selecting the best individual, but I certainly don't. I don't care which guy it is.

Soft on Hispanics

JT: When I was going through my trial, the Anglo journalist gave me much better ink, but Rubén Navarrete [*Arizona Republic* columnist] did not. When I asked him why, he said, "Because I don't want to be seen as soft on Hispanics." You guys shake your heads, but that's real life. [Just because they are Hispanic] doesn't mean that they are the best candidates. At this point we have an option—some of the people who have been placed in those positions have forgotten. How can you live in a vacuum and not forget? We see that with the church.

My job is to tell clients what they're going to hear in court or what they're going to face, so I'm not going to smooth it over. Politicians stroke people. I don't. I don't kiss anybody's ring. Often you see people in suits who ought to be saying that we're not equal, but yet are sitting back. I'm not going to sit here and tell everybody what they want to hear. My perception—that's the only thing that counts. If you don't think that you deserve everything that everybody else has, you are never going to get it, and I appreciate what all of you do for the community, but you have to also do for yourself [in order] to do well for others, to get to a place to do that.

Awards and the Chicano Community

MEC: I appreciate your frankness, and you have a level of integrity that I know some folks don't, and half the time I look at those Valle del Sol awards and say, "Hey, sometimes it's a joke, a complete joke."

JT: The people that got [the award] the year that I got it, most of them were representing APS, Salt River Project [utility companies], and they're the money people. I got it because I drew that line in the sand and said, "What these cops did to three Mexican kids was wrong." I was lucky. I litigated, I won, and then somebody put me in for this award, and boom, I got it. I didn't even know Valle del Sol gave an award. I was just like, "Damn, this is nice, a bunch of Mexicans in a room all dressed up at the Biltmore. I'm ready."

Circles of Friendship

MEC: Sometimes, just because we're brown doesn't mean we're qualified. I've been supported more by my Anglo, African American, and Asian Pacific friends than I have by my own race. I was confronted by three of my peers who are sitting pretty in their nice offices saying, "María Elena, you haven't paid your dues yet." It made me think of a few superlatives. They've got to be kidding!

A group of Chicanas has created a circle of friendship; we meet once a month. We're facing this male/female issue: the guys are getting these nice jobs, they're supporting each other in corporate America, and guess who is supporting them? It's the high-profile Anglo women who want to see them go places. And it's not the Chicano men who are in the positions that are supporting us, so we're going to do this on our own.

Doing Your Own Thing

RC: We don't have to love each other, but because I don't agree with another Chicano doesn't mean that I'm a sellout. You talked about Navarrete. I have a hard time with his politics, but he went out and maybe he did it so that he could make a name for himself. It's okay to do that. We need these discussions more often. We don't talk about issues. I'm interested in what the people that haven't spoken think. In our classrooms, the kids don't know how to talk; they just sit. They can't see tomorrow, and sometimes as adults we can't see tomorrow. What am I going to do today to get to tomorrow? A lot of times we model that as adults.

Educating Youth

CL: The census indicates that most Latinos are under eighteen, but they are not finishing their education; they are dropouts and in our criminal system. I know it's negative to say, but we need to make them aware that they don't have to be statistics. These are issues that affect us. I don't think that our older generation is doing a good job of telling them. They just say, "Don't drop out of school." But why? I've learned about some of the issues here at college, I didn't learn about them in high school. I just think that the older generation does need to reach out.

Reaching Out: The César Chávez Institute

MEC: I run the César Chávez Leadership Institute, a one-week summer program for incoming high school juniors and seniors. Students are awakening to what it is to get involved, to be educated on the issues and what they have to do to find their place. They don't know that they're a year or two from having to register to vote or with Selective Service. Again it comes back to education. [Students from the Phoenix Union High School District] tell me, "I don't even meet the requirements to come to the university because I was told I just had to graduate with however many credits." So it's a lack of education.

The Parental Role

JT: What happened to the parents? Who propelled me to go to ASU? My parents said, "You are going to get an education," and I wonder where have we lost that in our community? I saw Raúl [struggle for a second] to say "Chicano" 'cause sometimes there's a generation that doesn't like that term, and so you kind of have to hedge that, but when I was born in '57 and all through the sixties, my parents were like, "You are going to go to school." Where did that get lost?

RC: It's an unspoken rule that we don't talk about learning in our communities. I've mentored at Garfield Elementary, and the first thing that I ask is, "How many of your parents ever went to school?" None! They don't talk about school and don't talk about money. These immigrant youngsters think $10,000 is a lot of money. "Do your parents talk about education?" No. Either you are going to work on the farm or work in the family business, selling tacos and evading taxes for the rest of your life. That's their education.

Misperceptions

BS: There are perceptions and misperceptions. ASU, Univisión, and the City of Phoenix did a phone bank program—A Su Lado—where university staff answered questions from the Hispanic community about coming to the university. We took 1,200 calls over a five-hour period. The vast majority of the calls were from new immigrants wanting to know about educational opportunities for their children. The fact that their children didn't have the documents, they didn't have Social Security [cards] proved to us at the university that we have to do a better job of getting information to segments of the community interested in their children going to school. They see some barriers because maybe they don't have the documents, they don't have the Security numbers, but the university has ways to get around things. It proved to us that the perception that new immigrants are not interested in education for their kids is a misperception—they're very interested in their children getting an education.

ED: You are right when you say that it starts with the parents. Where do Chicanos in Phoenix send their kids to high school? They send them to St.

Mary's and Brophy [private Roman Catholic high schools], but not to the Phoenix Union District. Why are those choices made? Is our community giving up on the public schools? Is religion and faith playing a strong role? What about cost? There are many reasons why parents do this, but you're right: our parents are our first educators, our first teachers.

Many families will sacrifice to get one child through school because they see the bigger picture, they see the value of education, and we have to build on it. In my experience in Latin America, it's the same thing; parents want that. A growing population is overwhelming us, and the sad part is that the majority doesn't want us here. All you're going to be is a Mexican. So you happen to be an attorney in the law firm. You will still be a Mexican in the law firm. Or you can be an academic advisor, and still be told, "But you speak with an accent." It's how we carry ourselves that makes a difference.

Just a Mexican

JT: I have a degree, but if I sat in front of twelve individuals for four and a half weeks, and they explored my entire persona, it basically would come down to "I'm just a Mexican." I could assimilate with that jury because I was taller than the normal Mexican [and] I spoke without an accent. They looked at all these things. So did I have to sell myself? Absolutely. I will do anything. I don't care because all I wanted to do was win. I can't change who I am, and one thing that came out of that trial and tribulation of my life was that I realized I was just a Mexican, first and foremost. My father owns a business, my brother went to Harvard Law, but we grew up on Fourteenth and Garfield. I don't forget where I came from, but do I want my kids to go to school at Garfield [an inner-city elementary school]? No! [Laughter].

Changing Schools or Changing Addresses

CL: That's the problem. What about the kids that are going to those schools? I went to Edison and Garfield. Most of my friends' parents [wanted] them to go to college when we were growing up. And the sad thing is that out of all my friends, I'm the only one here. At Edison Elementary I had teachers that would tell us, "You're a Mexican. You don't have to do as well." When I did well on the Iowa test, one of the sixth-grade teachers told the students who weren't Mexican, "How can you let an immigrant come and do better than you?" I think these are issues that people don't really talk about. It's a community in crisis. You said, "I'm not going to send my kids there," but what about them? Oh, it's like, *son pobrecitos*. But what are you going to do about it?

JT: Why are you here? Who did your homework? Who does it now? You do, and you got that emphasis from your family. You didn't get pregnant, or maybe you did; there are a lot of things that hold people back. You're right. I know that neighborhood, I visit my grandma; I want to leave at night. [Laughter].

Dropping Out

CL: How can you explain that such a great percentage of students drop out? It's not necessarily an individual factor.

RC: I think we all have a responsibility to bring somebody with us. I'm the president of the University of Arizona Hispanic Alumni. I have scores of people wanting me to advocate on their behalf. I can't be everything to everybody, but I will do something. We [have to] pick our battles, and one of our biggest battles is how to educate our Latino community. Everybody keeps talking about the growing numbers of the Hispanic minorities, but not about the fast-growing minorities that are uneducated. And that's the problem—uneducated minority Latinos.

Do Parents Care?

JT: I agree that parents care—100 percent. They just don't know. They don't understand the nuances that we learned. I know the keys to success; I know that whole game. We have a large population of students and parents who don't understand that. And we continue to let schools control the curriculum. They are not teaching our kids the things that are necessary. That's why I sent my kids to a different school; I know the skills they need to learn. As concerned community members [we all have responsibility] because we are all community—black, white, brown, red, they are all my community at one level, and I want a Social Security check. We all have a vested interest in making sure that the community is profitable.

It Ain't Calculus

JT: There are parents that don't know that students need to be taking four years of math. They may say it's important, but they don't understand that. Then they get into low math and think they're getting algebra—they think they're taking calculus. It may say "calculus" on the line, but if you look at that calculus, it ain't calculus. It may be ten years ago. Everybody was taking algebra, and it was a joke! No! It's a lie! And nobody was there to say anything about it. There have to be people who will advocate for a common cause. It doesn't matter what color you are, when you go to South Mountain High School and North High School, everybody is at risk there. Everybody.

CM: You don't have to sell out; you don't have to be a fence-sitter to get to where you want to go and serve your own purposes in life. I think that you have to be true to yourself, but at the same time, be true to the people around you. You should not only serve yourself, but those around you, so that one day they will have enough trust and faith to get elected.

Education

CEM: I love South Phoenix. I'm a product of that community, and how the heck am I going to send my kids, if I were to have kids, to a school in this community when the schools are being graded at an F? Our teachers are not teaching the students what they need to know. Parents are just saying, "Okay, do the homework," and they're probably pushing them to do homework. Teachers are saying, "I'm frustrated, because my kids are coming with uncompleted homework because they are too busy watching the *novelas* with their parents at night." There are people watching *novelas* with their families and calling us asking, "What is it that my kid needs to do to get into college?" It's a complicated issue. How do we address it?

Saving the World

JT: Look at this under-thirty crowd! They all are motivated, but it's leading by example. They are the example of tomorrow, and if these kids in South Phoenix don't see that, then they're blind. I'm just a firm believer in that you just can't save the world.

ED: True, we can't save the world, but we can take steps towards doing that. The world is not going to be saved, but human nature makes progress with every generation, and we are part of making progress and we're contributors to that progress—if we don't, what hope do we have?

JT: How can you not look at these eager young faces and not go, "Damn, we are in good shape"?

ED: That's the pleasure of working at the university and seeing that growth and development, but we still have to take additional steps to broaden that base. That's the opportunity. If politicians don't do what we [elected] them to do, we have every right to vote them out.

Supporting Politicians

JT: What political leader do you know that, first and foremost, [does not want to] get re-elected? That's the number-one goal. . . . I don't believe in politicians because they are self-serving.

ED: That's the animal that democracy creates. We function in society, and as long as we believe in the negative, our thought is going to be negative. Last term, we had an opportunity to elect four Chicanos to Congress. When in Arizona history has that ever happened?

Talk, Talk, and More Talk

MP: We had an opportunity to elect a Hispanic governor. I helped run Alfredo Gutiérrez's campaign, and only fifty thousand people in Arizona understood what Marie, Mr. Delci, Cristina, and I understood. That's why I stayed so quiet, I've been to one hundred meetings like this, where we talk and talk and talk, but we never do anything. We're lucky to have Congressman Pastor there, and he is almost gone. We need to start fostering qualified Hispanics, not just any Hispanic, to start running in those positions. When someone like Alfredo Gutiérrez has the guts to run and we don't even bother to support him, we're too scared.

LA: There are a lot of leaders that have an influence on departments—[like] education, health services. I wanted to make sure that we are involving them too. I'm not a politician. I never had plans on running, but I enjoy being a part of the process.

The Importance of Dialogue

MEC: This was a real beautiful experience. We don't talk; we don't create the relationships. It's okay to agree or disagree. That's the one thing our community cannot seem to get past. I just want to close with a story about the power of relationships. It's a story about César Chávez and three young organizers, eager to learn about his organizing experience so they drove all night to La Paz. They got there and said, "Tell us, please, the secret of being a good organizer," and he said, "Well, first you talk to one person, and then you talk to another person, then you talk to another person," They interrupted him and said, "No, no, we want to hear what it [is] that really works. What have you done that made the farmworker organization and the grape boycott so successful?" And he said, "Well, you first talk to one person, and then you talk to another person, and then you talk to another person." I think that's what we are lacking in our community, and what we have done here is exactly that. I think we forged this relationship now, and this is just the first step. I hope we continue to do this.

An Intergenerational Leadership Resolana: Generational and Gender Challenges

MM: Today's resolana is with Tommy Espinoza, Nancy Jordan, and Danny Ortega, longtime leaders in the Phoenix community, and the group of young leaders who attended the previous resolana. Its themes are the generational and gender challenges facing our community. We will start with opening comments from our guests.

Giving Way to the New

NJ: When I was young I used to think that older people who had had their time were out of step and had not done much to connect with others. I now view it as a natural evolution; perhaps each generation has to push the other one aside and take their place. It is a kind of Darwinian philosophy. I am not sure that is bad because leadership has to be earned [from previous leaders and peers]. It is here that this gets played out in the larger society. It is sad to see.

Women and Men

NJ: The issues have not changed for Hispanics, and [they] will get worse as we become more of a threat—more prominent. It has always been an issue with Chicanas. There are so few who have the opportunity to move forward, but I am not convinced that it is always the males' fault. To some extent it might be our fault. It is easy to slide into the trap of being complacent, taking the more accepted way out, and there is a lot that you put up with if you are outspoken, or if you stand up for yourself. You can be ostracized very quickly, and those rules are communicated [to young women] from the time you are brought up. In some ways, there is a greater risk in stepping up to a leadership role if you are a Chicana. We look to men for leadership, and we don't always support other women leaders. There has been a lot of change, and when I look at the people who have supported me, there are more Chicanos who have supported than opposed me.

Bridging the Generation Gap

DO: I was impressed [by a presentation by Chris Marín on the history of leadership of the thirties and forties in our community] and the things they did in this state and in Phoenix that were helping shape our community long before I was born. People were making sacrifices, taking risks; [people] were passionate about change and made it their life's work. I would like to think that what we are *not* sharing with you is part of our problem [as was] the lack of sharing of those people.

I got started as a very young man, a junior in high school, [with] a group of students from the university. They were very active in organizing. They were busy knocking the hell out of the older guys, the "LULACers," the "Vesta Clubbers"—the people who were the leaders of the thirties, forties, and fifties. I am amazed at what they were able to accomplish. I did not know it then. I have to figure out how it is I am going to have some impact on your life that will make you want to create change, to have a passion for the things that the leaders in the thirties and the forties had. You will be the leadership of the new millennium.

Taking Stock

TE: I started to come to terms with [my] formation as an individual. I looked at religious experiences and family, and what caused the anger that I drew on to concern myself with community issues.

My mom formed the stability and kept whispering in my ear, especially when I was in trouble, that I was going to succeed, that I was going to do some great things. It allowed me to have some self-confidence. My father early on said to me, "When you were born you had stamped on your ass "Mexican American." Don't ever forget that! You have a beautiful culture and language and you are an American." He was speaking as an ex-Marine. What angered me most [was seeing] how my father was discriminated against by the utility company [APS]. I did not fit [the role of a model person], but I was wise enough at that age [fifteen] to know that he was being discriminated against. He would sit at dinner every night and I saw him [over the years] dejected because they did not promote him as foreman.

Taking on the System

TE: There are certain things that triggered my wanting to work for Chicanos Por La Causa, to "take on the system." This is in the sixties, seventies, and eighties. When you talk about leadership, you have to ask yourself, Can I analyze my life and look at those points in my life that have formed me as a person? And what is it that triggers my anger, my love, and my passion to want to move things for the better of the community? When you can grab hold of that and understand it, it allows you to give of yourself. I concluded that leadership is giving of yourself. Leadership is about forming yourself to realistically position yourself to fulfill [your] passions.

The Most Important Thing in Life

TE: Last week I sat in front of my ex-father-in-law who was dying of cancer. He was not the warm and fuzzy type. He was a very traditional, macho kind of father. I went to console him because we knew he was going to die. He was skin and bones and was crying because he had said some things to his son that really bothered him. He humbled me because he asked me to forgive him because I had divorced his daughter and he had ill feelings toward me. That was powerful; it took me to my knees. He was not worried about how much money was in his bank account, about whether he was driving a Beemer, or about wearing Armani suits. He was worried about his legacy of loving. You are not going to take any of it with you; you are only going to take those emotions that you have in your heart about who you loved and who you did not [love]. He was a leader that day. By the way, he died Monday and we buried him today. Life moves very rapidly. Don't waste it.

Sharing Experiences with Young Leaders

MN: The generation gap [notion] really struck a chord with me because [many] projects I work on are trying to fill in that gap. I'm not completely clued in to the history of our community, even though my parents have always been involved for a long time. I'm working on a project called "Campesinos," and we're trying to collect the histories of living campesinos. Benny A. said that one of his biggest regrets was that he didn't share what he knew with the younger members of the community. My question is, Do you feel that you shared your experiences with the young members of the community?

Talking (or Not) Talking about Yourself

DO: No. I think that we're going to get to an age when we will worry about the things we didn't do. I worry a lot about that—it's a driving force. That no matter how hard I try, it's never enough. If you're true to the commitment for your community, the last person in the world you want to be talking about is yourself. And the moral of my story is: Never talk about myself, unless someone is asking me a question or wants to know. And I want to humble myself to a greater cause and to a greater purpose. And so, it's very, very hard to share in that regard. That doesn't mean that I was that way when I was younger. I was the total opposite.

We have a technological gap, not just a gender gap, not just a leadership gap, but until we reach out to learn how to use those computers, the gap is only going to get greater. I don't think that we are making enough effort on how to connect better with you guys. I do it through others—this is my way of sharing my life, through others. And so it's a combination of things. I think that you have to reach out, and I have to be willing to deal with you not from a demeaning standpoint, but from where you are in life.

MN: What would it mean, if you did share? Is it that you don't want to come across as too arrogant or is there pain involved? What is it?

All You Need to Do Is Ask

DO: The bottom line is, if you come to me and say, "Danny, talk to me about x, y, and z; talk to me about the sixties, talk to me about my dad" (and I got stories to share about your dad); it has to come from you guys. And I'll jump at the opportunity. The best advice you can give is the advice you're asked for, and if you're not being asked, why give it?

The Hispanic Women's Corporation as a Teaching Tool

NJ: I'm not sure how much I can teach. I think the growth is in the process, and these are all very personal experiences. I want to talk about the Hispanic Women's Corporation; [they] try to create opportunity. The conference is what you see, but the actual model behind it is actually one that creates an opportunity for women to try things that normally they don't get the opportunity to do—to organize an event that has a budget of over $300,000. How many women really have that as part of their job? Not many. So I think it's the idea of taking the initiative to create opportunities for others and to mentor them as they're learning [in] a safe environment for people to try these things. And I think that that's the secret of why the conference and the corporation have been successful. There is something very empowering about the process of participation.

Had we not come together as a group, I don't know that we would be in the kinds of positions that we are today. And if I look at the group that was part of the core, we've all achieved but we did it, I think, in a very safe environment, helping each other. . . . I think that there are ways of passing on information or ensuring opportunity, but I don't know that I feel comfortable about saying that that was an individual thing. And there have been people that tried to take individual credit for that, and it isn't, it never was, and it never will be [an individual thing] because the effort of one individual will die.

Individual or Group Efforts and the Difference They Make

MN: But the flipside of it is that you [made] an individual contribution. And there is nothing wrong with declaring that.

NJ: What's to be gained by that?

MN: It's where it all came from. When I talk to people about the kind of movement in Phoenix and Arizona, the history of CPLC, I hear, "I didn't know that. Why didn't someone tell me?" I get that everyone contributed to a group effort, but there's an individual story that should be honored.

NJ: I can't say that one person was more important than the other. So I also think leadership is for the times. What worked ten years ago may not work today. And if you try to take the person from ten years ago and put them in a position now, they may not fit. I feel very strongly that we shouldn't focus on the individual. I'm much more comfortable with the idea of a group.

Changed Organizations

TE: The question is a good one. Sometimes we don't realize that we do mentor younger people and, in fact, engage them. Obviously, some become very personal relationships—you bond as friends. I don't think it is fair to say that it hasn't occurred. It has occurred. In fact, at one point CPLC was known nationally as one of the organizations that produced young leadership. But there was a period where everybody knew you didn't stay much longer than three, four, five years and then you were out. . . . It was a place to grow; it was a place to experience; it was a place to get exposed to the world and politics. It was a safe environment.

You weren't going to get fired if the banker yelled at you, if you got kicked out of City Hall, if you boycotted Phoenix Union High School— that was part of the experiment. But institutions change. [There is a] void in our communities [for] a vehicle that allows that kind of discussion [and] exposure that allows you to make mistakes. The reason I succeeded at CPLC was [because] I couldn't fail. We didn't know how to build houses; we went out there and built houses. We didn't know how to make small business loans, but we certainly learned real quick. We didn't know about education, but people were learning about education and we ran great programs giving folks scholarships. Danny was on the board of directors, a junior lawyer going through school, formulating policies and forming decisions that were going to impact our community. In my viewpoint, that vehicle does not exist inside our community right now. Back then that's the only vehicle we had, and I would argue that now we have many more vehicles than we did back in the seventies.

Culture Clashes

ED: There is a culture clash in what you are asking, because we're raised not to praise self. Yet we function in a society that only focuses on recognizing self. We volunteered to do the coaching [in the summer heat] without expecting anything in return. [The same applies to] teachers who put in extra time with their kids. We don't traditionally work at self-identifying the qualities that we contribute. The leadership role means doing by example.

MN: What happens if we forgot these stories? What if people didn't know?

NJ: It's the interpretation of the story. I think it's vital to tell the story. I'm [asking], Why does it have to be an individual story?

Jabón: Washing Your Mouth Out with Soap

MN: As a community we do tend to downplay our achievements. Why? I will give you an example. Nancy, you told me an interesting story about Alfredo: that he got his mouth duct-taped when he was a kid for speaking Spanish. To me that's a really powerful thing. I'm working on a play called *Jabón* that collects these stories, and I guess I do it because I'm so worried that I'm going to forget, that I'm not going to know. I care about the community. What about people who don't care about the community? What if they don't know that this happened, that we have a history here that's pretty strong? And if nobody shares it and we don't talk about it, we don't let it rise to the surface. I don't know what would happen but my sense is, that's a dangerous thing.

TE: Well, the exciting part to life is [that] we can do it. Your generation may be the one that says we need to write our history. We're really bad at doing that. We don't write the history of how the generation of the fifties and the forties impacted our community to allow us to be radical in the sixties and the seventies. I don't know what happened before that. I could tell you what happened in American Legion Post 41 because my dad spent a lot of time in there, but I wouldn't be able to give you the historical impact. I know about Maclovio Barraza because he was bigger than life when I was coming up, but I'm not sure that there's a central place where you can get that kind of information and data. And maybe it's time to do that.

Preparing New Leaders

DO: In sharing the principles of leadership, I've got to talk about the virtues that make up the kind of individuals that are going to take us beyond anything we've ever dreamed of. It's an issue of values, passion, and how we create change. [It's not about] values from an ethical standpoint, because if your parents didn't take care of it, I can't do anything with it—it's going to be a little late. How to create change is more important to me than to share history about what I've been through or my parents went through, because ultimately you're going to be motivated by self-interest. People in the *movimiento* got where they are because of self-interest, and that's not a bad thing. I [need] to figure what your self-interest is and then build upon that.

I think it's also a matter of priorities. There are those who want to talk to you about the virtues of God, and how that takes us to the next step in the transformation that we need to have as a community; those that are going to talk about hard work, and what they did in their lives; those who talk about service to country. But for me it's a matter of priority: [my] hope is to have an impact on your life.

MN: If we came to you and said, "Hey, talk to me about. . . ."

DO: We're dying to talk about those things. Not about ourselves [but about] our experiences.

MM: We are all part of an era, an epoch that to a great extent determines who we are. That's what Nancy was saying: if you don't watch it, you can become an anachronism. And you've got to change with the times, and sometimes the times are not the best, so you have to stay back.

No Longer a Minority

BS: From your perspectives, what do you see as the possible new frontiers in our community?

NJ: The biggest challenge is learning to accept the new role in our community where we are not a minority. This changes the definitions of everything, and it implies responsibilities that we will have—not to act like others have acted towards us. I'm not sure what it's going to be like.

TE: I will tell you that the future for your generation is going to be really exciting and challenging. One is [that] you are no longer a minority. In the business world it's called "general market," which means you're going to run this country. There are studies indicating that Latino communities, especially Mexicans, are not assimilating into the traditional models that have been categorized as part of this country. It's called balkanization. It scares [people].

We're already changing the character of this country. People and businesses are starting to market to us. They're concerned about their labor force, whether they understand the culture, where the markets are going to grow. If we're not astute as to where our market is growing and the kinds of languages that we need to have, then we're going to lose out. Our next generation will lose out in foreign policy, in forming markets, in forming what kind of educational systems are put in place across the country for our children and our grandchildren. So it's an exciting time, but also a very challenging time because [we're] living in a WASP model that's not working for us.

We are no longer second- and third-generation Mexican Americans. Your generation is going to have to wrestle with cultural changes . . . the language issue, but more importantly, an educational issue, where children from Mexico and Central America aren't prepared to go into our educational systems. So those are challenges that we're going to have to embrace and move forward. It's a great time to be alive in the movement.

The Need for "New" Organizations

YM: You mentioned that in the late sixties, early seventies, there were organizations that provided a safe environment for young people to take risks. Do you think that we have those kinds of organizations or opportunities for young people now?

DO: Let me start with the yes. I think we have enough influence over organizations like Valle del Sol, Chicanos Por La Causa, Friendly House, NCLR, and United Way that we're capable of bringing young people into these organizations to develop them into the leaders of tomorrow. [And] No, because we're your biggest problem. We stifle your leadership growth because you [have to] fit into a model. We never fit into anything. We made our own. And so sometimes our effort to help young people is the worst thing that we can do, because we don't let them fly.

We don't let them take risks, and we're very protective of their need to succeed. Our model worked fine for us, but young people today have to create their own model. You have to take your own risks. You also don't need to have the jobs that we created—they're stifling [you]. Chicanos Por La Causa, Valle del Sol, and Friendly House are service organizations. One of the heroes of the thirties and the forties was Placida Smith, the founder of Friendly House. She's dead [but] she's still serving people.

I would like to see young people be more adventurous, take more risks, create their own nonprofits, and fall on their face; just the way we fell on our faces. Do something on your own.

TE: The models that we had don't work anymore—they cannot address the issues of our time. There isn't a model out there that I could point to now that would fit what you need to succeed—it is a combination of business, politics, and immigration—everything was opened for us [after the civil rights movement].

The New Majority

MHD: I was a nontraditional student when I went to college. [I learned] that eighteen-year-old students don't want programs like affirmative action. I saw this complacency. So I started losing hope, but sitting here tonight, I hear discussions [about] creating new models, doing it on your own, and the new frontiers. We are the majority. But so what? We're still the least educated, the poorest group, we have the highest dropout rate, and the highest teen pregnancy [rate]. Maybe that's what's going to mobilize the young people and take them out of their comfort zone. Maybe those are going to be the models you're going to have to create.

Enter New Leaders

DO: I don't think your generation is going to be the generation that is going to take us to the next level. It's the first generation of those Mexican immigrants that are going to be the leaders of this community because they understand hunger. And they are not complacent. And they understand the work ethic in a much different way. I will be close to seventy before we see the kind of transformation that we need to see in leadership in this community. This is going to come from a different generation of young people that are first-generation, from families who have immigrated recently to this country.

Power and Change

CM: I am under the impression that to create change one needs power, and to have power one needs money. [However, we should] think [that] that's not the way to be. . . . Giving of our time in a benevolent manner should be the way we give back to our community. I thought, "Oh, yeah, I'm going to make a lot of money and that's going to get me to a good position." Well, it's gotten me nowhere by being supported by a wealthy father. When our generation stops thinking about how much they have in their bank account and realizes that money really doesn't buy them a place at the table, then they're going to believe that they can affect our community, not by their wallet, [but] by their actual selfless nature, to give back.

MN: You're saying that the only way you can effect change is by being rich?

CM: In my age group, people believe that. I'll be someone because I have the money to be there with the other people who are making decisions.

CL: I disagree with you. I come from a different background where my family wasn't wealthy, and in my family it was never about "once you get to a position where you have money, you will be able to effect change." . . . I'm not at that position right now either, but ever since I was in high school, and even in college, it's always about giving back to your community. Not later, but now. I guess because of my different experiences from yours, I see the complacency, but I don't think I have to wait until I get money.

CM: I see it around my own personal group of friends, and I do believe that my group of friends is very socially conscious. I believe that they truly do have a passion; they do care. They seem to think that money is the way to do it [though], and it's not.

The Complacent Generation

MN: I think that if we forget that our community had to fight to get to a place where we could be complacent, that is bad. What María and you guys are saying is that we are not going to do anything. We might never effect change because we have no cause to. We're fine.

NJ: If you think that the greater community, regardless of how light you[r skin] may be, thinks of you as anything else than a Chicano, you are sadly mistaken—they do not. I think that that is one of the big delusions that the younger generation has—that somehow because they're educated, that they're going to be admitted to the right clubs and things. Forget it!

MN: I don't think that we can let ourselves rest in that space.

TE: We all have free will. So what are you going to do with your lives? You have three elders telling you to get to it. All you need to do is decide that's what you want to get done. But you have to be willing to sacrifice.

If the Kennedys Did It, Why Can't We?

DO: What about the Rockefeller and the Kennedy model? They did it. I'm talking about tons of money. [They raised] some of the greatest people that this country's ever had in philanthropy. If you take the next generation of leaders and those with a lot of money and all these people in between, we can transform those models.

And by the way, there are no absolutes in this game, folks. I don't have the answer. And I have all the trappings of American culture. There's no model in that regard. But I do think there is a model about what it means to give and live for others and the greatness that comes from doing that. You don't have to sell everything according to Scriptures because not even Tommy is doing that.

We have to deal with the modern realities and with the realities of our culture. Take the hand that's been dealt to you and ask, How can I achieve greatness beyond the material things in life? You've got to take care of your own needs based upon your cultural upbringing—the way I've done, because my dad didn't drive a Jaguar. You know what leaders of the forties talked about? The great things they did with the time they had and the devotion they had to care for others.

Moving the Older Generation Aside

TE: I'm not going to wait around and ask somebody to give me "empowerment." I don't even understand what that means: [that] "the old guard needs to move over so we can take over." I'm thinking, "You better push real hard, buddy." By the way, power is not shared. Power [is] a rough game. You'd better be ready to fight because no one is going to give it to you. You've got to get out there and roll up your sleeves and fight for it.

DO: I'm telling you that people are better off getting it on their own.

LA: You have to be responsible, like you're saying, for what you believe in and not wait for somebody to hand you something.

Inheriting the Passion

LA: What we are saying is [that] we're not just going to stand around to tell stories, so unless you ask, you won't find out. I see the value in having these dialogues. [It] is really good because I think that it helps people light up, spark up [a] flame.

MEC: This is great information to be exchanging. I had the opportunity to work with these individuals so I feel privileged to say, "You know what, you get Danny somewhere and he can talk your ear off, if you ask him the right questions." I have the support of Nancy, I can pose questions and she can provide me with information. Wow, forget the Woodrow Wilson Fellowship, I'm getting the Tommy Espinoza Fellowship so people can learn grassroots organizing.

Hispanic Culture

DO: One of the worst comparisons that we can make is to compare ourselves to another community because we have to set our own standards—communities are different like families are different. And as a group [you need] to decide what makes up who you are, what's going to take you to the next level in terms of community service, in terms of building political power, in terms of building economic power.

Today, if somebody runs for public office and wants to be elected in an area that's predominantly Hispanic, he has to know Spanish. When we were being raised we didn't have to. The difference [then] was [that] we were trying to preserve culture and language, today you must *have* it. See the difference? I'm living a dream right now. My Spanish is what's gotten me where I am. So you guys have to begin to think about the language, and Spanish is the one you speak the least of, quite frankly. If you compare now to what we had, to what's there now, the transformation is unreal. And guess what? I'd love to take credit for preserving our culture. It happened on its own. And now you've got to deal with the reality of it.

NJ: Across the border is what happened.

DO: It happened on its own. And whether it was because of hunger, poverty, NAFTA, *maquiladoras*, cheap labor in this country, whatever the reason was, "You got a problem with us? Get used to it."

Embracing Success and New Identities

TE: I'm finding that Latinas are becoming much stronger in their positions. They are much better educated and more aggressive in moving forward with their careers. I challenge Latinos to embrace manhood, fatherhood, and be proud of it. That doesn't mean you try to dominate; it's about a balance in your life. The last point is that making money is okay. I remember the days when we felt guilty if we made money.

I'm the first one to walk into Chicanos Por La Causa with a tie. And they laughed and laughed. You need to understand that money is not evil. In fact, the Bible says very clearly it's the love of money that is the root of all evil—you need money to move things. We need bankers, we need MBAs, we need financial types, and we need those folks that understand how to run that part of business. And the last point is balance. Life is about balance—physical, mental, and spiritual. Make sure you look inside of you as to why you even want to lead. Sometimes it's okay to be a follower.

Doing Instead of Intellectualizing

NJ: I'm concerned that you may over-intellectualize this process, because in the end it's about doing. And too much angst over what should I be doing, how should I be doing it, is just going to cripple you and all your energy. It's about looking at things and addressing those things that you have a passion about.

DO: [I want to finish by] telling you that it's very simple to do because all it means is caring for others, and there are lots of things—children, the elderly, education, economics, organizations. There's a need out there for you to contribute your time and your talents for others. And it's really simple: from that caring and giving you will grow beyond your wildest dreams. While I'm taking care of myself, I can take care of others, and I can commit time to this project or to this person to do good for others. Think about it. If you don't feel like you're over-committed in doing community projects, then you are not doing enough.

A Final Community Resolana

In the fourth and final resolana, Atencio, Mares, and I presented summaries of our essays, fielded questions, and listened to the audience's stories about community life. The stories focused on issues that had come up in previous resolanas: leadership, the generation gap, wanting in, power. Younger people seemed to express different values than the older generation—they sought respect whereas their elders had sought money and had "wanted in." One young person spoke of her grandmother telling her to get an education "in case you get a bad husband." The important point raised in these discussions was that Hispanics could not be viewed as a cohesive entity separate from mainstream Americans. Hispanic ancestry is multidimensional and multicultural: it includes George Washington as well as Pancho Villa, Sor Juana Inez de la Cruz, La Malinche, professors and mentors, and Hispanic opposition to abuses of power; it includes the Declaration of Independence, the Bill of Rights, the good and the bad. The discussion on the need to know more about one another continued from previous resolanas; "we need to take biographies and oral histories and in the process work across generations; young people are itching to be involved, but they need to know that there are people available to help," one participant commented. One person summed up the importance of la resolana: "when you dialogue you have authentic regard for the truth; we are all equal before God's eyes, and uncovering this truth is our most difficult task in life."

The issue of gender was revisited. One of the participants talked about how gender issues loomed large within Hispanic culture, as many Hispanics were raised in families where fathers could do no wrong and women were not treated as well as they deserved to be. "Many of us also wished we had not learned many things that our fathers taught us. We are very good at telling Anglos how they should treat us but not so good at examining how we treat our women." Fragmentation exists also between first- and second-generation Americans, as expressed by a Mexican national who talked about feeling like an outsider within the Chicano community. She saw a need for healing and for learning about one another. There was talk about strength within the poverty of Chicanos and their love of family. It is important to engage the broader society "with a set of values that are consistent with Hispanic values of family and spirituality; we either sit back and complain or engage the world."

Cordelia Candelaria, eminent scholar turned university administrator, is a women who has engaged the world, and it is with her words that we end our resolana:

> One story that I have never told in public is one of the best pieces of education that I have ever learned: I graduated from college with the intent of becoming an English teacher when I was selected as a Woodrow Wilson Scholar. I went to the University of Notre Dame in 1970—it was Catholic and had a football team. Notre Dame was an all-men's school, but they did admit women in graduate school. One of the requirements was to have a threshold interview with the direc-

tor of graduate studies, a leading scholar in the area I wanted to study with. His office was right below Father Theodore M. Hesburgh's, the president of Notre Dame. I am talking here about power, leadership, and education, and how it is used. I was so excited: I dressed up, wore hose (It was hot and muggy in August), and waited twenty minutes. His secretary showed me in, and walked backward facing him not wanting to interrupt anything. He put his glasses up, did not say good afternoon. This was my first meeting, and I did not know what to do. This great man that I had wanted to learn from, the director of graduate studies at this prestigious university, said, "Mrs. Candelaria, I want you to know that I do not approve of women at Notre Dame." I absolutely could have wept. I was devastated. We talked about my program of study, but never sat down. There was someone who was leading and teaching who was setting a very bad example. And here was someone [me] not knowing what to do. But that is power and how it is used sometimes in a very inappropriate way. This was a brilliant man whose growth had been stunted in a place where that type of behavior was accepted. I stayed at ND and got my degrees. Later *Mechista* students raised other issues with Father Hesburgh about the treatment of nuns, who were working in the kitchen as maids and cooks, and were cleaning up after the priests.

Conclusion: What to Do?

There is a shared perception that the dominant society does not "take us seriously." Why is that? At one level one can argue that it is because the community is "fragmented" and does not act in unison. There are divisions between Chicanos and newly arrived immigrants (some legal, many undocumented, and others that have overstayed their visas), particularly among the working class, who view immigrants as competitors for jobs. Differences in language and customs also create divisions. The dialogues reveal growing rifts among immigrants from the various Latin American countries, many of whom come from the upper classes, and Chicanos who have been here for several generations (many rooted in the Southwest before statehood) and feel that these immigrants operate in opposition to their interests. The most dramatic differences seem to be between refugees who arrive with proper documentation, such as Cubans, and so-called illegals. Clearly, there are also differences in identity. Not everyone is in favor of a "Hispanic nation."

In *The Clash of Civilizations and the Remaking of World Order,* Samuel Huntington, a Harvard political scientist, identifies another level of fragmentation on a more global scale. He argues that the fundamental differences among peoples in the world today are not of rich versus poor, north versus south, east versus west, but rather of a clash of civilizations: the overall way of life of a people that includes their language, history, religion, customs, institutions, and self-identification. Western civilization incorporates ideas handed down from the Greeks and Romans and from Christianity, Protestantism, and the Reformation. Its distinctiveness lies also in the separation of church and state and other traditions that are taken for granted. Huntington claims that Latin America's "Corporatist" and Catholic religion makes assumptions about the world that explain the differences in political and economic infrastructures between Latin America and the United States. We wonder, along with him, whether Mexicans and other people from Latin America are adherents of Western civilization. Is it true that there is a conflict between Hispanic family values and the values of Western culture and capitalism, as he claims? After you read the dialogues (and the Mares essay that follows), I leave you to decide.

The issues that have been discussed—immigration, education, leadership, political participation, and the threats to family life—all point to the demographics of a frequently young, poor, and uneducated population. The importance of strong families is mentioned in every interview and is emphasized in the dialogues. These ideals, however, must be made congruent with the realities of family life in a Hispanic community that finds itself under pressure, particularly among its young people. Schwartz tells us that the "pressures of teenagers numbers will be so immense that it will reshape the world" (and it will reshape the Hispanic world and family even more). If not cared for, these children probably will end up "uneducated, unemployed, and in the hopeless end, street criminals."[11]

One of the strong messages in these dialogues is that young people need to feel valued, to feel that they are central to the story of their community. In *The Denial of Death*, Ernest Becker once suggested, "If everyone honestly admitted his urge to be a hero it would be a devastating release of truth. It would make men [and women] demand that culture gives them their due—a primary sense of human value as unique contributors to cosmic life."[12] How is this to be done, and is it the responsibility of leaders to insist that our youth be given their due? The answer lies in the connection between "not being taken seriously" and the life experiences of the participants, between America's "Western" values and the knowledge and experiences of Chicanos.

What are we to make of the revelation that a teacher forty years ago told her student that he did not need good grades because he was going to work in the mines, and that today a teacher tells her students they should be ashamed of themselves for letting "an immigrant" score better on an achievement test than they did? What are we to make of schools channeling students into vocational programs because they have no faith in their abilities, of teachers allowing students to advance without knowing how to read, of children watching their parents' despair over not being able to provide adequately for their children, of schools so ignoring the history of the Mexican experience that students do not know about the Treaty of Guadalupe Hidalgo or about their immediate history, of a Hispanic student leader being placed in a segregated environment upon arriving at the university, or of young Hispanic adults being told not to expect invitations to exclusive clubs controlled by Anglos? The No Child Left Behind policies reinforce to Hispanic children that they are failures and surely are connected to a long legacy of reminders to previous generations. What are we to make of smug college professors of Spanish telling Chicano students that their Spanish is not "correct"? Today's Hispanic schoolchildren are victims of constant media bashing: their parents are depicted as criminals; authorities pass laws and build walls to keep them out; immigrant children are barred from getting a college education while at the same time they are overrepresented in the criminal justice system.

Is it possible that "we are not taken seriously" because the knowledge and experience of Hispanics is subjugated, unworthy of consideration by the dominant society? This is a central theme of Atencio's essay and a position championed by scholars like Velez-Ibáñez and Greenberg, who argue that "public schools often ignore the strategic and cultural resources" which they refer to as "funds of knowledge."[13] If policymakers understood, truly understood, that by not validating children and their past, they are condemning them to a dismal future, they might reassess the consequences of their policies.

In this study we learned about the importance of shock in people's lives. For many of the interviewees, a seminal event shocks them into another reality. Bertolt Brecht's 1928 play *The Threepenny Opera* exposes the middle class, the bourgeoisie, for rewarding criminal behavior, and at the end of the play, the lights are turned on the audience to show them in all their bourgeois glory. Members of the audience don't know where to hide. Is there a way to shock the community (and us), as was done in that play?

It is important to reflect on the importance of myth in providing a framework for understanding behavior. A ready-made myth in our society revolves around materialism and success. Ronald Reagan, our modern-day Horatio Alger, when asked whether he was for the rich or the poor responded, "What I want to see above all is that this country remain a country where someone can always get rich."[14] This vision may be important, but clearly it is not the central preoccupation of the participants in this project. There are hints about what could be done to begin a search that will lead Hispanic people toward a healthier way of life.

I think the way out of these dilemmas begins with a positive attitude toward life in which people don't become embittered, and tragedy and disappointment are transformed into personal power. Two ideas seem central to these narratives: most of these individuals take responsibility for their lives, they don't blame others for their circumstances, and they are able to use their gifts of intelligence and courage to act on the world. The fragmentation in the community is what prompts the cry for unity and for greater concern for one another. In their quest for community, these stories reflect heroism, solidarity, and caring.

In my view, little can be transformed in the Hispanic world without an acknowledgment of the subjugation of knowledge and experience. There is always a certain tension between political and social visionaries, such as were found among the Chicano leaders of the sixties, and persons who are more pragmatically concerned about immediate life issues. The Chicano visionary would like the Chicano/Latino community as a whole to think more, to analyze more, to dare more, and to keep a communal, or tribal, design in mind. This is very difficult, although not impossible, in an individualistic society such as the United States. This individualistic orientation is now coupled with a narrow and highly idealized version of capitalism advocated by a strong neoconservative movement. Chicanos are not immune to the pull of this conservative ideology towards a social construction and a politics that mitigate against group cultural identification. Chicanos need to remind themselves and others that they are heirs to rich intellectual and cultural traditions, part European, part Iberian, part Mexican and mestizo, and part indigenous. There is also much in Hispanic daily life that merits attention: culinary skills, mechanical and construction skills, farming, and much other knowledge and skills that could and should be validated by mainstream American institutions. There are bound to be points of contention as Chicanos wrestle with their heritage and their current position, as a culture, in the United States.

Some of the values clearly highlighted in these dialogues are beacons for productive living. The subjugated knowledge includes both positive and negative aspects of Mexican culture. The important point is that living with "secrets" and not knowing about one's past make one vulnerable to manipulation, whether at the level of the family or the society.

We believe the ideas of "being born again" into "Western" culture or of waiting to become rich simply won't do for Hispanic children. They should be able to feel they are the center of the world *now*, not when they undergo some magic transformation. One person's advice was "to maintain the balance between a strong cultural identity and the Anglo world," a balance between "the Lexus and the olive tree."

Is it possible (and is there a willingness) to create communities in the image of Paul Tillich's new being: "more in harmony with nature, less driven, more perceptive, more in touch with [their] own creative energies, and who might go on to form genuine communities to replace the collectivities of our time, communities of truer persons in place of the objective creatures created by our materialistic culture"? Tillich recognized that this idea was a myth, an ideal that one might work toward and only partly realize.[15] We believe that the Chicano experience as articulated in Atencio's essay as "una vida buena y sana y alegre" and in these dialogues can be a productive part of this dialogue.

A Resolana on Networks

Chicanos, Connections, and Culture

E. A. "Tony" Mares

In chapter 1, Tomás Atencio analyzes rural Hispanic communities and their survival in terms of the metaphorical concept of la resolana, the idea that through dialogical exchange the members of a village come to understand their issues and problems and work toward solutions that maintain the cultural integrity of their community. In chapter 2 Miguel Montiel examines accomplished Indohispanics' struggle to succeed in the United States. He posits Atencio's idea of "resolana in action" as a basis for examining the notion of "success." These essays form the background for my more general consideration of Chicanos in relation to the socioeconomic forces at work within Western civilization.

Throughout, I use the terms *Chicano, Mexican American,* and *Indohispanic* interchangeably to refer to Mexican Americans who, with respect to their individual or communal identity (to the extent they still have one), form part of a spectrum of people. At one extreme on the spectrum are persons and communities who see themselves as indigenous, or fantasize themselves as such. At the other extreme are those who fantasize themselves as pure Spanish, whatever that is, or who think of themselves as Spanish American. My favorite term for those Hispanos who share cultural traits with indigenous communities is Indohispanic, because I cannot think of a clearer or more inclusive term to convey the breadth and depth of this cultural complex.

I raise the question, Are Indohispanics part of Western civilization? If they are, to what extent, and how do the members of this culture relate to the processes of self-identity and group identity, community, nationalism, and globalization? How do networks link Indohispanics with each other and with those outside their immediate interest spheres? While the forces of tribalism, nationalism, and globalization of the world's economy form the deep background of many of the issues discussed in these pages, I intend to pursue a distinct approach and analysis of these forces by emphasizing the role of networks in the contemporary world.

My first experience of networks occurred within my home community of Old Town, Albuquerque, New Mexico. Before I turn to this early background, I will briefly examine network theory, a specialized branch of mathematics known more generally as graph theory. The origins of this theory go back to 1736, when a Swiss-born mathematician by the name of Leonhard Euler showed that there was no continuous path across the bridges connecting several landmasses in his home town of Konigsberg, Germany. He called the landmasses "nodes" and the bridges "links." He was able to show that there was no continuous path across all the bridges (that is, connecting the nodes and links) without crossing at least one bridge twice, because *it was a property of the graph*. As Albert-László Barabási said, "Euler's unintended message is very simple: Graphs or networks have properties, hidden in their construction, that limit or enhance our ability to do things with them. . . . The construction and structure of graphs or networks is the key to understanding the complex world around us. Small changes in the topology, affecting only a few of the nodes or links, can open up hidden doors, allowing new possibilities to emerge."[1]

Although scholars after Euler studied the properties of graphs, it wasn't until the mid-twentieth century that mathematicians came to understand the practical and social implications of networks. They discovered that whenever there is a collection of nodes—say the nodes are strangers in New York City gathered around a tamale stand—links will form between the nodes. When the average number of links per node is one, something unique happens: the collection of nodes (strangers) forms what sociologists call a community. Physicists describe such nodes as having gone through a phase transition from being a collection of independent nodes to becoming a cluster. For example, the strangers gathered around the tamale stand might realize they are all immigrants from Mexico, and for a brief period they form a temporary cluster, one type of a random network.

Who We Are: A Network Perspective

Networks are seldom random, however. Our families are networks of persons linked by blood, affection, class, legal considerations, and often religion. We have workplace networks of associates and collaborators. There are also designed networks of highways and skyways for transporting people and things from node to node. The Internet is another example of a constructed network. In all these cases, the network has properties independent of the individual nodes. Network theory may also help us understand, in connection with the specific networks of the Latino community, one of its thorny issues: politics. For a political system is also a complex network. Small changes in the topology of Indohispanic communities can open hidden doors to social change.

My childhood world had many hidden doors. I could not see their network connections at the time, but they were there. These connections, in turn, were situated within a historic frame, without which nothing can be understood about Indohispanics. Here, a brief review is really necessary to place my later comments in a historical perspective.

Many cultures, of course, played significant roles in the spiritual and aesthetic development of the United States, its material construction, and its rise to political hegemony. Speaking in very broad terms, however, there are four major groupings of people whose cultural origins and development were key to the discovery of the Americas and the eventual founding, growth, and expansion of this country. These people and their varied cultures are the Native Americans, Europeans, African Americans, and Mexicans or Mexican Americans who now live in all regions of the United States.

Native Americans form the first category. These are the indigenous inhabitants of the Americas, and their roots in North and South America go back many thousands of years. From the Bering Strait to Tierra del Fuego, these early peoples occupied and populated the Americas. Whatever conflicts they had among themselves, and there were many, the indigenous cultures learned how to survive, and some of them eventually developed extensive civilizations.

Southern Europeans, and later their northern brethren, chanced upon the Americas in their quest for a safe maritime route to the Indies. The Europeans form the second group of concern here. Driven by the dynamics of their own economic and hegemonic needs, the Europeans conquered, exploited, enslaved, and destroyed most of the indigenous cultures, and tried to reconstruct the natives in images more suitable to their own Judeo-

Christian visions of the world and the cosmos. In the process, the Europeans seized and more or less permanently occupied the ancestral lands of the indigenous populations. In connection with this second group, my fellow contributors and I are aware of the European impact on our own thinking; we know that we cannot objectively stand outside the European conceit, but we can at least examine it with the perspective gained from our immersion in the deep roots of our own Mexican and Mexican American culture.

Variously known as whites or, usually inaccurately, as Anglos, Anglo-Americans, or simply Americans, the descendants of primarily northern Europeans have by and large documented and written the history of the United States. Not surprisingly, the history textbooks with which most Americans are educated have traditionally reflected, and continue to reflect, a Euro-American bias. As this story goes, America was founded by settlers who landed at Plymouth Rock, survived great adversity, tamed the wilderness, civilized the Indians, and conquered and settled the North American continent "from sea to shining sea." In the process, the American nation developed a representative democracy based on the ideas and ideals of the European Enlightenment and on primarily English and French models of institutions and governance. They expanded relentlessly toward the Pacific, fought a bloody civil war, and emerged as an industrial giant by the late nineteenth and early twentieth centuries. By the end of the twentieth century, the United States had become the most industrialized, technologically advanced, and undisputedly most powerful nation on earth.

Missing from the narrative, or appearing only in muted form, is the thread of racism woven into the fabric of this account. Missing, too, is the story of the extermination of native tribes; the brutal mistreatment of African Americans, Chinese, and Indohispanics in the westward expansion; and the rounding up of what was left of the indigenous people onto reservations, where they became wards of the U.S. government. Also missing is the story of the rise in the contemporary United States of a malignant form of fundamentalist ideological capitalism that Naomi Klein refers to as "a worldview that has harnessed the full force of the U.S. military machine in the service of a corporate agenda."[2]

African Americans form the third key group in the development of the United States. The story of how they were enslaved by fellow natives in Africa, sold to slave traders, and transported to the Americas is well known. Although the American Civil War ended legal slavery, their struggle for equality, justice, and full participation in the American political, social, and economic systems is far from complete and continues to this day. Throughout their struggle, the African American contribution to all the arts and sciences has been enormous.

The least-known story among the predominant peoples and cultures that make up the United States is that of the Indohispanics, whose ancestry is partially European and partially indigenous. The Vikings briefly visited North America, but the first Europeans to leave long-term footprints in the Americas were the Spaniards. Although Christopher Columbus was a master Italian sailor, he was in the employ of the Catholic King Ferdinand of Aragon and his co-ruler, Isabella, when, in 1492, he "discovered" the Americas for Spain, Christendom, and the rest of Europe. This is not the place to review the long, complicated history of Spanish conquest and colonization of Latin America, but I would like to make a few observations.

The Spaniards were harsh in their conquest and administration of indigenous cultures. Nevertheless, they concluded early on that the Indians were human beings with souls and could not be treated as animals. This may seem a quaint and condescending idea today, but in the sixteenth century it ensured that the indigenous populations had at least a foothold on legal and humanitarian claims for better treatment that would not be possessed, for example, by slaves in the southern United States. Although exploitation of native cultures became the norm throughout Latin America, there were also extensive sexual relations, liaisons, and marriages between Spaniards and native women. No doubt, many of these relationships were exploitive in that the Spaniards held all the power. Be that as it may, eventually this process led to the emergence of a numerically substantial class of mestizos, or people of mixed Spanish and Indian blood. In some Latin American countries, particularly in Mexico, the mestizo class came to predominate in terms of numbers, if not always in terms of political, social, and economic influence.

Given that a vast stretch of what is today the American Southwest was originally inhabited by Native Americans and then became, respectively, part of the Spanish Empire (1598–1821) and the Mexican nation (1821–48), the cultural and linguistic boundaries of Latin America do not end at the Rio Grande or at the current political boundary between Mexico and the United States. The Treaty of Guadalupe Hidalgo, which ended the Mexican War in 1848, established a border between the two countries that for much of its length was nothing more than an arbitrary line drawn on a map. Mexicans on both sides of the new border and their newly created Mexican American or Hispanic brothers and sisters on the northern side of the frontier have never paid much attention to what is for them a culturally ambiguous border.

When to this Indohispanic presence the Cuban and Puerto Rican populations in the United States are added, collectively they form a large bloc of people who culturally and historically have their deepest roots in the Hispanic and indigenous worlds. "Latin America" includes millions of persons who live in the southwestern United States. Latinos extend far beyond *la frontera*, the frontier, into the interior of the United States. They are, in fact, to be found in significant numbers in almost every state of the union. While these Latinos do not agree on everything, for the most part they share a similar Indohispanic historical formation. Although Samuel Huntington claims in his essay "The Hispanic Challenge" that "there is no Americano dream . . . there is only an American dream,"[3] it is patently clear that for millions and millions of citizens of the United States, theirs is a profoundly Americano dream.

Given the porosity of the U.S.–Mexican border, the historically relatively recent acquisition of slightly more than 50 percent of Mexico's national territory as a political result of the Mexican War (1846–48), and the huge social and economic impact of Indohispanics on the United States, the wonder is that Mexican Americans, including those who call themselves Chicanos, are so easily dismissed in the national discourse.

When I was growing up in Old Town, *la plaza vieja*, as everyone referred to it, I was most aware, of course, of my immediate and predominantly Mexican American community. Old Town differed from New Town in many ways. New Town was laid out in the 1880s on a grid that extended east and west as well as north and south from the railroad station and the tracks, about two miles east of Old Town. In contrast, Old Town, also called Old Albuquerque, was not organized on a grid but rather centered on a square, a plaza, in front of the church, San Felipe de Neri. This pattern, mandated by the Spanish crown in colonial times, of a town developing around a square, with the church at one end and governmental administrative offices (the *cabildo*) at the other end, is present to this day throughout Latin America.

Old Town had a variety of architectural styles and building materials, but adobe predominated. There was a definite nineteenth- or even eighteenth-century flavor to Old Town. New Town was all bustle and new construction. Pitched roofs and Victorian homes appeared more often in New Town, in contrast to the flat roofs and pueblo style of most Old Town homes.

Central Avenue ran east and west, from the valley of the Rio Grande where Old Town was located, through New Town clustered around the railroad station; the street crossed the railroad tracks, and then ascended toward the Sandia Mountains to the east. The rising landscape was referred to simply as "the heights."

Culturally speaking, Old Town and other Indohispanic or Mexican valley communities such as Barelas were on the "wrong side of the tracks," while the heights were on the "right" side of the tracks. There were exceptions to the rule, but generally the heights were Anglo while the valley was Hispanic. Although I wasn't aware of them as a child, strict neighborhood zoning laws forbade Mexicans, Indians, and Negroes (the term then in use) from living in areas where Anglos predominated. These zoning laws were active until they were abolished as a result of the civil rights movement of the 1960s. Anglos could, of course, live anywhere they desired.

Geographically, then, my childhood was more or less restricted to the streets of Old Town with occasional forays into New Town to shop, go to the movies, or see medical and eye doctors. I was small for my age, asthmatic, and nearsighted, so I became quite familiar with doctors' offices. There were also picnic trips to the nearby mountains and several visits per year to Santa Fe, where I had many relatives on my father's side of the family. For the most part, however, I spent my time in Old Town.

My family consisted of my mother, my aunt, my maternal grandmother, a younger brother, and myself. My father and mother were divorced around 1945 but later reunited. During the period when he was away, my mother; my brother; my dog, Lassie (a gift from my dad); and I simply moved out of our rented house and into my grandmother's home, about one block away. When my parents remarried, our family continued to live in my grandmother's home until my parents bought a small house not too distant from Old Town. My parents, my two brothers (one born after my parents reunited), me, my grandmother, and my aunt remained very close until death separated us one by one. Lassie was the first to go.

The center of my family was my grandmother. She ruled as a fierce but friendly autocrat. She was the connector, the hub of the family. Our home consisted, in effect, of seven nodes closely linked to one another; we were a small cluster. There were many similar clusters in Old Town. Most, if not all, were closely linked by kinship, by good friends and *vecinos* (neighbors), and by both formal and informal institutions. All together, Old Town was a giant cluster of closely linked families, friends, and neighbors.

At the heart of this giant cluster were two formal institutions: the church and the school. These institutions were the hubs of Old Town, linking together the various community clusters. San Felipe de Neri was the locus of daily religious celebrations and time-honored ceremonies that followed the calendric year. No season went by without its appropriate religious celebrations. There were Lent and Easter in the springtime; the fiestas or celebrations of saints' days, especially the feast of San Felipe Neri,[4] in the fall; and Christmas in the winter. Social life was to a great extent organized around the church. Parishioners frequently gathered for mass, baptisms, confirmations, first communions, weddings, and funerals.

During the fiesta de San Felipe there were *maromeros*, or acrobats, who entertained the spectators, *teatro de carpa y bailes de carpa*, tent theater and dancing in tents. At a funeral, the body of the departed one was laid out in the family's living room or a bedroom. A *velorio*, or wake for the dead, was held. Women would pray fervently around the dead person and prepare the food for those who attended the wake. The men would gather outside the deceased's home, reminisce about the person, smoke and drink (sometimes heavily), and generally have a good time. I remember these things.

The San Felipe School was a smaller hub, subordinate to the church but a social gathering site not only for the children of the school, but also for their parents who attended child conferences, school plays, and graduation ceremonies. There was also a secular Old Town Elementary School that served a similar subordinate hub function for a minority of Protestant families and for Catholic families who either could not afford the tuition of San Felipe or for personal reasons were disaffected from the Catholic Church.

I am not trying to romanticize Old Town as seen through the haze of the past. There were many social tensions in the community. The men of Old Town worked at mainly menial jobs, when they worked. Incomes were generally low. Due to our poverty, inexpensive beans, chile, and tortillas, with occasional meat and vegetables, usually canned, were the staples in my family's diet day after day, week after week. Most of the families I knew in Old Town lived very much as my family did. Where there is poverty, high unemployment, and low incomes, as in the Old Town of my youth, life can be difficult and sometimes very dangerous. The people of Old Town were caught in the transition from an agrarian community to an urban one. They were also caught in the throes of transculturation. Their normal ways of doing things extended back to a Spanish colonial and Mexican past. Under the dispensation of the United States, however, they had no choice but to adjust to the capitalistic, entrepreneurial reality of the new system while at the same time trying to consolidate their own evolving identity and retain a cultural consciousness of their language and customs, of who they were, what their origins were, and where they were going.

Eventually, Old Albuquerque was incorporated into New Town. Albuquerque became one city. I remember the bitter arguments in my home about incorporation. My mother and aunt wanted the incorporation because it would bring utilities to Old Town. My grandmother saw it as a death threat to her culture, her world. She was partially right. After incorporation, we eventually got gas heat and indoor plumbing. Gone were the wood-burning stove and the outhouse. Gone also, or at least weakened, were the strong ties of both the formal and informal hubs of the community as the tourist industry followed the modernized infrastructure into Old Town. La plaza vieja became more commercialized; one by one, as the older people died, their heirs sold their property to businessmen, and the living reality of their community became increasingly replaced by a Disney-like simulacrum of what Old Town had once been.

Prior to incorporation, there were thriving informal institutions in Old Town. One of the most important was the plaza. It was the gathering site for the men of the community. These were Old Town's resolaneros. They would gossip, exchange news, discuss politics, and compare the Anglo ways of doing things with their own. These resolaneros formed an informal but important hub linking the present Anglo-dominated world to an earlier Indohispanic and Spanish-speaking reality. For networks, indeed, have a vertical, or historical, dimension, linking the past to the present and serving as bridges to the mysterious and unknowable future.

From the Bottom Up: Networks and la Plaza Vieja

Before using network theory to explore Indohispanic issues, I want to describe more of the details of the network within which I lived in my earliest years. For within Old Town were strong personalities, eccentric characters, and close community ties that made this small community resemble something like a living organism.

An unusual figure, the pícaro, played a significant connective role in Old Town. The pícaro, a cultural figure who came to Mexico and New Mexico directly from Spain, is like the Russian yurodivy, or holy fool. Yuri Buida's comments about the yurodivy could just as well be made about the pícaro: "From the social point of view, a yurodivy was outside the society and was not afraid to act and say what nobody else would have dared to openly . . . a yurodivy was a free person."[5]

One of the oldest literary genres, the picaresque novel, developed in Spain, and the term pícaro is the source of the English word picaresque. Cervantes wrote picaresque novels, including the greatest of them all, Don Quixote de la Mancha. Often mistranslated into English as "scoundrel," the pícaro is more accurately viewed as a person who has learned how to survive by his or her wits (for there are also pícaras), more often than not on the fringes of society and the law in a hostile environment.

In terms of network theory, I view the pícaro (or pícara) as a *connector*. The pícaro knows his community. He is in close contact with all levels of the local society. In order to survive by his wits, the pícaro has to know the nodes (his contacts) within his community and how he links to them. He is the conveyor of gossip and news, and in return, because he lives on the fringes of society, he is allowed the freedom pretty much to dress, act, and speak as he wishes. Living on the fringes of society, the pícaro retains a certain objectivity as he views the forces of cultural change at work. The pícaro embodies a form of street theater. His role is to remind the community of its roots, its language and culture. He is also at times an upsetting figure because he is not a good bourgeois; he does not blend in—and he doesn't want to.

We had at least two notable pícaros in Old Town: Román and Florinto. I'm sure there were others, but I recall Florinto the most clearly. He was the garbage collector, a role that put him in contact with all elements of the local community. He had a cart and donkey, long after automobiles were common. If he spoke any English, I never heard him do so. Florinto's laughing and joking and carrying on in the streets considerably amped up the social electricity. He administered a sort of cultural shock treatment to the neighborhood. His insistence on Spanish, his loud voice and bizarre manner of dressing in the ill-fitting, cast-off clothes of others, and his mode of transportation recalled an earlier, culturally more vibrant and secure time. He was a constant reminder of another imaginary. He helped Old Towners dwell in what Homi Bhabha refers to as "beyond,"[6] a realm of memory and dreams that was far away yet very near.

Women also kept memory alive, especially when they would get together for social visits in their homes. My grandmother had a set of elderly friends who would occasionally gather in her small living room. They would play card games, smoke, sometimes have a little glass of wine, and discuss the entire gamut of local social relations. They would tell stories for hours on end.

My grandmother was an important focal point in Old Town. She was not the only one, to be sure, but she was significant. During World War I, for example, because she was fluent in both English and Spanish, she was the person designated to read the English-language newspapers with their death notices from the Western Front. The families, especially the mothers of soldiers, would gather around her as she read the names of the deceased. She spoke to me often of how difficult and painful it had been for her to see a death notice in the newspaper or to read the telegram bringing the bad news, with the mother or the family of the deceased in front of her, hanging on to every word she read.

The local barbershops were also small but important hubs in the Old Town network, as they are in other communities as well. There was gossip, an exchange of news and information, sometimes of the bawdy sort. And finally, there were the cantinas, the gathering places mostly for men and ladies of the night. There was a great deal of drinking in Old Town. My grandmother powerfully disapproved. Yet, even here there was a significant community network factor. I remember more than one night when a drunk would invite himself onto my grandmother's front porch and make all kinds of noise there, singing to himself, crying, and carrying on. My grandmother wouldn't have called 9-1-1, even if such an emergency number had existed then; she didn't even call the police. She would simply get out of bed in great irritation, march out to the porch, and inflict a tongue-lashing on the drunk (usually someone she had known since he was a child), and order the hapless and usually apologetic wretch to leave, which he promptly did. Such a thing is almost unthinkable today. I recount this anecdote because it illustrates how closely knit the community was: even the drunks were part of an extended family. They were kin.

What I have portrayed here is the network structure of one small community, la plaza vieja de Albuquerque, in the large Hispanic or Indohispanic Southwest. This community had clusters, families, hubs, and many nodes connected internally by a variety of links. There was even a power law distribution of wealth in this community inasmuch as a mere handful of people controlled the major economic activities, mainly construction, farming, and commerce. Communities like Old Town were found all over the Southwest in the period 1846–1950. I choose 1950 as the cutoff point because it was in the aftermath of World War II that accelerated change accompanied by a huge increase in population occurred in this region, although in fact cultural change had been accelerating since 1846.

The network context of Old Town was rather clear, even if I only dimly perceived it when I was growing up. Those of us born into the Hispanic culture of la plaza vieja had to interact with the larger world, but much of our psychological and emotional attention was devoted to our small world. As a child, I was not aware of our intellectual and cultural isolation. We Old Towners had been almost severed from our indigenous, Mexican, and Spanish roots. Like so many nuevomexicanos, our elders almost desperately insisted we were Spanish, not Mexican. With hindsight, I see this as an adaptive communal and collective attempt to buy time, to buy breathing space from the aggressive juggernaut of Westernization.

My classmates at San Felipe Elementary School, just like the children at Old Town Elementary, knew next to nothing about indigenous America or the artistic, literary, and scientific heritage of the Latin world extending to Iberia. While Spanish was tolerated in our schools, it certainly wasn't encouraged. As I remember, however, we were not punished for speaking Spanish. In many other communities like Old Town throughout the Southwest, children were routinely beaten or publicly humiliated for speaking Spanish. On the one hand, then, in Old Town we had weak ties extending into the larger, English-speaking world that surrounded us. On the other hand, our weak ties to Mexico and Spain, and to our indigenous heritage grew ever weaker.

We had no choice but to interact with the outside world. There was a sawmill in Old Town that served as an important economic hub. It had links to construction activities outside our community. The principal sources of jobs in other parts of the city were the Santa Fe Railroad shops; construction and trucking; and eventually, during World War II, Kirtland Air Force Base and Sandia National Laboratories. These military sites had strong links to Los Alamos, where the first atomic bombs were assembled. The University of New Mexico, very small in the thirties and forties, also offered some employment. Jobs and the numerous commercial interactions of the larger city meant that Old Town families had to take into account culturally different ways of constructing the world. Our families *had* to communicate with the outside world, interact with it, exchange information about faraway places like California and Colorado; and family members *had* to migrate if they wanted to be in a better economic position in this new world, even if the migration was temporary. Often the migration to California and elsewhere was permanent.

Here the idea of transculturation is particularly relevant because what happened, I believe, is that the people of Old Town lived as much of their Hispanic culture as they could under very negative circumstances. To put it simply, Old Town was overwhelmed by forces in the form of new hubs such as the railroad, the university, the health industry (a major factor in Albuquerque even in the early decades of the twentieth century), Kirtland Air Force Base, Sandia National Laboratories, and the tourist industry. Far from being a model for an isolated village, Old Town serves as a model for how a local culture subjected to such pressure by change agents loses much of its original identity and integrity.

That original identity to which I refer was not static. For more than a century, from the founding of Old Town in the early decades of the eighteenth century until 1846 and the entry of Union military forces as conquerors and occupiers, this community had evolved with the influx of new families, expanded agricultural activities, a variety of contacts with indigenous cultures, and the influence of the Catholic Church as a major hub with its missions, schools, and year-round religious celebrations and rites of passage.

The United States, by the imposition of its will through military force, altered this path of development and turned it onto new and unfamiliar avenues. Whether the changes were good or bad is not the question; the changes occurred and new network elements were either added on to the older network models or substituted for them. I would argue it was the property of the new networks introduced by the U.S. takeover that channeled the later and current sequences of developments in Old Town.

Old Towners did not so much acculturate or assimilate to the United States as undergo the experience of transculturation. They had no choice but to blend, to meld their own values and lifestyles with this Anglo worldview. As part of this process of transculturation, Old Town had diminishing feedback mechanisms, intellectually and culturally speaking, from Spain, Mexico, and Latin America. "Spain" was mythologized throughout the Southwest as a medieval wonderland from whence came kings and queens, *hidalgos* (nobles), land grants, and a false European pride. "Mexico" was reified almost as it was in the Anglo stereotype: as a backward land filled with oppressed people. The Spanish language, once dominant in Albuquerque, gradually withered away in Old Town and elsewhere in New Mexico.

Tragically missing from the fantasized picture of Spain, in my opinion, were the variegated cultures and peoples of the Iberian Peninsula and Mexico. In the distorted images of Spain and Mexico with which we children of Old Town were raised, we had little if any knowledge of the rich historical, political, and literary traditions produced by the multiplicity of cultures lumped together under those deceptive oversimplifications called "Spain" and "Mexico."

The sense of the past as a continuum for Indohispanics all over the Southwest was interrupted by the American incorporation of northern Mexico into the United States. Despite the interruption, many memories of the past were preserved in language, customs, family lore, and constant comparisons of the old ways with the new American ways. In other words, the *older Indohispanic networks did not entirely disappear*. Vertical, that is, historical, connections remained and survived through memory and storytelling.

Family and linguistic clusters may have scattered, even disintegrated entirely, but some survived, and network properties made it possible to reconnect to the past and to the future at a later time. That time is now.

My grandmother was one of the preservers of memory and also one of the connectors to the new Anglo-American occupation. When my grandmother recounted tales about young children being taken from the outskirts of Old Town by Comanches and narrated the stories about Texas invasions and how the people of Old Town hid their gold from the Tejanos, I cannot help but wonder if she had any idea that she was preparing me, her grandson, for a future in which I would always know my deepest cultural origins. I wonder if she knew she was ensuring that the past, as she conveyed it to me, would acquire a new dimensionality that would live in me and through me as I passed that knowledge on to others. Although the sense of the past as a continuum was interrupted, it was not entirely destroyed.

Memory offers a dimensional space to unite past and present in a new synthesis. This idea is close to Homi Bhabha's view that "being in the beyond . . . is also . . . to be part of a revisionary time, a return to the present to redescribe our cultural contemporaneity; to reinscribe our human, historic commonality; to touch the future on its hither side." In that sense, then, "the intervening space 'beyond' becomes a space of intervention in the here and now."[7] Memory synthesizes the past with the present on a continuum that becomes the future.

This is a dynamic notion of the interaction of memory with the ongoing rush of history. I mean by it, to return to my example of Old Town, that the inhabitants of this village, which was transformed within a few years after 1846 from being the center of a Spanish colonial outpost into an ethnic curiosity on the outskirts of New Town, had to dwell psychologically in a "beyond" space of memory where they could re-create their remembered past within the new American imperatives. New Town was the brash child of Manifest Destiny and the new Albuquerque was much like any other Midwestern town in the United States. I am not a determinist, but to some extent the choices the people of Old Town made were more or less constrained by the very properties of the evolving networks within which the web of their lives was being spun.

As Mexican Americans, we claim the right to know who we are—what has happened and is happening to us—and the right to reflect on all this and become better-informed agents on our lives, rather than remaining passive, manipulated observers of the changes occurring so rapidly in the postmodern, postindustrial world. The Mexican American writer Richard

Rodriguez observed in an interview that "the principle of merely preserving one's culture . . . is part of my problem with the Chicano culture. . . . It seems to me to be much too interested in preservation and not enough in acquisition. Acquisition is the great modern principle."[8] Acquisition may be one of the "modern principles," but this opinion primarily reflects Rodriguez's personal stance in relation to older Indohispanic cultural values. There are, after all, other traditions, Western and non-Western, that share the contemporary stage with the consumer-oriented notion of acquisition. I agree, however, with Rodriguez insofar as the idea of preservation is concerned: a preserved culture is one destined for the museums and dusty bookshelves. There is always the faint odor of formaldehyde about anything that is preserved.

I assert that Indohispanic culture is alive, developing, expanding, and interacting with all the cultures of the United States and the world. There is no simple Chicano culture or Mexican American culture, but rather there are "many Mexicos," as Lesley Byrd Simpson wrote several decades ago.[9] A multitude of Mexicans and Mexican Americans in communities, villages, towns, and cities across the United States are interacting and connecting with each other and with the larger world around them. These interactions and connections form intricate networks of persons and communities. Some of us who are Indohispanics are now in the earliest stages of examining network theory, the kinds of networks in which we participate, and the implications of networks for our own future.

Networks in a World Not Flat

One of the most pressing issues confronting Indohispanics in the United States has to do with politics. The two major political parties assiduously court the Latino vote. Yet large numbers of recent migrants from Mexico and Central America have different political experiences than U.S. voters. In their countries of origin, as in much of Europe, there are leftist, centrist, and rightist political parties. Yet the terms *leftist* and *liberal* have become demonized in the American political idiom. Political discourse has been reduced to a narrow, centrist song-and-dance routine. Apologists for globalization, and even such a discerning journalist as Thomas Friedman, assure us that it is better this way. Bedazzled as he is by the Internet, near-instantaneous worldwide communication, free-market economics, global capitalism, and the global market, Friedman argues that politics is essentially disappearing. Instead of the Marxist withering away of the state, we have the withering away of politics:

As your country puts on the Golden Straightjacket [free-market economics, privatization of the economy, business deregulation, no government corruption] . . . your economy grows and your politics shrink. . . . On the political front, the Golden Straightjacket narrows the political and economic policy choices of those in power to relatively tight parameters. That is why it is increasingly difficult these days to find any real differences between ruling and opposition parties in those countries that have put on the Golden Straightjacket. Once your country puts it on, its political choices get reduced to Pepsi or Coke—to slight nuances of taste, slight nuances of policy . . . never any major deviation from the core golden rules.[10]

Given the corporate corruption scandals such as Enron, the uncertainties in the global economy, the ineptness of the American government's response to Hurricane Katrina, and the general insecurities associated with the war in Iraq and the threat of more wars to come, some of Friedman's optimism about "golden rules" already seems outdated. The "gold" in the Golden Straightjacket seems to have been for those who exploited their corporate advantages, and the "straightjacket" was for all those workers and middle-class investors who lost their life savings.

In his most recent book, *The World Is Flat,* Friedman continues to sing the praises of globalization. By "flat," Friedman means that modern communication technologies, specifically information technologies, have leveled the economic playing field on a global scale. Reporting a conversation he had with Nandan Nilekani, CEO of Infosys Technologies, an Indian technology company, Friedman states "What Nandan is saying, I thought, is that the playing field is being flattened. . . . Flattened? Flattened? My God, he's telling me the world is flat!"[11] Friedman has chosen a humorous although fatal metaphor, for the idea of flatness implies infinite extension. It would have been more accurate for Friedman to have referred to the world as a web, because the world is round, finite in extension, and interconnected by information technologies and a growing global awareness of societies and cultures from "the bottom up" as opposed to "the top-down" perspective in Friedman's work. The bottom-up perspective is important because most of the people and their cultures in this world are poor, and their view is from the bottom up. This is certainly true for the majority of Chicanos.

For most Chicanos, Friedman's flat-world perspective offers little hope. The economic straightjacket has always been present for them, and it has never been golden. Chicanos rank low in education and income, and high in birthrate and crime. At one end of the Indohispanic spectrum there is, via intermarriage and social mobility, an ongoing loss of Chicanos absorbed into the American mainstream. That mainstream is itself undergoing constant change and becoming increasingly diversified through rising birthrates of minorities and the global movement of people from second and third world environments seeking better economic conditions. It is via this other end of the Indohispanic spectrum, the more or less constant inflow of Mexicans and other Latinos into the United States, that the great urban areas are becoming increasingly Latinized, Hispanicized, Mexicanized. For example, more than 2.2 million Hispanics, many of them undocumented workers, now live and work in New York City, where there is a strong demand for their unskilled and semiskilled labor. In the state of New York there are more than 2.8 million Hispanics.[12]

This Latinization of the United States is reflected at the popular level in the increasing number of Spanish-language newspapers and books published in the United States, in Spanish-language radio and television, and Latino-oriented advertising, often in Spanish, in the media. The English only movement seems to have slipped into oblivion despite a frantic nativist reaction to the rise in the use of Spanish in the United States. A Puerto Rican medical professional I met made this casual comment in relation to this movement, "Eso ya lo hemos dejado al lado" (We've already put that aside).

The dramatic increase in urban Latinos carries important social and economic issues in its wake. While the global phenomenon of mass migration is seemingly ongoing, in the wake of the September 11, 2001, tragedy, the Bush administration's focus on terrorism has had a very negative effect on cross-border issues in relation to Mexico. Prior to 9/11, President Bush had touted his friendship with President Vicente Fox of Mexico. Fox, a conservative like Bush, had been elected as the leader of the moderate-conservative Partido de Acción Nacional (PAN), unseating for the first time a federal government headed by the Partido de la Revolución Institucional (PRI), the self-styled heir of the programs of the Mexican Revolution of 1910. President Bush said Mexico was his "top priority." With two ideologically related heads of state who were personal friends and the firming up of democratic institutions in Mexico with the election of Fox, the prospects seemed bright for a NAFTA (North American Free Trade Agreement) accord stressing mutual benefits for the two nations. Mexico was about to get a better deal, or so it seemed, on immigration matters. The events of 9/11 changed all that.

Reacting to the attack on America, the Bush administration imposed controls on or shut down entry routes all along the U.S. border. This was an understandable reaction to such an assault. However, Mexico was one of the unintended victims of the new American emphasis on homeland security; the attack of 9/11 put on hold a possibly constructive agenda on migration. The U.S. insistence that Mexico support the invasion of Iraq and the Mexican refusal to do so further soured goodwill between the two nations.

This terrorism-tainted mindset has led many Americans to react fearfully to the phenomenon of immigration. The southern border has become increasingly militarized and a hindrance to normal transactions between the two countries; there are long delays and disruptions at the crossing points. The negative effect on the U.S.–Mexican border economy has been severe. No similar militarization of the Canadian border has occurred. I leave it to the reader to reflect on underlying agendas in the United States.

The high demand for drugs, legal and illegal, in the United States, combined with the enormous amounts of money supplier nations like Mexico can make in drug transactions, has formed a serious complicating factor for any constructive resolution of border issues. At the same time, it is hypocritical for the United States to blame its domestic drug problems on the suppliers when the demand is so great in this country.

Traditionally, the United States has been one of the countries most welcoming to immigrants. Indeed, it has one of the best track records on immigration of any country in the world. International terrorism has thus led to a marked about-face in American attitudes toward immigration. And yet Americans depend on immigrant labor for the performance of many tasks, from farm and factory work to highly skilled work in technical, scientific, and professional areas of the economy. Most but not all Mexican immigrants work in the lowest-paying, lowest-skill jobs that are available. The United States is painfully discovering that it can't have its cake and eat it too. Without undocumented Mexican immigration, available labor pools would be exhausted and the price of produce would almost certainly skyrocket. On the other hand, public and private institutions face collapse if they do not deal with Mexican immigrant issues. Health provider institutions and educational programs and institutions, as well as other public- and private-sector entities need at least adequate financial resources in order to function, and immigration places a drain on these entities.

Mexican immigration consists not only of emigration from Mexico but also of strong internal migration throughout the United States as Mexican and some Mexican American migrants follow the crops, seek better work opportunities, and eventually establish their communities throughout the United States. But not all Latinos are immigrants. Many Mexicans have been in the United States for generations, some for more than a century, and are American citizens. These Mexican Americans may or may not relate well to the new arrivals, but many of them will share significant cultural traits such as a belief in strong families, the use of Spanish (to a lesser or greater extent), and the desire to advance their economic interests. Mexicans and Latinos in general do not form a cohesive political force. Undocumented workers cannot participate in American political processes, while Latinos who are citizens often do not. Why this is so and how it can be turned around are not idle questions and are in fact difficult to answer, but they have to do with deeply held cultural attitudes.

The thread of my argument here is that the tragedy of 9/11 complicated already difficult transborder relations between the United States and Mexico. These relations have been and continue to be complex because of issues of transborder family ties, citizenship, drugs, and terrorist activities and immigration control. It is astounding, for example, that in a recent survey of more than 4,800 Mexican migrants in major urban areas in the United States conducted by the Pew Hispanic Center, 82 percent of all respondents had relatives in the United States other than a spouse or child, and for those who had been here more than fifteen years, the figure rises to 90 percent.[13] Entire villages in the interior of Mexico have been depopulated, with only the very old and the very young remaining, because of the exodus to the United States.[14]

Since 2005, rising hysteria about Mexican immigration has been fueled by the fear of terrorism, by the media, by political opportunism, and by plain old-fashioned racism. After the U.S. House of Representatives passed a mean-spirited bill that criminalized undocumented workers and all who help them, there was a powerful reaction from the Mexican and Mexican American communities and their supporters from all ethnic groups in the United States, including Anglos. Millions took to the streets in demonstrations protesting such harsh legislation. Many news commentators began to say that the anti-immigration hysteria had awakened a "sleeping giant," that is, the general Latino community. An estimated 500,000 persons took part in one demonstration in Los Angeles.[15] Culture matters. And so do network relations across the dense web of Latino contacts within and outside of their cultures.

Networks and Border Thinking: It's All in the Graph

I have mentioned how random networks can form but how in real life networks are seldom random. In the 1920s the Hungarian writer Frigyes

Karinthy, and later in the 1960s the American sociologist Stanley Milgram, explored the issue of human interconnectivity. Karinthy wrote fiction whereas Milgram was a social scientist, but both came to the conclusion that we are never more than a few links, or degrees—six degrees according to Milgram—of separation from any other person on the planet. While this may be an exaggeration, the actual number of links appears to be very few in terms of our individual separation from any other person in the world. Put in a slightly different way, we are all part of a global human network, and if we move along a path of links to others in the network, with a few weak ties thrown in, within a relatively few nodes, we will potentially be in contact with any other person in the world. In this sense, the world really is small. This idea became the basis of John Guare's Broadway hit *Six Degrees of Separation*. Possibly more than anything else, this play popularized the idea of networks.

From reading the popular literature on networks, I gather that network investigators have made at least four critically important discoveries since the initial insights of Euler in the eighteenth century.[16]

Importance of Random Links

Randomness is a key to understanding social networks. A few random links can convert any linked network into a small world. Randomness, nevertheless, is not a characteristic of social networks.

Strength of Weak Ties

Weak links, or ties, are often more important in identifying networks than strong ties are when it comes to interacting with networks outside our immediate family and social networks. Rather than being random, social networks are in fact highly clustered. We do not know our immediate family circle or close friends at random. Society is organized in clusters, often very tight clusters. However, clusters do not exist in isolation. If we lived in a world of only clusters, we would know our immediate circle of family and friends, and that would be it.

In the real world, with few exceptions, we have links with other people and with institutions outside our immediate familial and social relations. These links may form critically important weak ties with other clusters. If I am looking for a job, for example, my weak tie to a local university might certainly be more important than a strong tie within my own family.

Here is a thought experiment. I have a friend, a Mexican from Ciudad Juárez, who lives in the neighborhood and has some ties, or links, to my immediate friends—my "cluster," as it were. He makes frequent trips to

Juárez, where he has many relatives. Imagine he has a close cousin who drives a truck from Juárez to Chiapas in southern Mexico. The cousin buys fruit from a Zapatista who works closely with Subcomandante Marcos. Now, I have never met Subcomandante Marcos, but according to network theory, my immediate friends and I are only four to five links, or weak ties, removed from him. This imaginary small world, in fact, closely resembles the real small worlds, and their extremely important weak ties, within which most of us live.

Of course, we need not rely on only imaginary worlds. Recently, the Santa Fe columnist David Roybal, writing for the *Albuquerque Journal*, demonstrated a real-world situation where weak ties are extremely important. According to Roybal, a Santa Fe–based food vendor, Roque García, has attracted national attention for his savory *carnitas*, which he sells on the Santa Fe plaza. But there's more to the story. Roque García has a home in the Mexican state of Nayarit, in an impoverished village north of Puerto Vallarta. He discovered a desperate need for computers in a local school in his community and approached the Santa Fe City Council to see what, if anything, could be done to help.[17] Here is an example of a weak tie (Roque García) between a wealthy community (Santa Fe, New Mexico) and an impoverished village in Mexico. This one weak tie, as sociologist and social network theorist Mark Granovetter would no doubt agree, has tremendous strength in this kind of international relationship.[18]

Random Links Greatly Reduce Degrees of Separation in a Network

Just a few random links can have a huge effect on the degrees of separation in a network, converting it into a small world. As Mark Buchanan says, "With no random links at all, this number [degrees of separation] had been roughly 50; now, with a few random links thrown in, it had suddenly plummeted to about 7." Duncan Watts and Steven Strogatz added random links to many different kinds of networks, and no matter what they did, "the lightest dusting of random links was always enough to produce a small world."[19]

Role of Connectors, Hubs, and Power Laws

As the World Wide Web grew, investigators discovered "that the architecture of the World Wide Web is dominated by a few very highly connected nodes, or *hubs*."[20] Malcolm Gladwell, in his book *The Tipping Point*, popularized these highly connected nodes by calling them *connectors*. Whether the term used is *connectors* or *hubs*, it refers to those nodes that have many connections with less well-connected nodes. Airport hubs are good examples of connectors. So are personalities and institutions that funnel multiple connections between other persons and institutions. As Albert-László Barabási and his coworkers discovered, the hubs of the Internet or social hubs or any other kind of networked hubs "appear in most large complex networks . . . they are ubiquitous, a generic building block of our complex, interconnected world."[21]

The next discovery Barabási and his colleagues made is the critical one: *Hubs follow a power law distribution.* This means that a few well-connected hubs—be they persons, institutions, or services (for example, airport hubs)—have a large number of connections, while most nodes—be they small institutions or services (like an airport in Boise City, Oklahoma) or ordinary, everyday persons—have only a small number of connections to other nodes. To say the same thing in slightly different words, most of us are poorly connected in the world, while a handful of persons and institutions are very well connected.

Application to the Mexican and Mexican American Community

Now let's apply our insights about networks, weak ties, clusters, hubs, and power laws to Mexican and Mexican American issues. While there are Mexican immigrants and Indohispanic citizens in most towns and cities and in every state in this country, there are only a few sites that contain large concentrations of Latinos. I am thinking of hubs such as New York City, Atlanta, Los Angeles, El Paso, Phoenix, San Antonio, and Chicago. These hubs serve as jumping-off points for internal migration to the rest of the country or as sites for significant Latino social interaction and visibility. This kind of distribution, as in the examples of wealth, airport hubs, and many natural phenomena, follows a power law. At one end of the distribution are a few Latino hubs that are very well connected. Then there are the dramatically more numerous towns, villages, and rural communities where many Mexicans and Mexican Americans live and work under somewhat isolated conditions.

My use of network theory to shed light on the future prospects of the Indohispanic community is intimately linked to contemporary Western discoveries in mathematics and the physical and social sciences. These discoveries have led to the emergence of global networks in business, finance, marketing, transportation, telecommunications, and the World Wide Web. No culture or cultural entities are totally outside this all-encompassing global and technological loop. At the same time, however, postmodern, postcolonial, and deconstructionist studies have supplied us with new lenses, as it were, to analyze these developments from the perspective of the impacted cultures, such as the Indohispanic culture. Like my colleagues and other investigators, I am trying to use network theory to analyze Indohispanic phenomena in terms of a refocusing, or relocation, of the Western imaginary in a non-Western or only partially Western context, in order to achieve a deeper understanding of our own culture.

Borrowing a term from Walter Mignolo, the Western "imaginary,"[22] or "Occidentalism," has been at the heart of almost all discussions about Indohispanics. This imaginary is the totality of the ways a culture, through its members, envisions itself and, through its discourse, describes itself. The emergence of second and third world nation-states shifted the locus of the Western imaginary from Europe to the former colonies. The new nations of Latin America, in other words, continue to be dominated by hierarchies and educated elites who think in terms of the Western imaginary because this weltanschauung has been conveyed to them by their teachers and textbooks and by social norms and political institutions not of their making but imposed on them by Europeans or their satraps. This assessment is also true of Cuba, where a homegrown Marxism, certainly a derivative of the Western imaginary, holds sway.

This Western imaginary has become, in effect, a historical substitute for direct native observation and interpretation of the world. There is a saying in Spanish, *cada mono en su columpio* (every monkey on his swing), and that is the way power, prestige, and authority located in the Western imaginary have been transplanted to the New World. Every teacher, church official, military officer, or politician, clinging to his little seat on the swing of power, became an almost puppet-like source of the continuing project of Westernization of the natives. The very term *New World* illustrates the point, for it was, after all, a "new world" only for the Europeans, yet that term has endured to this day. As far as culture is concerned, Mexicans are the North American extension of the Spanish imaginary, while at the same time many of them carry within themselves an indigenous heritage.

There are few, if any, Latino commentators who stand intellectually outside this Western influence, yet we as authors resist it. We are aware of our limitations in trying to understand our culture—even though we are insiders to that culture—because our own perspectives have been partially shaped by an overwhelming force imposed from the outside long ago and now an inextricable part of our own thinking processes. So, like David facing Goliath, we will trust to our grasp of a truth, however small or fragile it may be, and aim it at the pretensions of Goliath, that milieu of Eurocentrism that wafts in the very air we breathe. We cannot, nor do we wish, to undo the benefits of Western civilization. We insist, however, that there are other ways of thinking, other ways of constructing a worldview, other ways of incorporating what is positive in the West into a more humane narrative of the world.

As a writer, I consciously locate myself as best I can within a non-Western tradition, as I have experienced it. From this vantage point I try to make better sense of the world and of the place of Latinos within it than I find in other accounts. I share with my colleagues what Mignolo calls a "double consciousness," or "transcultural consciousness."[23] We are consciously "border thinkers." Like Mignolo (and unlike Francis Fukuyama and Samuel Huntington), we know it is false to think of Latin America, Mexico, or the United States as homogeneous national states and do not even think it is desirable that they should be homogeneous. In Mignolo's words

> These conflicting homogeneous entities (Latin America, France, the United States, etc.) as we know them today are part of the imaginary of the modern/colonial world system. They reveal and they occlude. They are also a grounding . . . of hierarchical structures of meaning and knowledge. To think "Latin America" otherwise, in its heterogeneity rather than its homogeneity, in the local histories of changing global designs is not to question a particular form of identification (e.g., that of "Latin America") but all national/colonial forms of identification in the modern/colonial world system.[24]

I reject the notions that acculturation is a one-way street and that assimilation is the only desirable goal. Indohispanic connectivity within the modern world is a fact and will have growing importance. Ideas and theories I discuss here might very well be applicable to other global domains. My concern, then, is not restricted to Latinos or even more specifically to Mexican Americans, Chicanos, or Indohispanics who live within the United States; rather, I hope my efforts and those of like-minded colleagues will indicate to other individuals and other communities paths they may seek to lead them to a better understanding of themselves and their locus in the global community, and to a greater ability to change their conditions in the world.

In my own experience and that of my coauthors, the European mindset has been challenged by our individual and collective memories. In a sense, memory occupies a separate dimension. Whether history is linear, as it is in the Judeo-Christian cosmos, or cyclic or circular, as in the view of many indigenous cultures, it still has a primary mental dimension, which is memory. Mignolo relates that when he came to the United States, he was because of his Argentine background "particularly sensitive to issues of bilingualism and of cross-cultural understanding." Furthermore, Mignolo says, "becoming a citizen [of the United States] solves a great many practical matters but does not erase one's memories."[25] Mignolo was referring, I assume, to his Argentine memories. I remember a time when an Indohispanic worldview was a vivid and daily presence in my life. My geographic zone, or space, was where I lived, not a faraway place, as in the case of Mignolo's memories of Argentina. This space is still my home, and networks—both visible and invisible—connect it, culturally speaking, to the past and the future.

Networks and Naysayers

Not everyone agrees with a network approach to culture. There are two prominent commentators who have had so much influence on contemporary thinking about culture and the body politic that their perspectives merit extensive consideration. While this section is a digression from my main theme, I think it is necessary. One of those to whom I refer is Francis Fukuyama, a professor of public policy at George Mason University and the author of *The End of History and the Last Man*. In this work, Fukuyama argues that we have reached the end of history because there is a powerful evolutionary movement toward the emergence and ultimate stability of liberal, capitalistic democracies. The other commentator to whom I refer is Samuel P. Huntington, an influential Harvard professor and political scientist. I will discuss his ideas later.

Francis Fukuyama

As Fukuyama states in *The Great Disruption* "for the world's most economically advanced countries, there has been a convergence of political and economic institutions over time and no obvious alternatives to the liberal political and economic institutions we see before us."[26] Fukuyama thinks we have reached the end of history in the sense that we are on the verge of achieving a final synthesis of political democracy with economic liberalism. Nation-states have nowhere to go beyond this point of development. There may be fine-tuning here and there, like Friedman's adjustments within the "golden rule" and the disappearance of meaningful politics, but in this view the global triumph of liberal democracies is already a fait accompli.

Great social movements, however, rarely conform to academic theories and expectations. To give but one example of the recalcitrance of real events to conform to theory, at the very moment NAFTA was supposed to be triumphant in Mexico, the Zapatista movement opened up an entirely distinct social and historical vista. As Timothy Wise, Hilda Salazar, and Laura Carlsen have pointed out, "Seen from below, Mexico's Zapatista rebels fired the proverbial shot heard round the world that opened the current cycle of protest against top-down globalization. . . . Within Mexico, the rebels showed that history still matters and contributed directly to the national democratization process. They revealed that Mexico's neoliberal emperor had no clothes."[27]

Fukuyama's major thesis is that the shift from the industrial to the information age has been accompanied by a breakdown in morality and a loosening of the social ties that make for order. He couples what he sees as a decline in moral values with a disintegration of social bonds. He sees these general changes as "dramatic" and alleges they constitute "a Great Disruption in the social values that prevailed in the industrial age society of the mid-twentieth century." Furthermore, Fukuyama says, every society has a "stock of shared values," or social capital. Social capital, he argues, is created, used up, and re-created by humans in their interactions with each other. Nevertheless, he sees social capital as monolithic in a cultural sense, and as threatened by "the onslaught from a principled belief in multiculturalism" and ethnic concerns, which he views as dangerous to the stock of shared values, that is, the social capital found in the modern state. He identifies the nation-state, especially the United States, as a bastion for crucial moral guidelines. These guidelines are "universal obligations for tolerance and mutual respect." He apparently thinks it was a good thing that the United States, Britain, and France started out as "relatively homogeneous" states, "dominated by a single ethnic group and religion."[28]

Leaving aside the accuracy of his assertion that there has been a decline in morals and an unfortunate breakdown in the social order, the problem with Fukuyama's idea of the joy of hierarchy and monolithic culture is that it is a barely disguised version of a very old defense of the conservative preoccupation with social order. We have heard this argument before. There is a strong echo of Thomas Hobbes's *Leviathan* in both Fukuyama and Samuel Huntington. Fukuyama's attempt to distance himself from Hobbes amounts to a subtle and imaginative fig leaf. He rejects Hobbes's argument that the state of nature is characterized by a war of all against all, and he substitutes for this view the idea that as humans we have access to a wide array of sources for order, including the spontaneous emergence of informal order among ourselves. Although Fukuyama rejects Hobbes's famous dictum that life in the state of nature is "nasty, poor, brutish, and short," he asserts, "It would appear . . . that the state of nature was characterized by a war of 'some against some,' . . . and 'from the beginning early humans had rudimentary social organization that permitted cooperative enterprise and domestic peace.'"[29] This view amounts to a very modest amendment of Hobbes's thesis.

Fukuyama has updated Hobbes to take into account the primatological and archaeological knowledge gained since the seventeenth century. Like Hobbes, he is deeply concerned about the necessity for social order, and he is willing to make many sacrifices to maintain it. There is much of value in Fukuyama's analysis. He explores in depth the social impact and the demographics of crime, family disruption, and loss of trust in society. Unfortunately, he is willing to sacrifice all social, cultural, and linguistic identities other than a national cultural identity and a national language to maintain social order within the nation-state system. He is explicit about his monolithic approach to values: "Community is based on shared values: the more authoritative and widely held those values, the stronger the community and higher the level of generalized social trust."[30] While this is certainly true, a community may also have enough shared values with other communities beyond the nation-state anachronism so that trust may become more generalized than Fukuyama imagines.

Fukuyama has a very restricted view of networks. He considers them as a kind of social capital within which there are shared informal social values. In his view "a network is a moral relationship of trust."[31] I have no problem with this view, as far as it goes, but it is very limited in scope. Networks involve relationships where trust may be an underlying ethical or philosophical assumption, but the network itself functions independent of this moral overlay. For example, in the Enron scandal of a few years ago, no one would blame the financial networks for their conveying of stocks in such a way that Enron investors, including many employees of the firm, were financially ruined. The guilt or innocence of Enron executives is beside the point. Once certain transactions were put into motion, the networks in which those transactions occurred functioned normally. Networks, then, are neither good nor bad. Ultimately they exist as mathematical constructs and people use them or abuse them.

Hierarchy is the key to Fukuyama's social concerns. Ordinary morality based on biological imperatives is, he says, the source of social capital: "Ordinary morality is in some sense natural and the product of spontaneous human interaction." "Once human societies develop beyond the family or the small tribe, however, their interactions lead to problems of scale. The morality that worked so well with the family or the tribe breaks down. Large-scale communities begin to define themselves on the basis of race, religion, ethnicity, and other arbitrary factors and mayhem ensues."[32]

Now, under these changed social conditions, social capital is a private good that has a positive spin-off for the rest of society: "The view that social capital is a public good is wrong. Social capital will in fact be produced by private markets because it is in the long-term interests of selfish individuals to produce it."[33]

I do not think Fukuyama can have it both ways. If social capital arises at the small-scale level of human organization, then why does it become necessary to shift the locus of the creation of social capital to private markets? Private markets may indeed produce public good, but a change in scale doesn't necessarily imply a break in the continuum of social capital being produced as a public good. Private markets may enhance or retard the production of social capital for the general good, but social capital will still remain a social good grounded in human, social, self-organizational abilities, whether biologically based or not. In my view, social capital is the product of network relationships, and *networks always have their own properties as graphs.*

In order to maintain his dualistic notion of social capital, Fukuyama has to posit a dualistic morality. There is in his scheme of things an "ordinary morality" that works, so to speak, for ordinary people. For higher levels of social organization, as the hierarchical relations develop, other "virtues" are needed. While Fukuyama does not use the term *morality* in referring to his virtues, there is no reason to separate the two. Morality implies virtuous behavior. Personal virtuous behavior implies a moral backbone in the individual. Ordinary morality implies ordinary virtues for Fukuyama. These "virtues . . . are small ones that we have identified with social capital: honesty, promise keeping, reciprocity, and the like." But these small virtues aren't good enough to produce social order. "Leadership" and "charisma" are necessary in those individuals who can create social order, and these persons need other virtues: "Although they [the small virtues] are important to political order as well, the latter requires other, greater and less frequently observed virtues like courage, daring, statesmanship, and political creativity."[34]

Ordinary people, in this scheme, practice ordinary morality and share the small virtues. Those persons in the political and social hierarchy share other virtues, the big ones restricted to extraordinary people. This strikes me as an extremely naive view of persons who share power, wealth, and prestige. It flies in the face of how power was used by many nationalistic states in the twentieth century. Words like courage, daring, statesmanship, and political creativity might apply to Winston Churchill or Franklin D. Roosevelt, but what about Adolf Hitler, Benito Mussolini, Francisco

Franco, and Joseph Stalin? And what kind of virtues were Enron executives practicing recently?

Fukuyama sets up questionable dualities of society and history, of virtue and morality, to explain our prevailing historical condition. On the positive side, there is no doubt that he is hopeful about the future of humankind and that he sees history as developing in a progressive way. Yet Fukuyama really doesn't offer anything particularly useful in his views of the current historical moment. Instead, he basically proclaims the virtues of free markets, democratic institutions, and hierarchical structures. That's the end of history and that's all there is to it. We've heard this all before.

It would nevertheless be a mistake to dismiss Fukuyama. He remains an intelligent observer of historic processes. What he says in his recent book *America at the Crossroads* amounts to a rejection of his earlier neoliberal positions. On the whole, Fukuyama's views in this book are positive. Curiously though, he uses an odd metaphor that reveals his deep conservatism when he refers to the nation-state system as "the vertical silos we call states."[35] The rigidity of this view of nations needs no comment. Nevertheless, he rejects the outrageous doctrine of American exceptionalism so favored by the political right—the idea that the United States and its policies are morally superior to other nations, and therefore American power will always be used benevolently. For Latinos with knowledge of the way the United States has used the Monroe Doctrine to intervene in Latin America, the idea of a consistent, benevolent American exceptionalism is laughable.

For the most part Fukuyama also rejects preemptive wars, and he calls for the use of soft power, that is, persuasion and patient development of institutions, rather than military interventions, to further democratic causes. Yet I believe there is still a whiff of authoritarianism in him. He is preoccupied with hierarchies and their importance. I may be wrong, but I think he implicitly assumes that democratic, developed nations know what is best for underdeveloped nations.

My view is instead from the bottom up. I believe tribes, communities, small-scale associations, families, and individuals have the right and may someday acquire the power (because strong network connections are either in place or developing) to participate in the modern world on their own terms: to accept what is good for their communities, to reject elements of the modern world that might lead to their extinction, and to bypass entirely the nation-state system, even if this presupposes a more ideal and remote future than many can imagine at the present time.

Samuel P. Huntington

A scholar with a more conservative view of culture, society, and civilizations is Samuel P. Huntington. His approach to cultures and societies is far more tortured than Fukuyama's. Since his ideas are currently very influential in conservative think tanks and on national policymakers, I want to examine at some length his major ideas as they relate to Indohispanic interests. Huntington has advanced the ideas of core nations and collision-course civilizations in his book *The Clash of Civilizations and the Remaking of World Order.* He argues that "culture and cultural identities . . . are shaping the patterns of cohesion, disintegration, and conflict in the post–Cold War world." In Huntington's world, "the core states of the major civilizations are supplanting the two Cold War superpowers as the principal poles of attraction and repulsion for other countries." Such a state—the United States is one core, the Franco-German conglomerate is another one—"perform[s] an ordering function" for Western civilization and for other states within their respective civilizations "because member states perceive it [the core nation] as cultural kin."[36]

Huntington posits a rather inelegant typology of nation-states in his approach to civilizations. There are core states, member states, lone countries, cleft countries, and torn countries.[37] The first two are self-explanatory. Lone countries are those, like Haiti, that have little if any connection with other societies. Japan is another of Huntington's examples of lone countries. Japan may be "lonely" in the Huntington sense: "No other country shares its distinct culture, and Japanese migrants are either not numerically significant in other countries or have assimilated to the cultures of those countries (e.g., Japanese-Americans)." At the same time, however, Japan is a major player in communications and computer technologies. Its electronic networks tie it to every region of the planet. To the extent that technology, particularly computers, the Internet, and the World Wide Web, could be viewed as one form of an emerging global culture, then perhaps Japan is not such a lone country as Huntington would have us believe. A cleft country is one where "large groups belong to different civilizations," as is the case with India and Sri Lanka, among others.[38]

The word *cleft*, however, seems disparaging, implying a defect in these countries, an unhealthy cleavage, so to speak. It could very well be that in such societies two countries would be more viable than one nation state but Huntington's social contract, as rigid and hierarchical as Thomas Hobbes's, regards the breaking up of a nation with fear and loathing. Huntington's "torn country" has a single predominant culture and civilization, but its leaders decide that their country's civilization should change.[39] Examples would be, according to Huntington, the countries resulting from Peter the Great's attempt to Westernize Russia or Mustafa Kemal's efforts to Westernize Turkey. Once again, Huntington's choice of words is interesting. No one would doubt or deny the mixed results for nations whose leaders attempt to shift their civilizational base, but I dispute that "torn" is the appropriate word to describe this phenomenon. Why not call such states "ambiguous" or "complex" in terms of their civilizational self-identity? Why "torn" with its deterministic ring of inevitable violence?

To be fair to Huntington, he acknowledges that the rise of the West was not due to any inherent superiority in that civilization. Echoing Buckminster Fuller, Huntington states that "the immediate source of Western expansion . . . was technological: the invention of the means of ocean navigation for reaching distant peoples and the development of the military capabilities for conquering those peoples."[40] Implicit in Huntington's analysis is the geographic "gift" that was given to Europe. Europe is a subcontinent consisting mainly of peninsulas with relatively easy access to the sea. Great sailors became Great Pirates, in Fuller's expression,[41] and their profits from sea trade financed the European armaments that made expansion possible.

Huntington also states that "the West won the world not by the superiority of its ideas or values or religion (to which few members of other civilizations were converted) but rather by its superiority in applying organized violence."[42] Huntington's analysis of world civilizations is lucid and insightful. It is a sobering reminder that history should never be left out or slighted in any serious political, social, or economic analysis. Yet his views are also oddly shortsighted. It is as if Huntington's construction of the world had basically been carried out in the nineteenth-century ambience of realpolitik. He apparently will not or cannot go beyond a vision of the world that is hierarchical, static, and conflict driven. There is a crude Darwinian emphasis on clashes and conflicts in his analysis, as if no other models could be seriously considered for the growth and development of civilizations. There is little if any room in his world for concepts of harmony, cooperation, and problem solving.

The hierarchical and static nature of Huntington's views are clearly shown when he writes about the cultural identity of the United States. He asserts, as if it were fact, that "American national identity has been defined culturally by the heritage of Western civilization and politically by the principles of the American Creed on which Americans overwhelmingly agree: liberty, democracy, individualism, equality before the law, constitutionalism, private property."[43]

By reifying the most idealistic aspects of the "American Creed," whatever that is, Huntington conveniently ignores the dark side of American identity: the slaughter, and in some cases extermination, of indigenous people; the enslavement of Africans; the infamous aggressive war against Mexico that led, by 1848, to the acquisition of more than half of Mexico's northern territory (today's U.S. Southwest and California); and the well-documented legacy of violence, racism, and discrimination that set up the preconditions for the emergence of people like myself who fall culturally between an Indohispanic world and a New World variant of Western civilization.

Huntington's bête noire is multiculturalism. He asserts that the American heritage of Western civilization and the American Creed have "come under concentrated and sustained onslaught from a small but influential number of intellectuals and publicists." He quotes with approval Arthur Schlesinger Jr.'s lumping together of multiculturalists with "ethnocentric separatists who see little in the Western heritage other than Western crimes." Again, quoting Schlesinger, Huntington states the multiculturalists' "mood is one of divesting Americans of the sinful European inheritance and seeking redemptive infusions from non-Western cultures."[44] The sarcasm, arrogance, and unfairness of these remarks need little comment on my part. Yes, there are some ethnocentric separatists among Chicanos, but multiculturalism works *against* them.

Few if any Chicanos would want to belong to a separate state of Aztlán or a República del Norte if that state involved any sort of racist ethnic cleansing of Anglos, Native Americans, and other assorted folks. Furthermore, some multiculturalists, like myself, would argue the idea of a separatist ethnic state is "so twentieth century," to use contemporary jargon. We live in an era of rapid global communication, virtual reality, and mass movements of peoples and goods that was barely imaginable in either the nineteenth or twentieth centuries. In this century, national boundaries have become problematic, ambiguous, bothersome, and deadly. This hardly seems a propitious moment to reassert the tired nationalism of nineteenth-century Europe and its tragic and deadly offspring in the twentieth century. Millions of people have died in the name of nationalism. Does any sane person really want to add more numbers to that figure?

Huntington argues that the American multiculturalists "reject their country's cultural heritage." He states that these multiculturalists "wish to create a country of many civilizations, which is to say a country not belonging to any civilization and lacking a cultural core." There is a note of hysteria when he further asserts that "a multicivilizational United States will not be the United States; it will be the United Nations." Notice how fixed and hierarchical Huntington's views are. For him, the United States is identified as the core nation of Western civilization. He idealizes what for him are the best values of Western civilization and the United States, then he reifies these values. In turn, these values are no longer abstractions but become an identifiable ideology. Furthermore, it is the correct ideology. He approvingly quotes Richard Hofstader's comment on the United States to the effect that "it has been our fate as a nation not to have ideologies but to be one."[45]

These remarks express a deeply Anglocentric and xenophobic view of the world. More disturbingly, it doesn't take much insight to see in the remarks of Huntington and others like him a foreshadowing of the possible emergence in the United States of a Christian, missionary-driven, aggressive, corporate, authoritarian state in control of all major media of communication, masked by democratic rituals and ceremonies. If this foreshadowing were to become true, then our elections and our tripartite democratic institutions would become formulaic devices as devalued as Christmas and Easter are today when Santa Claus and the Easter Bunny serve as marketing hucksters for what are supposed to be meaningful religious celebrations.

With his "cleft countries" and "torn countries," Huntington has stitched together a Frankenstein monster's vision of the world. Ultimately, it is a defensive and deeply pessimistic vision. In Huntington's own words, "the prudent course for the West is not to attempt to stop the shift in power but to learn to navigate the shallows, endure the miseries, moderate its ventures, and safeguard its culture."[46] On the vast scale of historic change, Huntington's ideas express a kind of determinism that sees the inevitable rise, flowering, and decline of civilizations. He may, of course, be right on this score, but his solution to the West's predicament, as he sees it, is to shift the chairs on deck while the *Titanic* goes down. He wants to build a wall around the "best of the West," so to speak, in order to preserve it. He would make of the United States a Fortress America for Western civilization. I doubt not Huntington's intellectual integrity nor his deep knowledge of history nor his well-intentioned defense of the West. I do, however, think he is mistaken in his views on the world.

Atencio, Montiel, and I offer a more hopeful vision. First of all, we do not reject the finest elements of Western civilization, but we do attempt to moderate, if not entirely eliminate, its devastatingly negative consequences for Indohispanics and all other people and their cultures, including Anglo-American culture. Huntington would probably call our response to the West and modernization a "reformist" one, but he would be mistaken. He

defines reformism as an "attempt to combine modernization with the preservation of the essential values, practices, and institutions of the society's
indigenous culture."[47]

Indohispanics are already a mixed group in terms of their values, practices, and institutions. Huntington's idea of "preservation" is impossible unless the culture is already dead. It is possible, for example, to preserve remnants of Ishi's culture in history books and museums because the last of his
people, the Yahi, disappeared in California near the beginning of the last
century.[48] Unlike the Yahi, Indohispanics form a fluid and dynamic culture
that is versatile and highly adaptive. Rather than construct rigid categories
and definitions, my colleagues and I prefer to consider network theory as a
promising and revealing source of social analysis.

I have taken this digression from my main theme because both Fukuyama
and Huntington continue to be very relevant to contemporary American
thinking about culture, especially in conservative political circles. Despite
their many achievements, both have neglected or ignored the newest, and
possibly unwelcome, guests in the house of theory: the World Wide Web
and the Internet. Nowhere in their work will you find the insightful and
visionary language of Tim Berners-Lee, the man who created, or invented,
if you prefer, the World Wide Web: "Whether a group can advance comes
down to creating the right connectivity between people—in a family, a
company, a country, or the world. . . . The Internet and the Web have
pulled us out of two-dimensional space. They've also moved us away from
the idea that we won't be interrupted by anybody who's more than a day's
march away."[49]

A Network Conundrum: Los Alamos and Rural New Mexico

Network theory is now several centuries old. It has long been a powerful
analytic tool, first in the hands of mathematicians and then in the theories
of physicists. Only recently has it been applied to social phenomena. While
the jury is still out on the utility of this approach, I think network theory
is a fascinating lens to focus on the cultural issues of concern here. My
approach to networks is descriptive and narrative, and I can only suggest
how network theory might apply to the living conditions of Indohispanics.
My only objective is to point out new ways of participating in a constructive discourse about culture, language, and civilization.

The pioneering work of Tomás Atencio initiated the train of events
that resulted in this book. His contributions grew out of his many years'
experience as a social worker, philosopher, and Chicano activist. Here I

am interested in the way networks can be discerned in his essay and how a network analysis might highlight key elements of it.

Near the beginning of his essay, Atencio contrasts the high-tech city of Los Alamos, New Mexico, with the low-tech Hispanic and Pueblo villages that inhabit the same neighborhood. Los Alamos is the site where a team of some of the best physicists, chemists, mathematicians, and engineers in the world worked out the details of the first assembly of a fissionable atomic bomb. Since its halcyon years in the mid-1940s, Los Alamos has continued to be a center for scientific research and development, much but not all of it related to military uses. Los Alamos has the highest concentration per capita of PhDs in the nation, possibly in the world.

The Hispano villages and Native American pueblos, in contrast, are rural societies. Until Los Alamos was developed as a cutting-edge scientific site in the 1940s, these villages and pueblos had practiced their agrarian mode of existence for centuries. Long before the arrival of Europeans in the New World, the Pueblo Indians of the American Southwest had developed their civilized, village way of life with all the supportive social hierarchies and networks they needed to survive and thrive. The Hispano villages, beginning very early in the seventeenth century, shared the same water resources with the Pueblos and planted and harvested their crops in time with the eternal calendric cycle of spring, summer, fall, and winter.

U.S. annexation in 1846 initiated a process of adaptive change in the villages and pueblos. It was a relatively slow process, however, until the Great Depression in the 1930s and the eventual introduction of welfare, as Atencio discusses in his essay, led to a diaspora of Hispanic farmworkers following the harvests around the nation. The massive introduction of science and technology with the development of Los Alamos hastened the process of village and pueblo change. Over time, the old Pueblo and Hispanic village economies suffered and were distorted as young people left the agrarian way of life for the lures of Los Alamos and the larger cities.

Los Alamos looms large in this scheme of things. The village becomes vulnerable to both positive and negative contacts with a much larger world. The village cannot return to what it was in the past. Its only choices are to become a gentrified village, a tourist attraction of sorts, or to use the new resources, particularly the global electronic resources symbolized by Los Alamos, to reassert itself and its values in a new and global context.

It is the paradox of these choices that caught Atencio's attention when he returned to northern New Mexico. He did not accept the common wisdom that northern New Mexico could be adequately described, and dismissed, as an impoverished backwater. He perceived that the villages had an abundance of nonmaterial resources. The villagers did not care for the changes that were occurring in their world, but there was little they could do about them. What they could do was protect their identification by maintaining their traditions; by holding on to their memory, their family lore that kept their version of history alive; and by not accepting the common American vision of themselves as an impoverished and diminished people.

From experience, Atencio knew that the villages had informal associations of men who would gather on the sunny side of a wall, the south-facing side, or la resolana, where they would gossip and discuss virtually every topic under the sun. Atencio saw pure cultural gold in these small, informal groupings and he called them, collectively, el oro del barrio. This may sound romantic, but in fact it is not. The resolaneros were real; they were not conjured up in some novel about the Old West. La resolana was real. In fact, la resolana was a hub of highly connected individuals and village clusters. It was the village equivalent of an airport hub, or better still, a combination information center, living archive, and school. Trained as a social worker and community organizer, Atencio was able to put these concepts of la resolana and el oro del barrio to work as consciousness-raising tools in the villages.

It might be observed that la resolana emerged as a male-dominated and male-oriented phenomenon. That, however, was a product of the patriarchal nature of northern New Mexico villages at that time. The concepts of el oro del barrio and la resolana attracted the attention of women as well, and early on they became involved in resolana activities. Today, the influence of women on resolana is at least equal to that of men.

Drawing on his education and experience, Atencio took the abstract idea and informal associations of la resolana and converted them into a formal institution. Through dialogue, Atencio discovered that the stored memories of the villagers, their stories, their dynamic mental and oral reconstruction of the world, much as Bhabha and others have theorized, provided the basis for el oro del barrio. Through dialogue human experience is revealed and "brings about an understanding of life in the community. This process creates a body of knowledge understood within that experience related to universal knowledge expressed in other cultural and intellectual achievements."[50] The organization Atencio and his collaborators created, La Academia de Aztlán, completed the process of formalization. This vision attracted the attention of Paulo Freire, who spent some time in northern New Mexico with those of us involved in the early Academia. He was pleased with what he saw.

What Atencio achieved, in network terms, was the creation of a new, formalized, and organized cluster within the village community. This cluster, La Academia de la Nueva Raza and the Rio Grande Institute that evolved out of it, had and still has enormous potential for linkages with the larger world. The Chicano movement, centered for the most part in urban areas and drawing its intellectual support from Chicano studies centers in colleges and universities scattered around the nation, has been slow to respond to the Academia model. I attribute this to a general lack of insight into the potentially explosive nature of network expansion. The model Atencio developed transcends its rural foundation. The links and weak ties that result from the formalization of the model remain a largely untapped network resource for Indohispanics. Once fully activated, this resource could potentially result in a renaissance for all Americans, a veritable shower of literature, music, science, and the arts in general, and the opening of new vistas of political, social, and economic scenarios to enrich the entire spectrum of the American experience.

Euro-Americans need not hunker down in their Huntington bunkers or accept the Western triumphalism of Fukuyama's earlier books. The twin concepts of el oro del barrio and la resolana are not a threat but rather a promise of individual and community betterment for those untold millions of Americans for whom the American dream has become a cruel hoax.

Although possibly not fully aware of his role, Atencio was, in effect, a weak tie to the outside world for the village. His village interactions were in fact extremely complex but again, for my purposes, network theory says it takes only one node with one outside connection, a weak tie, to alter all the major relationships within a network of nodes, clusters, and hubs. The properties of the network connecting Tomás Atencio, the village, and many other sites, including Los Alamos, ensured that there would be significant interaction with the outside world that could not have occurred if either the village or Los Alamos had remained highly isolated from each other. This is not to say that Atencio was the only village link to Los Alamos and the world beyond. Many villagers worked away from their traditional domain and were very much aware of the wider world. Atencio, however, was able to provide the villagers with an approach drawn from their own rich historical heritage—el oro del barrio and la resolana—that could enrich their own network possibilities and deepen their understanding of their general contextualization in contemporary American society.

Notice that the network is entirely neutral. It could become the path for a creative approach to the village, such as Atencio's, or it could become the conduit for a highly destructive force. The clusters in a network, with a few random links, can convert the villages of an entire region into a small world. Again, the network is neutral: the small world might give rise to reform, revolution, or a descent into drugs and crime, or it might do all these things simultaneously. Keep in mind that networks are not explanatory devices. Rather, they are critical maps with specific properties that can be observed. Viewed as critical maps, networks make our choices about our actions clearer. The greater our understanding of the networks within which we live, the greater our opportunity to make wise choices for ourselves and for our cultures.

Atencio viewed real people in real social conditions and saw that they had untapped resources within their own history, their own culture and memory, and that they could use these resources to define, enjoy, and amplify their own world. There is no end of history here, no romantic clinging to the past, only another facet in the unfolding of human consciousness nurtured by memory and the past, experienced in the indefinable present in perpetual transition toward the unknown and unknowable future.

There is no clash of civilizations here. Network theory makes this clear. Euro-Americans are as much impelled by their own networks as Indohispanics are by theirs. An examination of these networks would show points of contact, cooperation, and mutual benefit, as well as the possibilities for friction. It may be that force and violence are so deeply rooted in the human condition that Fukuyama's stress on hierarchy, what he calls *homo hierarchicus*,[51] and Huntington's cautious conservatism and cultural elitism are justified. Anything, after all, is better than a return to Hobbes's nasty state of nature. Or it could also be, as Simone Weil argued, that beginning with the *Iliad*, force is the dark and admired presence in Western civilization that must be recognized before it can be overcome.[52] Force is a reality, but what good does it do to allow it to shape all human aspirations, to throw in the towel, so to speak, and meekly take our designated places far down the table from our rich and powerful cultural hegemons?

Networks and Chicano Urban Culture

An examination of the dialogues collected by Miguel Montiel reveals that his subjects have not been cowed by the force that initially changed their cultural relationship to the United States, the conquest and occupation of northern Mexico formalized by the Treaty of Guadalupe Hidalgo. Since 1848, the Chicanos Montiel describes, just like Atencio's northern New Mexico villagers, have lived out their lives in a continuous dialogue with their historically fractured cultural cosmos.

Montiel and his team of seven interviewers carried out their work as part of and prior to an educational seminar at Arizona State University in the fall of 2000 and in collaboration with the Profiles of Success project sponsored by a community-based organization called Valle del Sol, in Phoenix, Arizona. The interviewees were asked about their life's accomplishments and their struggles to succeed; about the forces, trends, attitudes, and influences that shaped their lives; and about the lives of Latinos in general (see chapter 2). Several themes emerged from the interviews: family, church, identity, assimilation, immigration, and social problems.

The analysis of the interviews was based on a variation of Atencio's oro del barrio concept: the search for cultural meaning in the lived experiences of these Hispanic leaders as they related what was significant to them through dialogue, myth, oral history, and storytelling. What emerges from an analysis of these interviews is an extension of el oro del barrio and la resolana from the rural to the urban Indohispanic experience.

The physicist David Bohm defines society as "a link of relationships" among people and institutions, so that we can live together.[53] The quotation is interesting for what it says and does not say. Bohm clearly implies a network relationship by his use of the term "link." Notice, however, that he says nothing about the quality of the linkage. People and institutions that are linked may live together in peace and harmony or in friction and misery. As I said earlier, the network is neutral. Although the network may restrict the zone of human freedom, particularly if it is highly clustered with few if any outside links, as might occur in a restrictive cult, for example, there is still freedom for some kind of human choice. As Ortega y Gasset put it, "We are not launched into existence like a shot from a gun, with its trajectory absolutely predetermined. . . . [Life] instead of imposing on us one trajectory, imposes several, and consequently forces us to choose."[54]

Montiel discovered the importance of myth, or at least one way of looking at myth, quoting May as "self-interpretation of our inner selves in relation to the outside world." This view of myths as "the invisible anchors of our existence,"[55] reaffirms the insights of Walter Mignolo and Homi Bhabha, among others, into the ways memory is used to give significance to the past. Our self-interpretation is like a continually running motion picture, a story, inside our conscious and unconscious mental processes. The cast of characters changes, at least slightly, from time to time, the plot has many nuances, and these are constantly fine-tuned as the story unfolds, moment by moment, until we die. What makes it all worthwhile, of course, is the unfolding story; the way we fill Peter Brook's "empty space" to construct the story, the drama, of our lives.[56] The invisible anchors of myth keep us in dialogue, through memory, with all that is significant in our culture, unless some extreme violence has destroyed the mythic ties to that unseen but experienced world.

Montiel's essay shows what a powerful force memory is. He and his team interviewed sixteen subjects. Two of these subjects were born and raised in Mexico, came to the United States, and through hard work overcame many barriers and became successful in this country. The majority, however, were born in the United States. They also overcame negative social conditions, worked hard, and experienced personal success in their careers. Nevertheless, there are significant differences between these two groups.

Dr. Elizabeth Valdez, one of Montiel's interviewees, was born in Mexico, educated in medical school in Guadalajara, and after much struggle went on to become a highly respected psychiatrist and director of a health clinic for Latinos. Dr. María Vega, another interviewee, was also born in Mexico and completed medical school there. On immigrating, she was unable to get her credentials accepted in the United States and became instead a teacher and early leader of bilingual education. Turning first to Dr. Valdez's network connections, Montiel writes that she "visits her family in Mexico on a regular basis and is a keen student of life on both sides of the border" (see chapter 2). It is interesting that from her well-connected cultural perspective, she sees Latinos who are educated, have social status here in the United States, and at the same time identify with their culture. She also sees Latinos who are "lost, marginalized, and neglected." Between these two extremes, she sees an identity crisis in many Chicanos, and she says this about people like herself, with a strong cultural base in Mexico: "We who came to the U.S. already educated and with a sense of who we are or what we can accomplish or what we can give back to society don't have to struggle with what a lot of Mexican Americans have to struggle with." Dr. Valdez suffers no crisis of identity. A glance at her network shows that she has strong cultural ties on both sides of the political border. She nurtures these ties through her work, her family, and her interests. She is connected to, and is a connector to, powerful hubs on both sides of the border.

The network connecting Dr. Vega to her culture on both sides of the Mexican border is slightly different from Dr. Valdez's network. Dr. Vega came from an impoverished Mexican family that placed a high value on education. Despite her early poverty, she received an advanced education in medicine. When she came to the United States, however, she was not able to practice medicine for linguistic and other reasons. Rather than accept defeat in her new environment, she became a noteworthy educator in Texas and Arizona. Like Dr. Valdez, Dr. Vega had a powerful cultural inner strength that enabled her to overcome the negative treatment she received at Arizona State University and elsewhere. Although her network connections in Texas and Arizona brought her into contact with very racist persons and social conditions, she had a strong enough sense of herself to overcome these barriers and eventually become successful.

The stories that emerged through the interviews were nuanced in slightly different ways. Some stressed a defining moment that ignited their determination to succeed. Others placed more emphasis on the core values or moral foundations handed down through their families or culture. Most of these stories, as Montiel points out, had elements of both.

The network structures of Dr. Valdez and Dr. Vega both exhibit strong core values in their Mexican backgrounds. The stories of three other interviewees, in contrast, reveal that they experienced a cultural shock or series of shocks that strengthened them by forcibly reminding them of who they were and what they were about.

Jess Torrez and Mary Rose Wilcox both experienced defining moments that led them to become outstanding persons. Sophia López-Espindola is a special case among those interviewed. Her story, unfortunately, is not atypical.

Jess Torrez came from a strong working-class family. His father was an upholsterer; his mother worked for the Arizona Civil Rights Commission. He had a number of discriminatory experiences in his school and at the community swimming pool. Nevertheless, he went to college and eventually became a police officer. While he was employed by the Scottsdale Police Department, he witnessed fellow officers violating the civil rights of three Mexican youths who had made the simple mistake of crossing an invisible line into the "no n***** zone" that police forces use to keep people of color out of white upper-class areas. Torrez was fired for blowing the whistle on this practice. Rather than meekly withdraw, however, he sued the police department and won. What interests me here is the network structure of Torrez's world. At the center is a strong cluster consisting of his family. So powerful was this cultural influence within the wider Mexican American community where he lived that it overcame the negative influences he encountered in school and at times in the community itself. The more adverse his circumstances, the stronger Torrez became. When we look at the nodes, clusters, and links on his network, we need to remember that events also occur *within* it. In his network, Torrez had access to powerful support mechanisms in his community that strengthened him for a confrontation in court. He won his lawsuit.

There is a striking resemblance between the formative network structures of Mary Rose Wilcox's world and those of Jess Torrez. Wilcox had
a strong family cluster at the center of her life experiences. She learned
about unions and organizing from her father. She realized how protected
she was in her own Mexican American community when she went to Arizona State University and was assigned to room with the only two other
incoming students of color. She never forgot this experience. After she left
college, she reinforced her family base. She had grown up in a large, loving
family, and had a stable marriage, children, and grandchildren. Educated
and with a rock-solid family foundation, she eventually became a successful elected official in Phoenix and Maricopa County, and she served on
various national boards and commissions. She demonstrated her fortitude
by continuing to serve in elected office even after she was shot by a man
upset over her vote on a tax issue.

In Jess Torrez's case, there is a triangular relationship between the
plaintiff (Torrez), the informal community standards that tolerated the "no
n***** zone" policy, and the defendants (the City of Scottsdale and its
police department). This triangle stands outside the network zone of more
normal relationships. It is the isolated nature of this incident that gave it its
shock value and galvanized Torrez's positive community social energies.
If Torrez had been a weaker person, however—insecure about himself or
where he stood in relation to his own culture—he might have found this
outside network force crushing. Instead, he was able to turn it into a positive contribution to his community.

Sophia López-Espindola's interview shows the dark, violent forces
at work in any human society. Fukuyama and also Huntington, I believe,
would probably argue that these forces are rooted deeply in the biological
and spiritual bases of the human condition. This may be so. Violence is a
force in every human culture. We must acknowledge this and somehow try
to channel violence in constructive directions for the benefit of humanity,
rather than make of it an icon, as in the *Iliad*.

Unlike our other examples, López-Espindola came from a strongly
dysfunctional family. She grew up in poverty in a problem-ridden family
and had to move into a foster home. Her father, and later her husband,
were both very abusive of her. Yet she never accepted their ugly, negative
views about her personal worth. Her son's killing in a gang-related incident
was especially tragic for her. Although she lived in a world of strong nega-
tivity, this world was contained within a wider Mexican American community. Somehow, the attitudes of those most immediate to her did not crush
her spirit. Her response to the tragedy of her son's death was to found a

community organization, Mothers Against Gangs, and become a positive, proactive member of that wider community. There are strong individuals in any culture who can transcend, or at least try to transcend, any and all difficulties in their environments.

Dr. Elizabeth Valdez and Dr. María Vega accomplished wonders through their use of network connections within both Mexico and the United States. Dr. Valdez was able to combine her medical knowledge with her observations of Indohispanics in order to direct a health clinic specifically responsive to Latino health needs. Dr. Vega was able to use her random connections in McKinney, Texas, to help found a school to educate the children of Mexican farmworkers. Both women had a deep sense of their own worth. Secure in their own cultural identities, both women were able to overcome extreme difficulties to lead productive and socially engaged lives in the United States. Whatever difficulties these women had in their own lives, they were able to direct their frustrations in positive directions. Each was able to become a hub in her respective community, and following the power law, both became connectors, super connectors, really, between medical and educational services and the needs of their respective communities. I think it is worth observing that both Dr. Valdez and Dr. Vega experienced a deep cultural continuity that started in their childhood years and continued into adulthood. Culturally speaking, neither experienced lasting negative psychological or social trauma. Culture matters.

For Indohispanics born on the U.S. side of the border, cultural experiences are quite different. At one end of the experiential spectrum is a person like Jess Torrez. His sense of family was very strong and he was part of a deeply embedded cluster within a large Mexican American community. Mr. Torrez's home community reinforced his cultural strength. He was able to resist whatever negative social pressures might otherwise have impelled him to lead a less constructive life. Mary Rose Wilcox, like Jess Torrez, had a strong sense of herself and her family, and that solidity enabled her to overcome racism in college, an assault, and other negative forces later in life. Torrez and Wilcox, I believe, are paradigmatic of Mexican Americans who have maintained their Spanish-language abilities and other elements of a Mexican culture while adjusting to conditions of life in the United States.

Sophia López-Espindola did not fare as well. She was surrounded by poverty, violence, and abuse from a very early age until well into adulthood. Her experience strikes me as paradigmatic of the experiences of many Chicanas. Yet as her network connections show, she was somehow able to find support and strength in the wider Mexican American and Anglo communities to make a success of her life.

What are the significant differences between the idealized networks of Dr. Valdez and Dr. Vega, on the one hand, and of Torrez, Wilcox, and López-Espindola, on the other, and the implied differences related to the experience of other Indohispanics? They are, I believe, the following: (1) Dr. Valdez, and to a slightly lesser extent Dr. Vega, had a fairly constant stream of cultural reinforcement from family in Mexico or from a strongly Mexican-oriented family. This means there was little, if any, loss of language, family values, and community solidarity. (2) Torrez, Wilcox, and López-Espindola did not have these strong cultural connections to Mexico, but enough of that Mexican identity had survived in their Mexican American communities to give them a sense of their own worth. (3) I am reminded that many Mexican American families and communities have lost virtually all identification with the Spanish language or with their Mexican roots. While a good number have made a successful transition and have become almost indistinguishable from other English-speaking citizens of the United States, many are lost souls who do not know what has happened to them in a cultural sense, and they lead dysfunctional lives. (4) Education is a significant factor in these various networks. When education is combined with a strong sense of one's own cultural values, as in the cases of Dr. Vega and Dr. Valdez, then successful, fulfilling life patterns have a good chance to emerge. Where that education is lacking or has been acquired painfully under difficult circumstances, then persons such as Torrez, Wilcox, and López-Espindola may have very difficult yet fulfilling lives. (5) Network connections made all the difference in the world for each of the interviewees. It was their network connections that enabled them to be positive, productive persons and to lead quality lives. Unfortunately, many Chicanos' network connections are decidedly negative. In either instance, positive or negative, an understanding of network connections might be helpful for individuals and communities who want to enjoy their cultures and not be trapped by their life circumstances.

Networks and Communities: Let the Harmony Begin

American triumphalism, as seen in the earlier work of Francis Fukuyama, and Western defensiveness, as seen in Samuel Huntington, are inadequate for a positive engagement of Indohispanics and other cultures within the United States. While American shoppers are kept happy with imported goods manufactured cheaply in third world countries, the social price paid in those countries is devastating to their cultures and even to their physical survival. Anyone who has visited, as I have, a *maquiladora* (a factory for assembling a variety of goods owned by foreigners, usually Americans, and operating in Mexico because of lower labor costs) will never be able to buy an inexpensive shirt in a shopping mall without feeling a tinge of guilt at the inequity of the transaction. If the American people were presented with a network analysis of how goods are produced, distributed, and priced, there might be widespread unease with this system and at least an attempt to find and implement a more just international economic system.

All the news about cultures and their interactions in the globalized world is not bad, however. One of the joys in writing this essay was the growth in my own awareness of the worldwide efforts of communities to determine their own future rather than leave it to the tender mercies of megalosaurian corporations and national governments hypnotized by a contemporary doctrinaire and sinister type of capitalism. Observers as distinct as the Egyptian Marxist Samir Amin and the Canadian journalist Naomi Klein have written extensively on this phenomenon. As Naomi Klein puts it, the fundamentalist capitalist economics of Milton Friedman, now enshrined as sacred writ in Western political and economic doctrine, created a social situation in which individual freedom became a "project that elevated atomized citizens above any collective enterprise and liberated them to express their absolute free will through their consumer choices."[57] Increasingly, the reappearance of the old scourges of mercenary armies and the use of torture has come to characterize the attempt to impose and sustain regime changes sponsored by this deviant type of capitalism. At least these old scourges are inspiring near-universal revulsion. In the words of Amin, "A model close to that of the mafia seems to be the one taking over in the business world as much as in politics."[58]

Even as you read these pages, resistance is growing to the Friedman-plus-torture model: In Mexico, the Zapatistas in the state of Chiapas continue to wage a peaceful, nonviolent struggle of cultural self-determination. Gustavo Esteva, an acclaimed author and grassroots activist, explained in a 2001 interview how the Zapatistas, who are very media savvy, are pioneering new horizontal, linked, network strategies in place of the traditional vertical modes of interaction: "So in many different ways [the Zapatistas] are destroying the idea of the great leader, of the party, of the organization, of whoever is at the top and creating the possibility of the people organizing themselves."[59] In the United States, the National Indian Youth Leadership Project applies indigenous knowledge to service-learning. In Canada, scholars such as Engin Isen are developing new concepts of citizenship.

He is interested in a cross-cultural and historical dialogue on citizenship.[60] Despite many serious setbacks, there are indigenous and popular democratic movements throughout Latin America—in Ecuador, Peru, Bolivia, Brazil, and Venezuela.[61] Then there are the relatively new and intriguing social movements such as the slow food movement, which promotes environmental sustainability and social justice in food production. With the motto "good, clean and fair," the slow food movement is one more bottom-up response to globalization and industrialized food production.[62] Around the world, many, many other grassroots popular organizations are asserting their right to have a major voice in determining their own future. This is not the time or place to explore these movements in depth, but communications about them accumulate in newspapers, magazines, newsletters, books, blogs, and Internet websites. There is reason, indeed, for optimism, for resolana, for light, in these dark times.

I draw five major conclusions from my analysis. Implicit in each is the analytic strength and wisdom of the resolana approach in trying to reach a political, social, and economic confluence where we may all enjoy *café para todos*—enough coffee for everyone, or justice for everyone, as this metaphor implies.

First of all, we live in a permanently linked world. It would take an unimaginable reversal of science, technology, and the human desire to communicate with others to undo our present networked world. Networks are so widespread, dense, and intense that all assumptions about the ultimate viability of the nation-state are up for grabs. Networks could be used in support of nefarious ideologies to control countless human lives across cultures; or, in contrast, they could offer a support system, the communications infrastructure, for a constructive approach to globalism that respects and celebrates cultures. Networks offer us as a species the possibility of breaking out of many of the dysfunctional and restrictive hierarchies inherited from the past and a chance to change the direction of history in fundamental ways.

Second, many Indohispanics have both strong links within their cultural communities and weak ties to other persons and cultures around the globe. As Granovetter and other network theorists have shown, such weak ties can be important for rapidly expanding a community's awareness of, response to, and impact on other societies. Also, it takes only a few random links between nodes for a phase transition to occur from isolated nodes into a community. Applied to a global scale, the possibilities for the emergence of community self-awareness or critical consciousness are breathtaking.

Third, networks are more important than hierarchies. I agree with

Fukuyama that people like hierarchies. Yet a glance at history reveals that longstanding hierarchies, like the Romanov dynasty, can disappear almost overnight when a serious revolution occurs. Russia's underlying networks survived the Romanovs and the Bolsheviks, and they will no doubt survive the current corrupt capitalist rule of Russia. Hierarchies come and go. Network structures are more deeply rooted in the human condition than hierarchies are. Indeed, it may very well be that the character of any network structure itself enables human communities to survive disasters and quickly reorganize around their needs and aspirations.

Fourth, an understanding of network characteristics might give us insight into why Indohispanics do not participate in politics as much as some people think they should. Assuming that there is a real difference between Indohispanic and Anglo voting patterns in terms of turnout at elections, a network analysis could offer insight. Mexican migrants who have become American citizens probably bring with them long memories of political corruption and deception in Mexico. Because of historic and cultural circumstances, there is a limited range of trust in Mexican society. The unresponsiveness of ruling elites in Mexico or their corruption or both do not inspire confidence in the voting process. For the documented and undocumented migrants to this country, given their Mexican political experience, as well as for the older Hispanic population that has had citizenship for a little more than a century and a half and something approaching equal voting rights only since the 1960s, the American two-party system may not seem worthy of much trust or even respect.

If Thomas Friedman is correct in at least one point about globalization's impact on politics, it is in the political pattern that has developed in the United States. Once upon a time, we had many political parties, but that is all but forgotten today. By the late nineteenth century, two major political parties emerged that were clearly distinguishable. No longer is that the case. To paraphrase Friedman, we have a national political choice, it seems, between Pepsi and Pepsi Lite. The more conservative party, the Pepsi party, has dominated national politics, with few exceptions, since 1980. The Pepsi Lite party, beginning in 1992, has started to look more and more like the Pepsi party.

Now, Mexican Americans are as observant as anyone else of the American political scene. They are accustomed to politicians coming into their communities, eating a few tamales, donning a sombrero, and then expressing some cliché in tortured Spanish. And for this they expect to receive the Indohispanic vote! Mexican and Mexican American social networks, strongly centered on family and community, may alert their members to the futility of voting for any such candidate. There may be other explanations for voter apathy, of course, but I believe neither the arrogance of the two virtually indistinguishable major political parties nor the lived political experience of Mexican Americans should be left out of consideration. Despite the negative attitudes toward politics that encumber Mexicans and Mexican Americans, if Chicano activists were to make political network connections clearer to the Hispanic community, the need to vote might become more apparent.

Fifth is the concept of network neutrality. Members of the Pepsi and Pepsi Lite parties may huddle around the frozen center of political and economic discourse. Theoreticians like Fukuyama and Huntington may set up models of conservative hierarchies and clashes between civilizations. Nevertheless, a network approach to all these issues offers a neutral arena for analysis. Networks have nothing to do with the politics of the left, right, or center. If we are dealing with a problem-ridden community of any culture, then a study of its network connections might reveal what is negative, dysfunctional, or destructive in the community, and it might also suggest constructive, humane ways of dealing with those problems.

I cannot think of a better way to end this essay than to refer to the words of Tim Berners-Lee: "Hope in life comes from the interconnections among all the people of the world. We believe that if we all work for what we think individually is good, then we as a whole will achieve more power, more understanding, more harmony as we continue the journey."[63] A saying in Spanish sums up the kind of world my colleagues and I envision for the future. However long it may take to achieve it, in that world there will never be perfection, a utopia, but there will be *café para todos* on our individual and cultural journeys. Long ago the seventeenth-century Japanese poet Matsuo Basho, as translated by Sam Hamill, expressed much the same thought: "The moon and sun are eternal travelers. Even the years wander on. A lifetime adrift in a boat, or in old age leading a tired horse into the years, every day is a journey, and the journey itself is home."[64] For Indohispanics, the journey has been long and hard, but it continues through the web of life, link by link, node by node. The interconnectedness of this web will allow Indohispanics/Chicanos to follow their own cultural paths on this journey while interacting with people of all cultures, and to share their lives, their stories, with all who make their home on this small planet. Indeed, there is hope.

Epilogue

Miguel: Let's end this book as we began it, with a resolana. Tomás, what did you learn from working on this project?

Tomás: Working on this book helped me realize that La Academia de La Nueva Raza's attempts in the sixties to create a body of knowledge from our culture's historical experience was truly an arrogant move. We had neither experience nor theory to direct us. Out of ignorance we began to use the people's response as our guide. We learned that just talking with people was better than asking questions. We learned that memory and imagination were as important as facts; we learned that oral history, personal histories, and folklore were excellent conveyers of knowledge and wisdom. We also learned that neither our history nor our ancestors' experiences were seen by the dominant society as valid foundations for knowledge.

Out of this we put together a theory-in-process—la resolana and el oro del barrio—arguing that this invalidated and subjugated knowledge was not only valuable to us but would be vital for the coming postindustrial age. Evidence of this is appearing as the Western mind turns to indigenous people in search of philosophical wisdom, meaning, and practical knowledge to address the challenges of globalization and the threats to the environment posed by a free-market economy. The dark side of this development is that indigenous and traditional societies and cultures are in danger of extinction by the same forces they could help humanize. Meanwhile their healing herbs, seeds, and traditional knowledge are plundered via copyright and patents.

Tony: In writing this book, I have learned that the three of us, like so many people and their cultures everywhere, are trying to throw off our cultural baggage of colonialism and assume our place in the universal search for meaning in the human condition. And we are looking for meaning in our history and our historical memories, in our family lore and folklore, and in our contemporary experience mediated by conflicting global narratives. This is a very positive voyage of cultural exploration and discovery. I am cautiously optimistic about where our voyage will take us.

Miguel: I also am optimistic, particularly about how dialogue can help expand cultural exploration. Through this project, I learned about the magic of dialogue. Read the resolanas in this book, and you'll experience the joy when the ideas and humanity of another person converge with your humanity. This book is not an anthology in the traditional sense; the essays are linked and we had, of necessity, to work with one another over a long period of time. There were many arguments, dead ends, and countless hours of work, but in the end, we managed to resolve our differences.

In the broad scheme of things, our goal is to get people with divergent views to dialogue with one another. Our society is addicted to formative thinking, everything is yes or no, conservative or liberal, black or white. We seem to be frozen into intractable positions, unable to listen to other points of view, incessantly trying to manipulate one another. My son-in-law told me a story about Bob Marley who once said that if he had been educated, he would have been the class fool—what people need is not education but inspiration. The Greeks have a wonderful word for what needs to happen to survive in a world of massive power devoid of personal responsibility: *metanoia*. It means change of heart.

I want to make one final point about subjugated knowledge. What has happened to Chicanos is not dissimilar to what is happening to the American people. Thanks to the concentration of power in a few corporations that control media outlets, knowledge of important issues—war, the economy, elections—is also being subjugated so that we as Americans are being denied important news and knowledge.

Tony, since Tomás and I had the first word in the prologue, why don't you have the last word in the epilogue?

Tony: It may be that a change of heart occurs only one person at a time. That sounds like bad news if you think globally. However, the good news is that if we apply our insights from network theory, then we realize that only a few personal network connections can transform isolated individuals and communities into small worlds and clusters. It is inconceivable to me that we would ignore the tremendous opportunity that networks—especially the largest network of all, the Internet and the World Wide Web—offer us as a transformative communication medium not only for Chicanos but for all people and their cultures.

So, I think we are three resolaneros of the future, but we are not ideologues, nor do we set up false gods, false icons, to mislead those less wary than us of authoritarian movements.

Notes

Introduction

1. Huntington, "Hispanic Challenge"; Fukuyama, *End of History*.
2. Friedman, *Lexus and the Olive Tree*, 105–6.
3. Friedman, *World Is Flat*, 7.
4. Arellano, *Entre Verde y Seco*; Atencio, "Academia de La Nueva Raza."
5. Padilla and Montiel, *Debatable Diversity*.
6. Freire, *Pedagogy of the Oppressed*; Habermas, *Theory and Practice*.
7. Bohm, *On Dialogue*, 1.
8. Spoto, *Hidden Jesus*, 64.
9. Huntington, "Hispanic Challenge," 11.
10. Mares, "Many Faces of Padre Martínez."

1. El Oro del Barrio in the Cyber Age

1. Pacheco, "Archetypal Image," 1–29.
2. Manito/as refers to New Mexican Indohispanics whose historical threads extend back to the colonial period. *Manito* is the shortened diminutive of *hermano*, brother. *Spanish American* is another self-designation of northern New Mexican Indohispanics. *Mexican American* is used for people whose roots are in Mexico but who settled in the United States around the time of the Mexican Revolution in 1910–1920. *Chicano* is a street term derived from colonial-period Aztec usage and adopted by Mexican Americans as well as manito youth.
3. This was drawn from informal conversations with Arturo Martínez y Salazar from Taos, New Mexico, between 1966 and the early 1980s.
4. Los Alamos employment was a boon to the subsistence farmer since he had his plot where he could build his home and continue farming while enjoying a relatively well-paying job. This created an illusion that one could succeed and become affluent without much education; unfortunately, this attitude has spread among young people, and education has been a low priority in many families.

5. The analyst Rudolf Ekstein (1912–2005) conducted weekly seminars for psychiatric residents, psychology interns, and social workers.

6. The community of interest model is discussed in National Commission of Community Health Services, *Health Is a Community Affair.*

7. *Pícaro* is usually translated as "rogue." In Spanish, he is an antihero who survives by his wits. He has been immortalized in Spanish literature from the anonymous publication in 1554 of *Lazarillo de Tormes* to Juan Estevan Arellano's 1992 novel of northern New Mexico, *Inocencio.*

8. Abt, *Progress without Loss of Soul,* 255–67. His study of the effects of industrialization and government policy on Swiss mountain villages offers intriguing parallels with the situation in northern New Mexico.

9. *Resolaneros* are the men who gather in la resolana.

10. "His mind is always on the story, the narrative account of things done. . . . It is not an accident that the highest philosophic teaching that Plato offers is not doctrine, but dialectic, a conversation in which ideas animate persons in search of wisdom" (S. Buchanan, *Portable Plato,* 6).

11. Atencio, "Survival of la Raza," 262–65.

12. Mumford, *Myth of the Machine,* 10; Theobald, "Cybernation Revolution," 5; Ellul, *Technological Society,* 428.

13. From 1972 to 1977, La Academia de la Nueva Raza conducted seminars on lifestyles in a postindustrial society at the Ghost Ranch Conference Center in Abiquiú, New Mexico.

14. The village's original name was El Puesto del Embudo de San Antonio, commonly known as La Plaza del Embudo. In 1904, a post office was established in the village, and the name of the postal agency became Dixon, named after Collins Dixon, a Civil War veteran who stayed in New Mexico and was honored for having taught children English.

15. The Stanford Chicano Fellows developed a special relationship with the Academia. A group of students initiated "el oro de la universidad," and an undergraduate student, José Padilla, conducted an oral history project in his home region. The Royal Chicano Air Force (RCAF) also had a very close relationship with the Academia. Among the "established university" *colegios* were Jacinto Treviño in Mercedes, Texas; La Universidad de Aztlán in Fresno, California; Colegio César Chávez, Mount Angel, Oregon; Deganawidah-Quetzalcoatl, (DQ-U) at Davis, California; and Escuela y Colegio Tlatelolco in Denver, Colorado. See Gómez-Quiñones, "To Leave to Hope or Chance," 153–66.

16. Vigil, "Marx and Chicano Anthropology," 21.

17. In the 1940s, the *pachucos,* Mexican American zoot-suiters, appropriated the term *Chicano.* Most adults, in contrast, shunned the term as it signified lower-class status and Indian identity. Some Chicanos became activists in the Mexican American civil rights movement.

18. Mares, "Myth and Reality."

19. Jaramillo, "Nueva Raza." Luis Jaramillo, a Roman Catholic priest from New Mexico, distinguished himself as a religious thinker and committed advocate for social justice.

20. Wright, *Nonzero*.

21. Huxley, introduction to *Phenomenon of Man*, 20.

22. Wright, *Nonzero*, 7.

23. Huxley, introduction to *Phenomenon of Man*, 20.

24. In 1973, Segura Granados published a summary of his work as "La continuidad de la tradición filosófica Nahuatl en las danzas de concheros" in *El Cuaderno (de Vez en Cuando)*, an Academia publication. In 1995, Segura Granados and Gonzales edited "La continuidad de la sabiduría y la tradición Nahuatl en las danzas de concheros," which corrected material in the earlier Academia publication.

25. Toffler, *Third Wave*, 137.

26. Based on my recollections of conversations with Eliseo Atencio in Dixon, New Mexico, in 1963.

27. Mumford, *Myth of the Machine*, 10, 19.

28. Theobald, *Beyond Despair*, xvii.

29. "The problems of the information society will be future shocks . . . the inability of people to respond smoothly to rapid societal transformation" (Masuda, "Computopia," 625).

30. Huntington, *Clash of Civilizations*, gives a detailed examination of the "clash of civilizations"; Friedman, in *Lexus and the Olive Tree*, is an apologist for globalization. See also Harrison and Huntington, *Culture Matters*.

31. Ehrenreich, *Nickel and Dimed*.

32. Drucker, *New Realities*, 25.

33. Theobald, *Guaranteed Income*.

34. C. Anderson, "Bioethics," 52–54.

35. Bezold, "Pharmaceuticals," 709.

36. Bell, "Introduction," xxxvi.

37. Foucault, *Power/Knowledge*, 78–108, discusses this theme.

38. Atencio, "Una vida buena y sana."

39. Kist, *New Literacies in Action*. Especially relevant to Chicanos is chapter 6, "Dot Com with Salsa," a case study.

40. Atencio, "Resolana," 9.

41. In forging the idea of a learning society, La Academia presaged Masuda's assertion that "the past developmental patterns of human society can be used as a historical analogical model for future society" (Masuda, "Computopia," 620).

42. Chávez, *But Time and Chance*, 45. The Penitentes are men belonging to a brotherhood known as La Cofradía de Nuestro Padre Jesús Nazareno. In 1833, Bishop Zubiría of the Diocese of Durango, Mexico, banned them from the Catholic Church for their excessive "corporal penances."

43. A connection was made between Paulo Freire and La Academia de la

Nueva Raza in a resolana in the Dixon Learning and Documentation Center and at the Ghost Ranch Conference Center in Abiquiú, New Mexico, in 1973.

44. Atencio, "Resolana," 9. *Snapeando,* a cognate deriving from the Anglo colloquialism "snap," means to see the essence of something by way of insight; *maliciandola* probably derives from *malicia,* the loss of innocence. The concept of "the sun shining on everything . . ." was used by O'Odham elders to describe full integrity in communication, wherein the sender of a message, the message itself, the receiver of the message, and the feedback to the sender, are all perfectly clear.

45. *Alabado,* translated by E. A. "Tony" Mares.

46. Atencio, "Resolana," 10–13.

47. Many issues were taken up through this process: (1) an action to bring the Bureau of Land Management to account for its claim to land that Mexicans had settled before the United States annexed New Mexico; (2) an organized opposition to a cheap housing project proposed by building contractors and paid for by the federal government; and (3) water issues and exploitive tourism.

48. From its earliest days La Academia had contact with scholars, including Dolores González, the late professor of education at the University of New Mexico; Stanford University Chicano Fellows; Professor Miguel Montiel at Berkeley and later at Arizona State University; Ernesto Galarza; Paulo Freire; and classes from various universities. In 1979, the National Council of La Raza sponsored the Resolana Project, funded by the National Endowment for the Humanities, through *Agenda,* their quarterly publication.

49. Adler and Gorman, *Great Ideas.*

50. Habermas, *Theory and Practice,* 9, 22–25.

51. Gordon Cook, e-mail message to Tomás Atencio, April 18, 1994. See Atencio, "Resolana," for a description of the pícaro.

52. Atencio, "Resolana." Upon reading this work, Ronald J. Grele, oral history scholar, suggests the term *reflexive sociology* to describe our process. He found similarities between la resolana and Pierre Bourdieu's concept of habitus. Although there may be some similarities between la resolana and Bourdieu's methodology, my use of *reflexive sociology* does not claim kinship with Bourdieu's work.

53. Atencio, "Crypto-Jewish Remnants," 60; see also Van Manen, *Researching Lived Experience,* 35.

54. Pedro David, a native of Argentina, is a well-known criminologist and is active in the International Phenomenological Society.

55. Heidegger, *Being and Time,* 54–59. I use Heidegger's definition of phenomenology because he breaks this word into *phenomenon* and *logos. Phenomenon,* "the showing-itself-in-itself, signifies a distinctive way in which something can be encountered" (54). Logos is the Greek root of the process of disclosure

"a definite mode of letting something be seen" (57). This understanding of phenomenology more accurately describes the resolana process of uncovering the themes in a story and discerning their meaning.

56. Van Manen, *Researching Lived Experience*, 1–46, explains phenomenology and hermeneutics in relation to the pedagogy of experiential learning.

57. Antonio Medina, a social worker, ordained Presbyterian minister, and cofounder of La Academia de la Nueva Raza, is a nationally respected leader and advocate for Latinos.

58. The work on streets and gutters had been recommended by a sector development plan approved in 1978 by the city council, but was not implemented until Gallegos became a councilman.

59. Suazo, "Grassroots Social Movement," describes the SAC experience in detail. Wesley Woo, a regional field representative for the Center for Community Change in San Francisco, came to Albuquerque to discuss ongoing community projects. Impressed by his visit to the old sawmill site and our group's vision for a housing development there, he assigned a community consultant who guided SAC through the process of acquiring the property and transferred it to the city for development as a community land trust.

60. The Institute for Community Economics in Massachusetts assisted the SAC in creating the Sawmill Community Land Trust.

61. See Gonzáles, "Bringing Telecommunications to Northern New Mexico," a dissertation on this topic.

62. The Internet dialogue of Resolana Electrónica was made possible by Robert Theobald's Transformational Learning Communities and Transformational Change program managed by Robert Stilger of Northwest Region Facilitators in Spokane, Washington. Stilger and Theobald responded to our need for an interactive Internet program that would allow students to dialogue among themselves.

63. *Dancing with Photons*, produced by Chain Reactions Productions, Santa Fe, New Mexico; broadcast as part of the "Colores" series on the Public Broadcasting Service's Albuquerque affiliate, KNME-TV, in October 1997.

64. Michael Morris was Academic Dean of the University of New England in 1989 when he launched an effort to create the College of the Twenty-First Century. He learned of the work of La Academia, and I joined the discussions and shared the concept of la resolana as a pedagogical and knowledge-building process for the cyber age. Morris also helped develop and implement the AmeriCorps "Resolana: Learning while Serving" project.

65. In earlier times, torreones were built at opposite ends of a village plaza as sentry posts to guard against attacks by Plains Indians.

66. G. Anderson, "Dimensions, Context and Freedom."

67. Atencio, "Journey in Self-Reliance," 34.

68. Mares discusses network theory as it applies to la resolana and globalization in chapter 3.

69. In 1986 I was appointed to serve on a committee planning a Hispanic museum in the Barelas barrio of Albuquerque. My contribution was to develop the concept of a cultural center that would include an oral history documentation center.

70. By 1969, Huntington, a Harvard professor of political science, had published three major books on national politics, but his focus on culture as an "explanatory variable" did not become apparent until the 1980s. See Foucault, *Power/Knowledge*, 81–92, on the subjugation and the insurrection of subjugated knowledge. In 1968 Foucault's work had not yet been translated into English, but his interest in the insurrection of subjugated knowledge seems to have developed during the political turmoil in France in 1968.

71. Huntington, *Who Are We?* 229.

72. Quotations from Brackenridge and García-Trejo, *Iglesia Presbiteriana*, 47, 47–48, respectively.

73. Brackenridge and García-Trejo, *Iglesia Presbiteriana*, 48.

74. Chávez, *But Time and Chance*, 92–100.

75. See Mares, "Many Faces of Padre Martínez," 18–47.

76. Torrez, "Los Alamos," 16–17.

77. Arellano, "Querencia," 31.

78. Petrini, "Carlo Petrini talks with Enzo Bianchi."

79. Van Dresser, *Landscape for Humans.*

80. Ortega y Gasset, *Interpretation of Universal History*, 28.

2. Resolana in Action

1. Atencio, "Oro del Barrio."

2. For a discussion of globalization and its impact on Hispanics, refer to chapter 3.

3. Schwartz (*Art of the Long View*, 121–27) identifies world changes that will impact the Hispanic community in the twenty-first century: the global economy and its burgeoning immigrant population; the nation's rapidly increasing population and commensurate changes in class, race, gender, professional, and other social relationships; the feminization of poverty, the stresses on family resulting from immigration, and changing family roles; and the gap between the educated and the uneducated. The 2000 U.S. census counted 32.8 million Hispanics (12 percent of the U.S. population: 66 percent Mexican, 14 percent Central and South American, 9 percent Puerto Rican; and 4 percent Cuban). Compared to Caucasian census respondents, Hispanics are more likely to be young, undereducated, poor, and noncitizens (see also Fox, *Hispanic Nation*, 17).

4. May, *Cry for Myth*, 20.

5. Selecting Hispanic leaders was not an easy task. There was the danger of romanticizing the Hispanic experience by confusing celebrity (or visibility) with heroism, as is often the case with sports and entertainment figures. Our

ideal was to identify individuals who lead lives of virtue. Refer to Ortega y Gasset, *Revolt of the Masses.* Several individuals who participated in the first resolanas were not part of the original group. They included Cristina Muñoz, ASU graduate student and president of the Greater Phoenix Chapter of the National Women's Political Caucus; Aurora Espinoza, executive director of San Juan de Dios Institute, a Catholic Lay Organization, and daughter of Tommy Espinoza; and Nancy Jordan, associate vice president of community development at ASU and one of the founders of the Women's Corporation, a woman's advocacy group in Phoenix, Arizona. Jordan was an active participant in several of these resolanas. MM refers to me.

6. The participants in this study referred to themselves in a variety of ways, revealing fundamental differences in how members of the Hispanic community choose to refer to themselves. Chicanos generally do not view themselves as Latinos; Latinos, the preferred label for people from Latin America outside Mexico, do not view themselves as Chicanos. In this study we make those distinctions clear, but when referring to the group as a whole we used the label *Hispanic* unless there was a specific reason for using another term, because this seemed to be the majority choice among those that participated in this study. Other labels, used in order of preference, included Latino, Chicano, Mexican American, and Mexican (Mexicano). We should note that the vast majority of the individuals who participated in this project were Mexican American or Mexican.

7. Ramos, *Perfil del hombre.* In the 1930s, Ramos referred to the *pelado* (literally plucked like a chicken) as the basic portrait of the Mexican character. Suspicion was at the core of the Mexican personality, and feelings of inferiority infected all his relationships. The pelado's "masculine protest" (an Adlerian term) was manifested by vulgar behavior and aggressive language tainted with an ideology of male superiority. Exaggerated macho masculinity was a mask to hide feelings of inferiority created by the conquest and domination of the Spaniards over the Indians.

8. Failde, *Latino Success.*

9. Montiel, "Chicano Family," 22–31. The literature on Mexican Americans, particularly before the 1970s, portrays them as not living up to the standards and values of U.S. culture. Today, the depictions of these new immigrants are couched in terms of the difficulties of assimilating them into Western civilization. Other expressions of these sentiments are manifested by politicians playing up to the frightened masses in their anti-immigrant posturing. These expressions are heard in talk shows all across the United States.

10. In selecting "young leaders," I simply asked graduate students in the School of Public Affairs at ASU to identify a diverse group of individuals that might want to enter into dialogue with the leaders interviewed previously. I was looking for young professionals involved in business and community affairs. Our intent was to engage these men and women in a series of resolanas with

leaders identified by the Valle del Sol process. We called the individuals on our list, and all but one participated. The participants included Ricardo Cortazar, co-owner of a real estate company; Monica Pérez, a student and employee at the Arizona Hispanic Chamber of Commerce; Bob Soza, ASU assistant vice president for student affairs and dean of students; Jess Torrez, owner of a private investigation company in Arizona; Mary Herrera Daniels, with Congressman Pastor's office; Miguel Montiel, ASU professor; Claudia López, ASU student in the Chicano Studies Department; Dulce Gonzáles, with Congressman Pastor's office; María Elena Coronado, ASU program coordinator of the César Chávez Leadership Institute; Raúl Cárdenas, with the ASU School of Business and former high school principal; Ed Delci, senior academic advisor, outreach counselor, ASU College of Liberal Arts and Sciences and community activist; Milton Dellossier, Wells Fargo Home Mortgage; Cristina Muñoz, ASU graduate student and president of the Greater Phoenix Chapter of the National Women's Political Caucus; Yvonne Montiel, PhD, instructor, South Mountain Community College, Maricopa County; Marcos Najera, actor and commentator on the NPR radio station KJZZ,; and Lydia A. Aranda, governor's executive director and small business advocate for Arizona.

11. Schwartz, *Art of the Long View*, 121–27.

12. Becker, *Denial of Death*, 5.

13. Velez-Ibáñez and Greenberg, "Formation and Transformation of Funds of Knowledge."

14. May, *Cry for Myth*, 18.

15. Becker, *Denial of Death*.

3. *A Resolana on Networks*

1. Barabási, *Linked*, 12.

2. Klein, *Shock Doctrine*, 15.

3. Huntington, "Hispanic Challenge," 11.

4. Although San Felipe Neri is the correct name of this saint, parishioners in Old Town Albuquerque customarily referred to him as San Felipe de Neri.

5. Buida, "God's Fool, Parfeni et al."

6. Bhabha, *Location of Culture*.

7. Ibid., 7.

8. Torres, "I Don't Think I Exist," 176.

9. Simpson, *Many Mexicos*, 10.

10. Friedman, *Lexus and the Olive Tree*, 105–6.

11. Friedman, *World Is Flat*, 7.

12. U.S. Census Bureau, "United States Census, 2000."

13. Pew Hispanic Center, "Survey of Mexican Migrants," 12.

14. Root, "Migration of Work-Age People."

15. Associated Press television news archive, "U.S. Immigration," April 11, 2006, available online at www.aparchive.com/index.aspx.

16. See Barabási, *Linked;* M. Buchanan, *Nexus;* Gladwell, *Tipping Point;* Watts, *Six Degrees.*

17. David Roybal, "Unpaid Ambassador More Than Just a Carnitas King," *Albuquerque Journal,* Tuesday, January 30, 2007.

18. Watts, *Six Degrees,* 49.

19. Buchanan, *Nexus,* 54.

20. Barabási, *Linked,* 58.

21. Ibid., 63.

22. Mignolo, *Local Histories,* 23.

23. Ibid., 167.

24. Ibid., 170–71.

25. Mignolo, *Darker Side of the Renaissance,* 6.

26. Fukuyama, *Great Disruption,* 10.

27. Wise, Salazar, and Carlsen, *Confronting Globalization,* x.

28. Fukuyama, *Great Disruption,* 5, 11, 281.

29. Ibid., 275.

30. Ibid., 90.

31. Ibid., 199.

32. Ibid. 199, 234.

33. Ibid., 256.

34. Ibid., 235.

35. Fukuyama, *America at the Crossroads,* 156.

36. Huntington, *Clash of Civilizations,* 20, 155, 156.

37. Ibid., 136–40.

38. Ibid., 137.

39. Ibid., 138.

40. Ibid., 51.

41. Fuller, *Operation Manual,* 21.

42. Huntington, *Clash of Civilizations,* 51.

43. Ibid., 305.

44. All quotations ibid.

45. All quotations ibid., 306.

46. Ibid., 311.

47. Ibid., 74.

48. Kroeber, *Ishi in Two Worlds,* 3.

49. Berners-Lee, *Weaving the Web,* 200.

50. Atencio, "Resolana," 2.

51. Fukuyama, *Great Disruption,* 227.

52. Weil, *Iliad, or the Poem of Force,* 37.

53. Bohm, *On Dialogue,* 16.

54. Ortega y Gasset, *Revolt of the Masses,* 47–48.

55. May, *Cry for Myth,* 20.

56. Brook, *Empty Space,* 9.

57. Klein, *Shock Doctrine*, 52.
58. Amin, *Liberal Virus*, 22.
59. Esteva, "Interview with Gustavo Esteva."
60. "Road to Congress."
61. Zibechi, "Indigenous Movements."
62. Slow Food Press Office.
63. Berners-Lee, *Weaving the Web*, 209.
64. Basho, *Narrow Road to the Interior*, 1.

Works Cited

Abt, Theodore. *Progress without Loss of Soul: Towards a Wholistic Approach to Modernization Planning.* Wilmette, Ill.: Chiron Publications, 1989.

Adler, Mortimer J., ed. in chief, and William Gorman, gen. ed. *The Great Ideas: A Syntopicon of Great Books of the Western World.* 2 vols. Chicago: University of Chicago Press, 1952.

Amin, Samir. *The Liberal Virus: Permanent War and the Americanization of the World.* Delhi: Aakar Books, 2005.

Anderson, Clifton. "Bioethics." In *Encyclopedia of the Future,* vol. 1, edited by George Thomas Kurian and Graham T. T. Molitor. New York: Simon and Schuster, 1996.

Anderson, Gregory T. "Dimensions, Context and Freedom: The Library in the 'Creation of Knowledge.'" In *Sociomedia,* edited by Edward Barnett. Cambridge, Mass.: MIT Press, 1984.

Arellano, Juan Estevan. *Inocencio: Ni pica ni escarda, pero siempre se come el mejor elote.* Mexico, D.F.: Grijalbo, 1992.

———, ed. *Entre Verde y Seco.* Introduction by Tomás Atencio. Dixon, N.M.: Academia de la Nueva Raza, 1972.

———. "La Querencia: La Raza: Bioregionalism." *New Mexico Historical Review* 72, no. 1 (1997): 31–38.

Atencio, Tomás. "La Academia de la Nueva Raza: El Oro del Barrio." *El Cuaderno (de Vez en Cuando)* 3, no. 1 (Winter 1973): 4–14.

———. "Crypto-Jewish Remnants in New Mexico Manito Society and Culture." *Jewish Folklore and Ethnology Review* 18, nos. 1–2 (1996): 59–67.

———. *Ghost Ranch: The First 25 Years.* [Commemorative pamphlet.] Abiquiú, NM: Ghost Ranch Conference Center, 1980.

———. "A Journey in Self-Reliance: A Report on the Status of the Papago Health Programs." Sells, Ariz.: Papago Tribe, 1973.

———. "El Oro del Barrio in the Cyber Age: Revitalizing the Mexican American Community." Paper presented for Motorola Community Revitalization Project, Department of Chicana and Chicano Studies, Arizona State University, Tempe, November 17, 2001.

———. "Resolana: A Chicano Pathway to Knowledge." Third Annual Ernesto Galarza Commemorative Lecture. Stanford Center for Chicano Research, Stanford University, 1988.

———. "The Survival of la Raza Despite Social Services." *Social Casework* 52, no. 5 (1971): 262–65.

———. "Una vida buena y sana: A Philosophy of Life." In *Thought and Action Papers*, 1–16. Albuquerque: Rio Grande Institute, 1991.

Atencio, Tomás, and Consuelo Pacheco. "The Concept of Resolana." *Agenda* [National Council of la Raza quarterly] 10, no. 1 (1980): 14, 34.

Barabási, Albert-László. *Linked.* New York: Penguin, 2003.

Basho, Matsuo. *Narrow Road to the Interior.* Translated by Sam Hamill. Boston: Shambhala, 1991.

Becker, Ernest. *The Birth and Death of Meaning.* New York: Free Press of Glencoe, 1962.

———. *The Denial of Death.* New York: Free Press, 1973.

Bell, Daniel. "Commission on the Year 2000." In *Encyclopedia of the Future,* vol. 1, edited by George Thomas Kurian and Graham T. T. Molitor. New York: Simon and Schuster, 1996.

———. "Introduction: Reflections at the End of an Age." In *Encyclopedia of the Future,* vol. 1, "edited by George Thomas Kurian and Graham T. T. Molitor. New York: Simon and Schuster, 1996.

Berners-Lee, Tim. *Weaving the Web.* San Francisco: Harper, 1999.

Bezold, Clement. "Pharmaceuticals." In *Encyclopedia of the Future,* vol. 2, edited by George Thomas Kurian and Graham T. T. Molitor. New York: Simon and Schuster, 1996.

Bhabha, Homi K. *The Location of Culture.* New York: Routledge, 1994.

Bohm, David. *On Dialogue.* Cambridge: Pegasus Communications, 1990.

Bourdieu, Pierre, and Loïc Wacquant. *An Invitation to Reflexive Sociology.* Chicago: University of Chicago Press, 1992.

Brackenridge, Douglas R., and Francisco O. García-Trejo. *Iglesia Presbiteriana.* San Antonio: Trinity University Press, 1987.

Brook, Peter. *The Empty Space.* New York: Atheneum, 1968.

Buchanan, Mark. *Nexus: Small Worlds and the Groundbreaking Theory of Networks.* New York: W. W. Norton, 2002.

Buchanan, Scott, ed. *The Portable Plato.* Trans. Benjamin Jowett. New York: Viking Press, 1971.

Buida, Yuri. "God's Fool, Parfeni et al." *New Times*. April 2006. Available online at www.newtimes.ru/eng/detail.asp?art_id=1019.

Cather, Willa, *Death Comes for the Archbishop*. New York, A. A. Knopf, 1927.

Chávez, Angélico. *But Time and Chance: The Story of Padre Martínez of Taos, 1793–1867*. Santa Fe: The Sunstone Press, 1981.

Drucker, Peter F. *The New Realities: In Government and Politics*. New York: HarperBusiness, 1994.

———. *Post-Capitalist Society*. New York: HarperCollins, 1993.

Ehrenreich, Barbara. *Nickel and Dimed: On (Not) Getting by in America*. New York: Henry Holt and Co., 2001.

Ellul, Jacques. *The Technological Society*. New York: Vintage, 1967.

Esteva, Gustavo. "Interview with Gustavo Esteva on the Zapatista Rebellion." *Zmagazine*. May 2001. Available online at www.zmagazine.org.

Failde, Augusto. *Latino Success: Insights from 100 of America's Most Powerful Latino Business Professionals*. New York: Simon and Schuster, 1996.

Foucault, Michel. *Power/Knowledge: Selected Interviews and Other Writings, 1972–1977*, edited by Colin Gordon. New York: Pantheon Books, 1980.

Fox, Gregory. *Hispanic Nation: Culture, Politics, and the Construction of Identity*. Tucson: University of Arizona Press, 1996.

Freire, Paulo. *Pedagogy of the Oppressed*. New York: Herder and Herder, 1971.

———. *The Politics of Education: Culture, Power, and Liberation*. South Hadley, Mass.: Bergin & Garvey, 1985.

Friedman, Thomas L. *The Lexus and the Olive Tree*. New York: Anchor Books, 2000.

———. *The World Is Flat: A Brief History of the Twenty-first Century*. New York: Farrar, Straus, and Giroux, 2005.

Fukuyama, Francis. *America at the Crossroads*. New Haven: Yale University Press, 2006.

———. *The End of History and the Last Man*. New York: Free Press, 1992.

———. *The Great Disruption*. New York: Simon and Schuster, 1999.

Fuller, Buckminster. *Operation Manual for Spaceship Earth*. New York: Pocket Books, 1969.

Gladwell, Malcolm. *The Tipping Point*. New York: Little, Brown and Co., 2000.

Gómez-Quiñones, Juan. "To Leave to Hope or Chance: Propositions on Chicano Studies, 1974." In *Parameters of Institutional Change: Chicano Experiences in Education*, 153–66. Hayward, Calif.: Southwest Network, 1974.

Gonzáles, Carmen Linda. "Bringing Telecommunications to Northern New Mexico Communities: Using On-line Resources to Extend Community." PhD diss., University of New Mexico, 1995.

Habermas, Jürgen. *Theory and Practice.* Boston: Beacon Press, 1973.

Hardt, Michael, and Antonio Negri. *Empire.* Cambridge, Mass.: Harvard University Press, 2000.

Harrison, Lawrence, and Samuel P. Huntington, eds. *Culture Matters: How Values Shape Human Progress.* New York: Basic Books, 2000.

Heidegger, Martin. *Being and Time.* New York: Harper and Row, 1962.

Huntington, Samuel P. *The Clash of Civilizations and the Remaking of World Order.* New York: Simon and Schuster, 1997.

———. "The Hispanic Challenge." *Foreign Policy* March–April 2004. Available online at http://cyberlaw.harvard.edu/blogs/gems/culturalagency/SamuelHuntingtonTheHispanicC.pdf

———. *Who Are We? The Challenges to America's National Identity.* New York: Simon and Schuster, 2004.

Huxley, Julian. Introduction to *The Phenomenon of Man,* by Pierre Teilhard de Chardin. New York: Harper and Row, 1965.

Illich, Ivan. *Deschooling Society.* New York: Pantheon, 1971.

Jaramillo, Luis. "A Modern Parable: Too Late Your Tears!" *El Cuaderno (de Vez en Cuando)* 1 (1971): 15–17.

———. "La Nueva Raza: An Introduction to the New Humanity." *The Centro LNR Bulletin.* San Anselmo, Calif.: El Centro de Comunicación, 1971.

Jung, C. G. *The Archetypes and the Collective Unconscious,* vol. 9 pt. 1. Trans. R. F. C. Hull. Princeton: Princeton University Press, 1959.

Kist, William. *New Literacies in Action: Teaching and Learning in Multiple Media.* New York: Teachers College Press, 2004.

Klein, Naomi. *The Shock Doctrine: The Rise of Disaster Capitalism.* New York: Metropolitan Books—Henry Holt, 2007.

Kroeber, Theodora. *Ishi in Two Worlds.* Berkeley: University of California Press, 1961.

Lummis, Charles F. *The Land of Poco Tiempo.* Albuquerque: University of New Mexico Press, 1966.

Mander, Jerry, and Edward Goldsmith, eds. *The Case against the Global Economy.* San Francisco: Sierra Club Books, 1996.

Mares, E. A. "The Fiesta of Life: Impressions of Paulo Freire." *El Cuaderno (de Vez en Cuando)* 3, no. 2 (Spring 1974): 4–16.

———. *I Returned and Saw under the Sun.* Albuquerque: University of New Mexico Press, 1989.

———. "The Many Faces of Padre Antonio José Martínez: A Historiographic Essay" In *Padre Martínez: New Perspectives from Taos,* 18–47. Taos: Millicent Rogers Museum, 1988.

————. "Myth and Reality: Observations on American Myths and the Myth of Aztlán." *El Cuaderno (de Vez en Cuando)* 3, no. 1 (1973): 33–50.

Masuda, Yoneji. "Computopia." In *The Information Technology Revolution*, edited by Tom Forester. Cambridge, Mass.: MIT Press, 1985.

May, Rollo. *The Cry for Myth*. New York: W. W. Norton, 1991.

McLuhan, Marshall, and Bruce R. Powers. *The Global Village*. New York: Oxford University Press, 1989.

Mignolo, Walter D. *The Darker Side of the Renaissance*. Ann Arbor: University of Michigan Press, 2001.

————. *Local Histories/Global Designs*. Princeton: Princeton University Press, 2000.

Montiel, Miguel. "The Chicano Family: A Review." *Social Work* 18, no. 2 (1973): 22–31.

Montiel, Miguel, and Felipe Ortego y Gasca. "Chicanos, Community and Change." In *Community Organizing in a Diverse Society*, edited by John Erlich and Felipe Rivera. Needham Heights, Mass.: Allyn and Bacon, 1998.

Mumford, Lewis. *The Myth of the Machine: The Pentagon of Power*. New York: Harcourt Brace Jovanovich, 1970.

National Commission of Community Health Services. *Health Is a Community Affair: Report*. Cambridge. Mass.: Harvard University Press, 1966.

Oldenburg, Ray. *The Great New Place*. New York: Paragon House, 1991.

Ortega y Gasset, José. *An Interpretation of Universal History*. Trans. Mildred Adams. New York: Norton, 1973.

————. *The Revolt of the Masses*. New York: W. W. Norton, 1932.

Pacheco, Consuelo. "The Archetypal Image and the New Mexican Indo-hispano." In *Thought and Action Papers*, 1–29. Albuquerque: Rio Grande Institute, 1991.

Padilla, Raymond V., and Miguel Montiel. *Debatable Diversity: Critical Dialogues on Change in American Universities*. New York: Rowman and Littlefield, 1998.

Petrini, Carlo. "Carlo Petrini talks with Enzo Bianchi, Part One." *La Stampa* [Italy], March 2, 2004. Available online at www.slowfood.com/sloweb/eng/archivo/lasso?pagina=8&cod/=007-31-k.

Pew Hispanic Center. "Survey of Mexican Migrants, July 2004—January 2005." Available online at http://pewhispanic.org.

Ramos, Samuel. *El perfil del hombre y la cultura en México*. 2nd ed. Mexico, D.F.: Robredo, 1938.

"Road to Congress: Engin Isen Reveals the Art in Citizenship." *Ylife*, York University, March 27, 2006. Available online at www.yorku.ca/ylife/2006/03-March/03–27/Isin-032706.htm.

Root, Jay. "Migration of Work-Age People Has Devastated Many Mexican Villages." *Knight Ridder Washington Bureau.* March 23, 2006.

Roybal, David. "Unpaid Ambassador More Than Just a Carnitas King." *Albuquerque Journal,* January 30, 2007.

Schwartz, Peter. *The Art of the Long View: Planning for the Future in an Uncertain World.* New York: Doubleday/Currency, 1991.

Segura Granados, Andrés. "Continuidad de la tradición filosófica Nahuatl en las danzas de concheros." *El Cuaderno (de Vez en Cuando)* 3, no. 1 (Winter 1973): 16–33.

Segura Granados, Andrés, with Gilberto E. Gonzales. *La continuidad de la sabiduría y la tradición Nahuatl en las danzas de concheros.* San Juan Bautista, Calif.: Gilberto E. Gonzales, 1995.

Simpson, Lesley Byrd. *Many Mexicos.* Berkeley: University of California Press, 1963.

Slow Food Press Office. "The Fifth International Slow Food Congress." Fall 2007. Available online at www.content.slowfood.it/upload/3E6E345B1 169F25A78TMD75F.

Spoto, Donald. *The Hidden Jesus: The New Life.* New York: St. Martin's Press, 1998.

Suazo, Mark. "The Grassroots Social Movement and Cultural Interaction." Honors thesis, University of New Mexico, 1992.

———. "Mobilizing in Defense of Community: A Case Study of the Sawmill Advisory Council. Master's thesis, University of New Mexico, 2002.

Theobald, Robert. *Beyond Despair: A Policy Guide to the Communications Era.* Washington, D.C.: Seven Locks Press, 1981.

———. "The Cybernation Revolution." Address to the 52nd Annual Conference of the Council of Southern Mountains. April 7, 1964.

———., ed. *The Guaranteed Income.* New York: Doubleday, 1967.

———. *Reworking Success: New Communities in the Millennium.* Gabriola Island, B.C.: New Society Publishers, 1997.

"The Threepenny Opera: Introduction." *eNotes.com.,* January 2006. Available online at www.enotes.com/threepenny-opera/introduction.

Tijerina, Reies López. *Mi lucha por mi tierra.* Mexico, D.F.: Fondo de Cultura Económica, 1978.

Toffler, Alvin. *The Third Wave.* New York: William Morrow and Co., 1980.

Torres, Hector A. "'I Don't Think I Exist': Interview with Richard Rodriguez." *Melus* 28, no. 2 (2003): 165–202.

Torrez, Robert. "Los Alamos: In Search of an Identity." *New Mexico Historical Review* 72, no. 1 (1997): 15–22.

U.S. Census Bureau. "United States Census 2000." December 17, 2007. Available online at www.census.gov/prod/2001pubs/c2kbr01–1.pdf.

Van Dresser, Peter. *Landscape for Humans: A Case Study of the* Potentials for Ecologically Guided Development in an Uplands *Region.* Albuquerque: Biotechnic Press, 1972.

Van Manen, Max. *Researching Lived Experience: Human Science for an Action Sensitive Pedagogy.* New York: State University of New York Press, 1990.

Velez-Ibáñez, Carlos, and James B. Greenberg. "Formation and Transformation of Funds of Knowledge among U.S.–Mexican Households." *Anthropology and Education Quarterly* 23, no. 4 (1992): 313–35.

Vigil, Diego. "Marx and Chicano Anthropology." *Grito del Sol: A Chicano Quarterly* 3, no. 1 (1978): 19–34.

Watts, Duncan J. *Six Degrees: The Science of a Connected Age.* New York: Norton, 2003.

Weil, Simone. *The Iliad, or the Poem of Force.* Wallingford, Pa.: Pendle Hill Publications, 1985.

Wise, Timothy A., Hilda Salazar, and Laura Carlsen, eds. *Confronting Globalization.* Bloomfield, Conn.: Kumarian Press, 2003.

Wright, Robert, *Nonzero: The Logic of Human Destiny.* New York: Pantheon Books 2000.

Zibechi, Raúl. "Indigenous Movements: Between Neoliberalism and Leftist Governments." IRC Americas Program, Silver City, N.M., International Relations Center, May 3, 2006. Available online at http://americas.irc-online.org/am/3257.

INDEX

O'Malley, Debbie, 48, 49
Oppression, 73
Organizations
  changed, 123–24
  community, 12
  need for new, 126–27
  strengthening, 105–06
Organizing, lost art of, 100–101
Ortega, Danny, 71, 81, 88, 119
Ortega y Gasset, José, 68, 72, 108, 176
Othón, Arthur, 71, 77, 78, 88
Outsourcing, 26

Padilla, José, 41, 42,
Parental role, 114, 116
Participation mystique, 15
Pastor, Ed, 71, 84, 109
Penitente Brotherhood, 31, 62, 63
Perspectives
  defining moments, 72, 78–82
  switching, 73
Pharmaceuticals, 27, 28
Phenomenology, 45
Phoenix, 111, 114, 117, 120, 123, 179
Pi'caros, 14, 44, 146, 147
Plaza Vieja, 146–52
Political participation, leadership and, 88–89
Postindustrial age, 23
Postindustrial cultural fallout, 12
Postindustrial society, 32
Power, 93–94, 128
Praxis, 46
Praxis learning, 32, 47, 52
Presbyterian, 62, 63, 64
Profession, knowledge-related, 25
Progress Without Loss of Soul, 67
Protestantism, 63
Protestant missions, 62
Psychoanalytic interview, 43

Querencia, 15, 22

Racism, 141
  as identity, 75–76
  as drive to succeed, 79–81
Random links, 158
Reflexive learning, 42
Refranes, 15
Religiosity, postindustrial rise in, 58

Resolana, 4, 70, 91–93, 173, 174, 187–89
  in action, 5
  applying to el oro del barrio, 8
  community, 131–33
  with community leaders, 93–107
  for the cyber age, 58
  and el oro del barrio, 13–19
  intergenerational leadership, 119–31
  new, 17, 34
  as pathway toward learning society for the
    cyber age, 30–42
  theory and practice of, 42–46
  with young leaders, 108–19
Resolana, La, 39, 54, 138
Resolana de Una Vida Buena y Sana, La, 46
Resolana Electrónica, 49, 50
Resolana Service Learning Documentation
    Center, 49, 52–60
Resolaneros, 146
Revolt of the Masses, 72
Rio Grande corridor, 51
Rio Grande Institute, 174
Rio Grande Railroad 63
Romero, Leo, 48
Ronstadt, José, 69
Rosales, Gilda Ortega, 71, 84, 89
Royal Chicano Air Force (RCAF), 19

Sandia National Laboratories, 51, 149
San Felipe School, 145
San Felipe de Neri 143–145, 149, 198
Santa Fe Railroad, 149
Santos, 35, 36
Sawmill Advisory Council (SAC), 47
Sawmill district, 52
Sawmill, 47–52, 149, 195
Scholar, becoming, 104–05
Schools, 115–16, 135, 144
Scottsdale Police Department, 78, 79,
    178
Segura, Maestro Andrés, 21, 40
Self-promotion, 73
Serfdom, modern form of, 26
Siete del Norte, 56
Slow food movement, 7, 183
Smith, Placida, 127
Social capital, 163, 165
Social linkages, 12
Social order, 163

About the Authors

MIGUEL MONTIEL is the Motorola Presidential Professor Emeritus in the Department of Transborder Chicana/o and Latina/o Studies at Arizona State University (ASU). He received his doctorate from the University of California, Berkeley, where he also served as an assistant professor. He came to Arizona State University in 1974 and held positions in the School of Social Work, the Honors College, the Hispanic Research Center, and the School of Public Affairs. In the 1980s he served as assistant vice president for academic affairs and as a visiting professor at the Universidad Autónoma de Guadalajara in Mexico. He also worked for the City of Phoenix as a loaned executive. Montiel is on the board of the Arizona Center for Public Policy and is a member of the Arizona Judicial Council. He has evaluated public programs and has consulted on initiatives with various public agencies. His early work on the Chicano family has been cited in numerous articles over the last thirty years. Montiel's work at ASU is documented in *Debatable Diversity: Critical Dialogues on Changes in American Universities* (Rowman and Littlefield, 1998). He is married to Yvonne and has two daughters, Aída and Maritza, and a granddaughter, Lea.

TOMÁS ATENCIO, a native of Dixon, New Mexico, is lecturer emeritus, Department of Sociology, the University of New Mexico, Albuquerque. He holds a master's degree in social work from the University of Southern California and a PhD in sociology from the University of New Mexico. Before entering academe, Atencio was a community mental health consultant and community activist in northern New Mexico. In the mid-1960s he was named executive director of the Colorado Migrant Council in Boulder, Colo., where he developed innovative adult literacy programs using farmworkers' own experiences as they followed the migrant stream. In 1968 he returned to New Mexico, where he conceived and cofounded La Academia de la Nueva Raza to uncover and reclaim subjugated Indohispanic knowledge. From that process Atencio developed the concept of la resolana as a metaphor for enlightenment through dialogue. In addition to his work on la resolana and education, Atencio has written on the history of Indohispanic Protestantism in New Mexico and on Crypto-Judaic vestiges in Indohispanic society and culture. His latest publications include an essay adapted from his doctoral dissertation about Old Town Albuquerque, in *Albuquerque: Portrait of a Western City* (Clear Light Publications, 2006). Atencio and his wife, Consuelo Pacheco, live in Albuquerque, N.M.

E. A. "TONY" MARES is professor emeritus of English, University of New Mexico, Albuquerque. His PhD (University of New Mexico, 1973) is in European history with an emphasis on Spain. He has published widely as a poet, writer of fiction, historian, and journalist. His poems have appeared in numerous local, national, and international publications. His most recent collections of poems are *With the Eyes of a Raptor* (Wings Press: San Antonio, 2004) and *Casi toda la música/Almost All the Music*, his translations of the poems of Ángel González (Wings Press: San Antonio, 2007). He has led poetry workshops for many universities and chaired the Literary Awards Committee for the 2004 National Hispanic Cultural Center of New Mexico Literary Prize.

While teaching at the University of New Mexico, Mares had his first experience with networks when he founded and directed what was probably the first university Internet outreach program in the United States for high school writers, The Writers' Inn. In addition, his research reinvigorated the study of Padre Antonio José Martínez of Taos, a key figure in New Mexican history. The book he edited, *Padre Martínez: New Perspectives from Taos* (Taos: Millicent Rogers Museum, 1988), and his one-man performance play based on Padre Antonio José Martínez of Taos, *I Returned and Saw under the Sun* (Albuquerque: University of New Mexico Press, 1989), are significant works in recent Martínez historiography.